90 0523286 4

KW-468-337

THE TIME OF
EUROPEAN GOVERNANCE

MANCHESTER
UNIVERSITY PRESS

EUROPE IN CHANGE SERIES EDITORS THOMAS CHRISTIANSEN AND EMIL KIRCHNER

already published

Committee governance in the European Union
THOMAS CHRISTIANSEN AND EMIL KIRCHNER (EDS)

Theory and reform in the European Union
DIMITRIS N. CHRYSSOCHOOU, MICHAEL J. TSINISIZELIS,
KOSTAS IFANTIS, STELIOS STAVRIDIS

The EU and the Cyprus conflict
Modern conflict, postmodern union
THOMAS DIEZ

Greece in a changing Europe
Between European integration and Balkan disintegration?
KEVIN FEATHERSTONE AND KOSTAS IFANTIS (EDS)

An introduction to post-Communist Bulgaria
Political, economic and social transformation
EMIL GIATZIDIS

The new Germany and migration in Europe
BARBARA MARSHALL

Turkey's relations with a changing Europe
MELTEM MÜFTÜLER-BAC

Righting wrongs in Eastern Europe
ISTVAN POGANY

Two tiers or two speeds?
The European security order and the enlargement of the European Union and Nato
JAMES SPERLING (ED.)

Recasting the European order
Security architectures and economic cooperation
JAMES SPERLING AND EMIL KIRCHNER

The Emerging Euro-Mediterranean system
DIMITRIS K. XENAKIS AND DIMITRIS N. CHRYSSOCHOOU

Magnus Ekengren

THE TIME OF EUROPEAN GOVERNANCE

MANCHESTER UNIVERSITY PRESS
Manchester and New York

distributed exclusively in the USA by Palgrave

The right of Magnus Ekengren to be identified as the author of this work has been asserted by him in accordance with the Copyright, Designs and Patents Act 1988.

Published by Manchester University Press
Oxford Road, Manchester M13 9NR, UK
and Room 400, 175 Fifth Avenue, New York, NY 10010, USA
http://www.manchesteruniversitypress.co.uk

Distributed exclusively in the USA by
Palgrave, 175 Fifth Avenue, New York, NY 10010, USA

Distributed exclusively in Canada by
UBC Press, University of British Columbia, 2029 West Mall,
Vancouver, BC, Canada V6T 1Z2

British Library Cataloguing-in-Publication Data
A catalogue record for this book is available from the British Library

Library of Congress Cataloging-in-Publication Data applied for

ISBN 0 7190 6155 5 *hardback*

First published 2002

10 09 08 07 06 05 04 03 02   10 9 8 7 6 5 4 3 2 1

Typeset in Minion with Lithos
by Northern Phototypesetting Co Ltd, Bolton
Printed in Great Britain
by Biddles Ltd, Guildford and King's Lynn

Contents

List of figures and tables   *page* vi
Preface and acknowledgements   vii
List of abbreviations   ix

1   The temporal dimension of European governance   1

2   The oligopoly of the future: the changed status of political promise   23

3   Back to the present: new conditions for political action   67

4   The recurring past: transformed horizons for policy planning   102

5   Institutional implications of European time   145

Bibliography   164
Index   177

*F*IGURES AND TABLES

Figures

1	The abstract 'calendar'	*page* 108
2	The Spanish presidency of the second half of 1995: 'Julio'	110
3	Agenda 2000: timetable	112
4	The ministry's internal timetable	114
5	The 'driving scheme'	115–116
6	The private EU timetable I (extract)	117–118
7	The private EU timetable II (extract)	119
8	Deadline-day	138
9	The European governance calendar	141
10	The European governance calendar (extract)	143

Tables

1	Meeting frequency in some EC organs 1985	76

PREFACE AND ACKNOWLEDGEMENTS

Why the time of European governance? My first experience with the time of Europe dates back to the early 1990s when serving at the Swedish representation to the Council of Europe in Strasbourg, France and, again since 1995, at various departments for European Union (EU) affairs at the Swedish Foreign Ministry in Stockholm. The most striking and surprising feature for my colleagues and myself was not that European cooperation and Swedish EU membership involved a broader network of actors both in Europe and at home – that was expected – but that we had much less time to prepare for our endeavours. The frequent contacts with European colleagues and the continuous preparation for European negotiations necessitated a different allocation of time and working rhythm that made us slightly uneasy about neglecting other tasks, such as strategic planning. Another creeping concern was that also the policy content unintentionally changed as a direct consequence of the compressed time framework for action and shortened horizons. In short, our working days were more stressful and sometimes summarised in exhausted sighs such as 'all these EU deadlines will eventually kill me'.

Returning to the university to finish my doctoral thesis I became puzzled by the neglect of this time dimension: perhaps the most significant expression of Europe for people with operational responsibilities and with such impact on policy-making. I entered the theoretical battlefield at a time when neorealism and neoliberal institutionalism were challenged by historical and sociological approaches to international and European relations, such as social constructivism and reflectivism. One of the main task of these latter – to which I soon adhered – was to show how not only preferences and interests but also the basic identity of international and European units and institutions change over time. Coming from the world of practitioners and having closely experienced a period of great transformation in European politics, the attraction of analytical approaches accounting for the possibilities of significant change was natural. It seemed important to see through old prefabricated 'structures' implying blind spots of post-state transformation, by means of interpretative and ethnomethodological approaches that cut the distance between the reality of European actors and the researcher. I wanted to turn my insights of change into reliable knowledge. Perhaps my theoretical choice was guided by a similar observation to that of Professor Ruggie, who has greatly inspired my writings, when assessing his tasks as Assistant Secretary-General of the United Nations: 'creative leadership in international organisation is social constructivism in action' (Ruggie, 1998: xii). The theories used in this book can be grouped under the label 'reflective approaches'. This was also the case for the theories of European governance that I, together with like-minded colleagues, used to open up new realities of change in an explorative study that broke new ground under the visionary intellectual leadership of Professor Knud Erik Jørgensen, University of Aarhus (Jørgensen, 1997c).

I started my study of a Europe in change with the help of the sociologists Anthony Giddens and Pierre Bourdieu. These were enthusiastically introduced to me by Professor Björn Wittrock at Stockholm University. The space dimension had for decades been thoroughly examined by others in terms of transactions, territoriality, networks and new levels. Time as a study object crystallised in the light of Bourdieu's writings on the importance of an understanding of the dynamics of time in all human practices for a full assessment of their meaning. The assumption was that Europe in change involves a transformation of time identity for the actors in European governance. The empirical task was to investigate how action changed not only over time, but also *in* time. The implications on policy-makers and institutions must be profound.

It is time, European or not, to extend my thanks to the people who have supported me in writing this book. The very existence of the volume is due to Professors Paul 't Hart, Leiden University and Bengt Sundelius, Uppsala University. I am indebted to Paul who not only encouraged me to revise my thesis into a book manuscript, but also took the time and effort to help me achieve it. His invaluable suggestions stretched from constructive thoughts on contents to references that I needed to look at, and editing proposals that helped to turn the dissertation into a book. All of this delivered with the same blend of intellectual frankness, well-meaning ironical remarks, openness for counter-argument and humour that is the characteristic of a good professor. As 't Hart also Bengt, my former supervisor, believed in the potential of the dissertation and spurred me to finalise the manuscript, as he put it. He urged me to take a leave of absence from the ministry for a few months and helped me to arrange the necessary practical conditions. I am most grateful to these two mentors for their faith, team spirit and friendship, on which I hope to be able to profit also in the future. I am also thankful to Professor Emil Kirchner, University of Essex, for his encouraging support and for including my book in the distinguished series *Europe in Change* that he edits, and to the anonymous referees of my manuscript for valuable remarks and suggestions.

I would like to extend special thanks to Professor Walter Carlsnaes, Uppsala University, for theoretical guidance and the initial encouragement in my choice of subject. I am also indebted to Donald Lavery for his excellent language editing that included valuable ideas for substantive clarifications, and to the officials of the ministries of foreign affairs of the United Kingdom (UK), Sweden and Denmark for disposing of some of their precious time in European governance by allowing me to interview them. My dissertation work was initiated within the framework of the project 'Transnational Interpenetration: Sweden in Western Europe in Sweden', supported by the Swedish Council for Research in the Humanities and Social Sciences. It was financed for three and a half years by a grant from the Special Programme on Foreign and Security Policy Studies at the Swedish Institute of International Affairs. I also thank the Board of this Programme for its confidence in my project that was expressed also in the support of the post-doctoral work required to complete the book.

Finally, I would like to express my warm gratitude to my Mia who has reminded me that there are times for other things than European time. I would like to thank my parents, Inga-Lill and Kristian, who have whole-heartedly supported my studies ever since first class in school.

Magnus Ekengren
Nyåker, Uppsala

Abbreviations

C	Centre Party (Sweden)
CEE	Central and Eastern Europe
CFSP	Common Foreign and Security Policy (EU)
CM	Council of Ministers' Meeting (EU)
CoE	Council of Europe
COEST	CFSP Committee for Eastern Europe and Central Asia (EU)
COPO	French for PoCo
Coreper	Comité des représentants permanents (EU)
COSEC	CFSP Committee for Security (EU)
DTI	Department of Trade and Industry (UK)
EC	European Community
ECJ	European Court of Justice
EEA	European Economic Area
EEC	European Economic Community
EES	European Economic Space
EFTA	European Free Trade Area
EMS	European Monetary System
EMU	Economic and Monetary Union
EP	European Parliament
ETUC	European Trade Union Conference
EU	European Union
EUD	European Union Department, FCO (UK)
FCO	Foreign and Commonwealth Office (UK)
Fp	Liberal Party (Sweden)
GAC	General Affairs Council (EU)
HLO	High Level Officials Meeting (EU)
HR	Human Rights
IGC	Intergovernmental Conference (EU)
IR	International Relations
Kd	Christian Democrats (Sweden)
Kds	Since 1996, Kd
LO	Swedish Confederation of Trade Unions
M	Conservative Party (Sweden)
Mp	Environmental Party (Sweden)
OSCE	Organisation for Security and Cooperation in Europe (EU)
PoCo	Political Committee (EU)
QMV	Qualified Majority Voting (EU)
R&D	Research and Development
S	Social Democratic Party (Sweden)
SAP	Social Democratic Party (Sweden)

SEA	Single European Act
UK	United Kingdom
UN	United Nations
V	Left Wing Party (Sweden)
Wg	Working Group (EU)

1

The temporal dimension of European governance

Why a new dimension?

The difference between the nation-state and European governance is not only one of scale. Conceptions such as 'multilevel', 'multiperspectival' and 'polycentric' place undue limits on our thinking about the character of European governance. By overemphasising the spatial dimension, those metaphors unintentionally hide the profundity of the change constituted by European governance. This aspect is not least of great importance in the on-going debate on whether and to what extent European governance and the European Union constitute something fundamentally new in world politics, or just a forum for traditional intergovernmental bargains.

As a means to investigate the implications of European governance and how it differs from governance in the state, this book takes as a point of departure the *temporal* dimension of policy-making. How does policy-making evolve *over* and *in time*? How is the 'future' conceived of in the formulation of policies in European governance in comparison to the nation-state? How does an altered concept of the future change the view on the capacity and potential for change of politics? To what degree is policy-making focused on the past, present and future? Are future concerns of the same weight as in national policy-making? Or are current issues of overriding priority? The purpose is to distinguish *the temporal logic* of European governance and to examine how it affects national policymakers and institutions. European governance is defined as a historically unique world view or practice of the legitimate management of political relationships and problem-solving institutions *beyond* the state (not above) in today's Europe (cf. Jachtenfuchs, 1997).

Furthermore, the book aims to show that the time perspective might be a more natural approach than others in the empirical investigation of European governance. The work indicates that it is in the dimension of time that European governance is most clearly expressed. Indeed, it shows that the more actors have to think about time, as in the case of European governance, the more politics and policy-making become time oriented. *Pace* and *time* are replacing *space* and *extension* in our understanding of how Europe is governed. It is time to discover that time is of the essence of politics in times of European governance.

By bringing the increasingly rich social sciences literature on time, particularly its interpretative–reflectivist branches, into the study of European governance, this book throws light on a dimension left in the dark by earlier theory. In this way the book purports to *complement* studies that mainly have come to deal with the spatial dimension of the transformation of political and administrative patterns.

The value of successfully demonstrating the replacement of the time of states by a post-state temporal logic of European governance can hardly be over-estimated. On the scientific side, we can think of the stimulation this potential finding would be for hypotheses breeding valuable investigations of changing organisational rhythms and styles of public policy and administration, and for specific areas such as the conditions for democracy in Europe. What is meant by 'democratic accountability' – the control in the future that today's promises have been fulfilled – if the 'future' is viewed differently? For theories of the historical significance and future of European governance, the temporal dimension is able to provide empirical facts that can match the results of spatial studies in a comprehensive understanding of European governance. Such systematic syntheses of change in time and space will greatly strengthen the arguments that the modern European state-based system is undergoing a fundamental transformation. In this sense, the temporal dimension has the potential to provide crucial support to the claim that the European Union and European governance may be the first post-modern international political forms. The temporal dimension opens up a qualitatively new window of analysis that, together with the findings of spatial studies, is able to generate a whole field of puzzling new questions and promising assumptions for the characterisation of the macro level. Can there be a European polycentric structure in a system of interacting units coordinated in centrally decided uniform time?

For the policymakers, there is an urgent need to understand the temporal context of politics in the European arena. They often feel that they resort to ad hoc solutions because of the short planning horizons in the European Union, which makes it difficult to foresee decisions. This feeling has been aptly summoned up as 'the need for Europe to win back its future'. There is also here clearly a need for a two-dimensional approach for an understanding of European governance.

For the sake of comparison, my investigation takes as points of departure analyses of the role of the view of the future (chapter 2), the present (chapter 3) and the past (chapter 4) for nation-state politics and policy-making. Does European governance give birth to any concepts of the 'future' in analogy to the strongly 'progress' oriented politics of the nation-state? To what extent is the century-long 'monopoly' of the control of the political future kept by the nation-states? How does European governance affect national policymakers' perception of what should be included in the political past? The differences that presumedly will be revealed will constitute the basis for a discussion of how they matter for policy formulation, action and planning. How do national policy-makers experience the time available for action in European governance? On the ground of which political past are political action and planning formulated? The institutional implications of European time will be discussed in the final chapter of this book (chapter 5). What are the implications of new horizons and rhythms on public policy and administration, European democracy and the general character of European governance?

Political time

Past, present and future in political history

Each epoch throughout history has been dominated by a certain focus with regard to the political past, present and future. Medieval time was the time of prophecies. All time was ultimately measured in relation to *the last judgement*. The task for the prophets was to estimate the time remaining to humanity. The particularities of each present were uninteresting in the sense that in relation to the mythological last settlements, they all belonged to the same time – they were timeless. That is why we often find anachronistic (in our modern view!) elements combined in medieval paintings (Koselleck, 1985).

In the so-called 'New time' (1500–1800) the absolute state struggled against all kinds of religious and local 'superstitious' predictions, in order to gain a monopoly of the vision of the future. To this end the philosophers made a distinction between the ecclesiastical history and *historia humana*. The main difference between the two was that the human history was not teleological. Thus, human wisdom and state action could play a role in the shaping of the future. The rulers could use rational political calculations to enhance their own and the state's power. However, the future was in the calculus only 'probable': unlike the 'final day' of medieval time nothing could be taken for granted. The statesman was recommended to be prepared for any possible event, and to have foresight in his *prognoses* of the future. Political time was perceived to be circular; the aim of the prognosis was to predict power struggles, wars and reigns of an eternally recurrent character (Koselleck, 1985).

The time dimension of modern politics (1800–) has been analysed in depth from many different angles. Koselleck has shown from a linguistic perspective how the balance between experience and expectation in people's consciousness of time changed in the modern era, compared to earlier times. A key concept in this perception has been 'progress', which implicitly tones down the importance of earlier experience and holds up the openness and expectations of the future. In modernity the future was made completely open and ready for definition and 'construction' by those with power. The reason for this changed balance and the growing importance of anticipation of an unknown future was, according to Koselleck, that earlier experiences lost their value in the modern period of very rapid industrial, social and economic transformations. Koselleck has argued that this 'temporalisation' of political concepts has existed since the French Revolution and will continue and accelerate in the future (Koselleck, 1989: 297–306).

Luhmann (1982) has modified Koselleck's picture of the modern notion of time to a certain extent. According to Luhmann, time in modernity is not just more future oriented, as Koselleck shows, but also more 'differentiated' than time in older societies:

> Complex societies build broader, more abstract, and differentiated temporal horizons than do simpler ones. They are surrounded by a 'world' whose complexity has become richer in possibilities, allowing them a greater range of selections in both experience and action. (Luhmann, 1982: 297)

Not only are time horizons in complex society more differentiated. They also seem to be shorter because the complexity limits the time for coordination and calculations of quickly changing relationships between actions:

> Time becomes scarce; … it predisposes some kind of 'packaging' or 'splitting'; it necessitates limitations and terminations, as well as agenda setting. Action in the end is always a 'time-binding' disposition that fills the memory beyond the moment and creates premises for future action. (Luhmann in Nowotny, 1992: 494)

Luhmann questions Koselleck's prediction that the temporalisation process will be a permanent phenomenon. He believes that it is rather characterising a period of transition to a new type of world society (Luhmann, 1982: 288). It was not only the view of the future that changed in modern conception of time, but also that of the past, i.e. the long-term historical memories or the so-called *longue durée* defined as designating

> The span of historically interpreted time, usually stretching from some originary point in the past (a beginning, a founding moment) down to the period of one's own lifetime. Depending on how the flow of time is conceptualised, this can mean a few generations, a few centuries, or even a millennium or two. (Gross, 1985: 54)

Modernity's progressive view of the future needed a new conception of the *longue durée*. In contrast to the circular, repetitive character of the *longue durée* of preceding centuries, modernity imposed a periodisation on the past that made it linear. The progressive nature of the future was made logical by a description of earlier periods as less progressive. Step by step, conceptualised as distinct historical periods, epochs etc. humanity climbed towards a higher degree of civilisation. This radical programmatic rewriting of the past was part of the modern state's ideologification and politicisation of temporality.

> By the nineteenth century, however, the ideologues of the state altered this theory ('theory of progress') in such way as to make the modern state central to the whole

idea of progress. When this happened, the history of progress became virtually syn-onymous with the growth of the centralised state, or at the very least the two were viewed as running parallel to and reinforcing one another. (Gross, 1985: 70)

According to Gross, the state politicised the modern concepts of time to its advantage in two ways. First, the state presented itself as the driving force behind social progress; 'progress' came to be identified with the extension of public state power. Secondly, the state defined progress so that it would seem as if progress was facilitated by the state, even though not a direct result of state policy. For example, progress came to be equalled with 'a complex and well-organised soci-ety' (Gross, 1985: 71–72). This monopoly over progress was further strength-ened by the state's monopolisation of a common 'memory' for the citizens of the nation-state by means of being society's main keeper of information. Indeed, this was a monopoly of history.

> By organising the time of the *longue durée*, the state gains a strong hand in deter-mining how the temporal dimension itself is experienced. And to the extent that an individual's conception of temporality necessarily affects his overall orientation in the world, it also affects his attitudes and intellectual disposition, and therefore per-haps his social and political behavior. (Gross, 1985: 68)

Luhmann (1982) has seen a development of this modern state temporality in the late Western welfare state. According to Luhmann, the basic traditional opposition between 'progressive and conservative orientations' in politics is today eroding. Because of the increased tempo of change in society, the roles of the two poles are often reversed:

> For example, for the sake of preservation the conservative position may require that many changes are made. And the progressive position depends on preserving things the way they are, at least on preserving those structures and measures through which it wants to create change. (Luhmann, 1982: 65)

The instability in politics, resulting from rapid change, makes expectations about the future more unreliable; 'the horizon of the future becomes shorter and more foreboding'. As a result the welfare state's optimistic and progressive view of the future has turned into some sort of short-term crisis management in order to counteract undesirable outcomes of earlier political action and plan-ning (Luhmann, 1982: 66). According to Ricoeur (1985), there is a 'crisis of the present' in contemporary society, owing to the fact that the gap between (often utopian) expectations of the future and tradition is so wide that the two can no longer be reconciled (Ricoeur, III, 1988: 216, 235):

> Today, time no longer symbolizes the knowledge of an appropriate time for action. Arrangements are made within time, but time itself is indifferent to what consti-tutes these arrangements. Temporal, social and factual dimensions are irrevocably separated … Time becomes anti-Utopian. (Nassehi, 1994: 60)

At another level, political systems display significant variations with regard to political rhythms and horizons. Politics in the USA has to large extent been shaped by the particular way of acting by each president in office *over* time (the sequence) and *in* time (simultaneously) at different layers of government and society. It is the cycles of the presidential leadership – the 'breakthrough', 'break up' and 'breakdown' – that to a higher degree than, for example, the periodicity of electoral politics explain political change (Skowronek, 1997). The temporality of the contemporary welfare state has been characterised by governments' sequencing of time in terms of planning events, their visionary long-range plans and the difficulties of coordinating the centre and lower level of government as regards temporal perspectives. Significant for these states has been the strong internalisation of governmentally created 'natural' deadlines ('the year 2000', 'by 1998 we will see the effects of our policy') and reform horizons ('the implementation of reform X during period Y'). One of the conclusions is that there is a crisis of the contemporary state's policy plannning (Schneider, 1991).

The recent time focus of politics could be seen as a consequence of the rapid expansion of new techniques of communication. Here, the objective of time analyses has been to define social and symbolic time in contrast to other forms of time, e.g. astronomical time. Linear clock time is today said to be replaced by the cyclical time of social rhythms, i.e. intersubjective time created through social interaction, owing to the fact that human beings exist in several social–political systems simultaneously (Nowotny, 1992: 483–91). Political scientists have developed new areas such as 'the politics of time' (Hernes, 1987). Time and democracy have most recently been constituted as an important area of research.[1]

The *circular* view of time is thus the oldest and, throughout history, the most predominant one. Influenced by the rhythm of the agricultural year, it dominated man's perception of time for millennia. Other cyclical times were religious and mercantile ones. This time changes in rhythm, intensity and meaning depending on the specific period of the cycle; a permanent cycle of qualities is brought up over and over again. The *linear* time perception is mainly associated with the modern era in history. Time is in this view like a straight line without a beginning, or end, and without any variations of rhythm. Furthermore, time is seem to be irreversible and cumulative with a homogeneous inexorable duration. Time has also been regarded as *distinct events*, or connected 'points'. Time in this sense is neither a continuum nor a duration. Compare, for example, when we say that 'time or history accelerates', thereby referring to particularly eventful periods when the 'density' of 'points' or events or actions is higher than usual.[2] Some researchers have also pointed out signs of a *multitemporal* situation. This concept may have two different meanings. On the one hand, multitemporalism means that all three perceptions of time referred to above always exist in various proportions in every period of history. On the other hand, the term has been used to characterise a notion of time particular to the post-modern era, one that stands in contrast to the linear time of the modern age. Owing to the fact that people in the post-modern era participate in an increasing number of systems of social interaction, there is a 'plurality of times', pluritemporalism (Nowotny, 1992: 483–91).

Bureaucratic politics of time

Temporal dimensions of administration have been investigated in more depth, particularly with regard to governmental terms of office and national budget processes. Schlesinger (1994) has examined how the transition from opposition to government, and the different phases between elections and the term of office of governments, have a great impact on the nature of the ambitions and actions of political parties (Schlesinger, 1994). When a government takes office it is under extreme pressure of time. The ministers soon discover that immediate concerns take up most of their time, leaving little over for longer-term questions and planning. At the same time, the possibilities of pursuing change are best at the beginning of a mandate period when the government's legitimacy is at its height, and before opposition and other interests have been effectively organised. Consequently, the government pursues different strategies in the different phases. Bergström (1987) found that the preparation of both the government and the opposition hardly extended beyond the mandate period. The parties did very little before an election to translate their programmes into plans for concrete action that could be taken in the event of an election victory. Thus, the recurrent phases of government did not significantly affect the predominantly linear planning horizons of the political parties for one term in office. In contrast to the party political level, there are important *circular* temporal rhythms *within* national government and administration, such as the annual national budgetary procedures. Owing to the very strict timetable and deadlines for decisions, these procedures put a strong time pressure on national politicians and civil servants, who feel they have very little control over the process (Brunsson, 1995: 21). During certain periods of the working year, the budgetary timetable functions as the main coordinating device in national policy-making. In order to present the budget to the parliament in time, the government sets a strict timetable that regulates when the ministries and the governmental agencies and their respective part of the procedures must be concluded. This timetable is translated into internal timetables at all levels of administration. What accounts for the repetitive and almost ritualistic character of the budgetary process is the fact that public administration is continuous, while budgetary resources are appropriated for only limited periods.

The strictness of budgetary deadlines in the relationship between government and parliament, which is of such crucial importance for the public administration and the state as a whole, often has considerable political consequences. It has, for example, been found that many contradictions in the government's declared 'rational' management and presentation of the budget process are caused by the need of giving priority to the meeting of the deadlines (Brunsson, 1995: 182–183). Never is time such a manifest and significant political factor in the modern welfare state as in the budgetary process. However, most parts of the administration are affected by this process during only a limited period of the year – mainly from September to November for the Swedish specialised ministries (Brunsson, 1995: 12–15). In terms of the definitions used in this book, the temporal dimension of the national budgetary process is as a political factor more one of form than of meaning. In the Swedish case, the governmental budget has not been used as a planning instrument *vis-á-vis* the public administration. Hence the budget dialogue between the cabinet and the bureaucracy concerns narrow fiscal issues of limited importance for the everyday activity of the civil service and the political time horizons. There is a sharp contrast between the language the cabinet uses to depict its long-term (progressive) goals and reforms, and the recurrent fiscal discussions it has with the bureaucracy about resources (Amnå, 1981).

In the search for a temporality beyond the modern administration, Ronfeldt (1992) has developed the concept of 'cyberocracy', which he bases on an investigation of how new communications technologies, and the acceleration in the diffusion of information, have affected Western state bureaucracies. One consequence is a change in the time horizons of bureaucrats, which results in officials' 'detachment from history' (Ronfeldt, 1992: 243–296). The behavioural and organisational changes within bureaucracy owing to the information technology revolution ('the information society') have been explained as a result of the 'overloading' of information, which puts pressure on bureaucrats to act as quickly as possible.

The result of the information revolution for national bureaucracy is, according to Ronfeldt, very difficult to foresee. What is clear is that both integrative and disintegrative, positive and negative tendencies are at work within bureaucracy (Ronfeldt, 1992: 267). On the one hand the new technology enables politicians and officials to 'conquer time' in the sense that the technology makes them more able to move in time and space between different issue areas. On the other, the high speed of communication has strong decentralising effects, leading to instability of bureaucratic organisations, demands for governments to strengthen centralised control and the constant adaptation of the central state administration. In Ronfeldt's view, one thing is certain: the changing possibilities for communication constantly alter the bureaucrats' perception of time.[3] Others have talked about how the revolution in information technology has made possible 'the colonisation of time' in analogy to the earlier colonisation of space (Carey, 1988). The characteristics of fast decisions in high-velocity environments are similar to industry and private firms. Fast decision-makers tend to use more information and develop more alternatives for action than do slow decision-makers. The shape of strategy and performance is to a very high degree determined by the speed of decision processes (Eisenhardt, 1989).

Edelman (1988) examines how the construction of a political 'event' largely depends on the *timing* of the presentation of a political initiative. In other words, what is of increasing importance is an understanding of *when* the construction of political language is carried out *in time*. The timing of the change in interpretation constitutes to a large extent the essence of political action. From these reasons, it follows that the calculation of potential political gains from a strategic act comes first in the 'chain' of change.

Statecraft: pace replacing space

Virilio (1984, 1986) has taken up the 'spatio-temporal' dimension in studies of the constantly heightened speed of communications within the area of war techniques. The techniques of war have to a large extent determined the institutional and organisational set-up of the state, as well as the cognitive framework of its decision-makers, including their time perspectives. During the cold war, the warning time for war diminished radically and resulted in an 'automation of decision' at the cost of 'political reasons'. The time for national security decisions contracted to between five and ten seconds:

> The transition from the state of siege of wars of space to the state of emergency of the war of time only took several decades, during which the political era of the statesman was replaced by the apolitical era of the State apparatus. (Virilio, 1986: 140)

The techniques of nuclear deterrence, or as Virilio puts it, 'the means of communicating destruction', replaced geostrategy with *time calculations* in war planning. Space was replaced by pace. The reduction of the margin of manoeuvre in the 'state of emergency', implied, for example, an 'extreme concentration of responsibilities for the solitary decision-maker that the Chief of State has become' (1986: 149–151).

> In this precarious fiction speed would suddenly become a destiny, a form of progress, in other words a 'civilisation' in which each speed would be something of a 'region' of time … The final power would thus be less one of imagination than of anticipation, so much so that to govern would be *no more than* to foresee, simulate, memorize the simulations; that the present 'Research Institute' could appear to be the blueprint of this final power, the power of utopia. (Virilio, 1986: 141)

Der Derian (1987) has developed the analysis of what he calls 'late-modern', time diplomacy, based on new techniques of power and 'representations of danger' for the constitution and mediation of estrangement between states. The techniques of communication have not only distanced the actors from each other. In addition, as a result of the growth of electronic media, 'images' have become the main sources of diplomatic behaviour, irrespective of both the distance between the actors and whether the image reflects the original meaning of the sender's message. Der Derian calls the new situation the 'hyper-mediated' diplomacy of late modernity (Der Derian, 1992: 7), a concept built on his analyses of the impact of media, particularly television, on decision-making: 'These new techniques of power are transparent and pervasive, more "real" in time than in space, and produced and sustained through the exchange of signs rather than goods' (Der Derian, 1992: 3).

Because of these techniques there are today, according to Der Derian, new forces and powers in the international system:

> To clarify: they [the forces] are 'chronopolitical' in the sense that they elevate chronology over geography, pace over space in their political effects; they are 'tech-

nostrategic' in that they use and are used by technology for the purpose of war; they
have a discursive power in that they produce and are sustained by historically tran-
sient discourses which mediate our relations with empirical events; and the problematic is late (or post-) modern because it defies the grand theories or definitive
structures which impose rationalist identities or binary oppositions to explain
international relations. (Der Derian, 1992: 3)

Furthermore, time and timing have also been extensively analysed within
the area of crisis management, e.g. as regards third-party intervention for mediation in conflicts and synchronicity in government actions (Zartman, 1985;
Kleiboer and 't Hart, 1995; Sundelius, Stern and Bynander, 1997). Ruggie (1998)
argues that foreign policy makers, as well as researchers, need to base their
analysis on 'conjunctural' and 'epochal', rather than 'incremental' and short-
term 'temporal forms', in order to cope with contemporary global problems
such as the sustainability of resource bases, the capacity of ecosystems, and
global population issues.

European temporality explored
The exceptions to the neglect of the time dimension in European governance
have been of an explorative nature. For example, Tilly (1994) argues that the
European Community (EC) threatens the heart of modern nation-state time,
which has been based on official clocks and calendars, the control of timing of
all kinds of activities (travel, holiday, payment of taxes, etc.), and demands for
citizens' time for state service (directly – e.g. military service – and indirectly –
necessary work time for payment of tax):

> Eventually, however, the Community most likely will resume steps that subvert both
> circumscription and central control at a national scale: common currency, mobility
> of capital, free movement of labor, enhanced flow of communication, ready transfer
> of technology, coalescence of educational systems, and similar forms of pooling
> mandated by the Maastricht pact. In all these regards, the influence of individual
> state actions on the overall timing of activity will greatly diminish. (Tilly, 1994: 16)

Furthermore, the high pace of the EU decision-making process owing to
demands for efficiency threatens national democratic participation (Sverdrup,
1996). Elements of a new sense of time have been found in perceptions and practices of politicians and civil servants within EU member-state administrations
with a stronger focus on *the present* in political action than outside European
governance (Ekengren, 1996a, 1996b). Jacobsson (1997) has also found that the
political 'now' has been given increased importance in the Swedish democracy
discourse of the 1990's relating to the European Union. The temporal effects of
Europeanisation on national democracy, and the predictability of politics, are
very similar to the consequences of internationalisation in general (Jerneck and
Stenelo, 1996).

As seen in this section, the weighting of politics towards the political past,
present and future has been dependent on the historical–institutional context

and of great importance in determining the character of policy-making. The way the political language is oriented towards the future in the modern state is certainly of fundamental importance for the logic of, for example, policy formulation. There is now a need to investigate in depth the difference for European governance and elaborate a framework for systematic empirical research. Why has the temporal dimension of European governance so far been ignored?

Towards a temporal perspective on European governance

The lost dimension

In the study of European integration and governance, most of the mainstream approaches[4] have conceived of change in terms of the '*limits* and *territory* of state sovereignty and authority', 'new *boundaries* between internal and external politics', spill over between, or overlapping, *(multi-) levels* and *fields* of competences and governance. On a closer examination it can be noted that these theories have presented only *one* dimension of change, namely 'real' and perceived alterations of the *spatial* delimitation and organisation of jurisdictions and sovereignty. The result is that these approaches have overlooked the possibility that the temporal dimension of politics has also changed with the emergence of European governance. These approaches have thus, in my view, tended to be based on the unwarranted a-historical assumption that the discourses and practices in terms of which European governance has been organised resemble those prevalent in the nation-states in most aspects except with regard to matters of *scale*. The point of departure of this study is the assumption that the political discourse and practices of European governance have also had a distinct evolution *in and over time*, and that the interpretation of this logic is as important for our understanding of the politics of European governance as the examination of its spatial content.

MACRO: LOST POST-MODERN EVIDENCE

Ruggie (1993), in a very influential article has drawn the conclusion that 'the [European] community may constitute nothing less than the emergence of the first truly postmodern international political form' (1993: 140). He argues that modern political forms are based on the Renaissance invention of the central perspective and on territorial thinking. Interesting to note is that the central (single) perspective originally developed within painting, the most spatial of all art forms.[5]

> From the vantage point of the present analysis, however, a very different attribute of the EC comes into view: it may constitute the first 'multiperspectival polity' to emerge since the advent of the modern era. That is to say, it is increasingly difficult to visualise the conduct of international politics among community members, and to a considerable measure even domestic politics, as though it took place from a starting point of twelve separate, single, fixed viewpoints. Nor can models of strategic interaction do justice to this particular feature of the EC, since the collectivity of

members as a singularity, in addition to the central institutional apparatus of the EC, has become party to the strategic interaction game. (Ruggie, 1993: 171–172)

von Bogdandy (1993) emphasises that the process of European integration represents a 'completely new form of stability in the international system' (1993: 23). This implies that European integration should not be seen as a transitory stage towards a more 'developed' form of political organisation (federation, state), but instead as a form in its own right. This form is in von Bogdandy's view characterised by its 'pluralistic and polycentric structure':

> The new structures cannot be understood in the traditional hierarchical sense. The old centres and the new centre in the political and administrative system form elements of a system of interaction without a clear apex. Rather, a weak political system which, unlike the nation-state, in no way claims to represent all of society is revealing itself. The same can be said of the relation between the national and the Community system of law which, contrary to all tradition, are understood as two systems of law working side-by-side on one territory. The extent of this polycentrism goes far beyond comparable processes within individual states. (von Bogdandy, 1993: 27)

What von Bogdandy seems to say is that we need several towers from which we can view what he calls 'the contours of integrated Europe'. One centre does not, according to von Bogdandy, seem to materialise. In this sense his perspective comes very close to Ruggie's. Hence, both Ruggie and von Bogdandy try to challenge the terminology of modern political organisation that has its basis in spatial conceptions and definitions. Nørgaard (1994) sees the Community's fragmentation of 'universal constructions', resulting in a pluralism of political and social institutions, as a typical post-modern phenomenon:

> The EC is a new configuration of international space, but it does not supplant the states. EC authority is functionally delimited, but by implication the post-1992 state has become a non-sovereign entity. EC politics represents authority without unity and policy-making without democratic legitimacy. Rather, centralisation through segmentation, rationalisation through technocratisation, and democratisation through marketisation have become dominant institutional characteristics of EC politics. (Nørgaard, 1994: 276)

As this quotation indicates, Nørgaard is cautious with regard to the historical significance of this spatial qualitative transformation of international relations. Similarly, Wæver (1994) is unsure about the character of the units that would make up a post-modern international world:

> These do not have to be necessarily one type of like units, but we need to have an idea of what kind of units we are talking about: distinguished in time or space, in territory or informatics, continuously or discontinuously, personalized or abstract, overlapping or exclusive, etc. (Wæver, 1994: 244)

Wæver's conclusions with regard to the new Europe are very similar to those of Ruggie and Nørgaard:

> this [commenting chapter] tries to draw attention to the centrality and radicality of the multilayered character for the new Europe. It challenges basic assumptions of traditional FPA [Foreign Policy Analysis]; it raises new questions, like the logic of interaction between state-like units at several levels (the motor of the neorealist integration scenario); and it asks for the kind of foreign policy that will evolve among units that are increasingly unlike. Differentiated as to function, and maybe implicitly acknowledging suzerainty-like hierarchies, they will develop kinds of diplomatic relations and foreign policies that we best anticipate by reading about 'proto-diplomacy' in Der Derian's *On Diplomacy*. (Wæver, 1994: 271)

A deeper understanding could, in Wæver's view, be reached by further empirical studies of 'the very basic ways of conceiving of political time and space' (Wæver, 1994: 243).

Jørgensen (1997b) defines his new unit of analysis, 'The Diplomatic Republic of Europe', by means of the informal rules, routines and standard operating procedures that the national foreign policy-maker has to learn when entering into it. The term 'Diplomatic Republic' is intended to point beyond the sheer sum of fifteen separate traditions; there is a process of learning 'the grammar of appropriateness in the diplomatic republic', which in its great impact is unique. This 'grammar' is presented as an expression of a new level of European foreign policy integration, which in the long run might create a new foreign policy identity. It has been concluded that polity ideas about the overall order of how Europe should be organised matters highly (Jachtenfuchs, Diez and Jung, 1998). Also here, however, the main qualitative differences between the new order and the nation-state seems to be that of level and scale.

Risse-Kappen (1996) argues that it is the 'multilevel' character of the Union that makes it unique. This type of governance differs from the single-level one with regard to the conditions for democracy, citizen participation and publicity. What accounts for these differences is the complexity involved in keeping the levels interlocked and the diminished possibilities of overview and accountability created by overlapping political layers. Recent analyses of the 'Euro-polity' have only confirmed that the uniqueness of the new patterns has to do with the interplay between the European and the state level (Majone, 1996; Marks *et. al.*, 1996; Scharpf, 1999). Terms such as 'Condominio' (Schmitter, 1996), 'multi-tier' (Kohler-Koch, 1997), 'multi-framework, multi-lateral and multi-purpose' (Wallace, 1999) have been elaborated in order to specify its complexity.

The claim that the Community/Union represents a fundamental change and 'uniqueness' in the international state system has been strongly questioned throughout the history of the organisation. Such doubts have been developed along two closely connected lines of argument, namely that the nation-state system is still rigorous, and that the empirical underpinnings of the claim have been weak. Some responses to Ruggie's 1993 article were telling:

> On the basis of my own empirical research, I must therefore conclude that states continue to adapt to ongoing changes in the world economy and that firms continue to value their national identity, since only the state can assist them in international

negotiations over such issues as market access and regulation. If this is true, it means that the old-fashioned language of political science, with its emphasis on 'power', 'interests', and the 'state', is still useful for articulating the nature of the international system (Kapstein, 1993: 503) ... Those, like Ruggie, who wish to make claims for some fundamental transformation of the international system by nonstate actors owe us more than a thought piece; they owe us a theory. (Kapstein, 1993: 502)

The argument above is very significant in the questioning of the claim that the change represented by the Union is a fundamental one. It quite convincingly pushes the question up to a more general level about what territorial unit remains the *dominant* one in the international system.[6] Few would also deny that in order to question the state as the building block of the territorial organisation of the international, or even the European system, more empirical studies are urgently needed. This book will provide not only meta-theoretical and empirical grounds to challenge the state-centric and intergovernmentalist view of change and European governance, but also a new dimension of change. The potential of a new dimension of change not rooted in territorial thinking is great. My findings will indicate that the strongest forces of change in today's European relations may be found in the temporal dimension of interactions. My study thus considerably strengthens the claim that a fundamental change has taken place owing to the fact that European governance also represents a post-modern logic of policy-making over and in time.

MESO: LOST SIGHT OF A NEW POLICY STLE

'Network' and 'network governance', have become catchwords for the new political–administrative organisation of Europe. Their main purpose has been to point out the *existence* and proliferation of networks between bureaucracies and economic actors.

One of the results of this research is that we can conclude that public policymakers *are* affected by a new network mode of governance in the European Union, that there is *congruence* of the actors' perspective on the principles of policy-making (Kohler-Koch and Eising, 1999). An adjacent area of investigation has dealt with the *extension* of today's European networks (Friis and Murphy, 1999; Wallace, 1999). We still know relatively little, however, about *how* the new patterns affect public policy and administration (Richardson, 1996; Börzel, 1997; Matlary, 1997; Jönsson, Elgström and Strömvik, 1998). It is widely acknowledged that the Union has acquired the policy-making attributes of a modern state, but the complexities of the processes and the variation between different issues, policy areas and sectors make generalisations about a distinctive type of governance very difficult (e.g. Richardson, 1996; Stone Sweet and Sandholtz, 1998; Kohler-Koch and Eising, 1999).

In sectoral studies, analysts of European policy networks have tried to remedy the weaknesses with regard to explanation of outcome (Wallace and Wallace, 1996; Armstrong and Bulmer, 1998; Bartle, 1999; Daugbjerg, 1999). By means of comparative approaches, differences of 'Europeanisation' between national administrations have been revealed (Wessels and Rometsch, 1996; Harmsen, 1999). Thus, there is still a need to ascertain whether politics and policy-making *function* differently generally in European governance, compared to the nation-state. What happens to policy-making in European networks and governance: what happens to the very nature of politics? A temporal perspective will show that the meso-level approach of sector-specific and comparative Europeanisation studies underestimate the convergence in the way Europe is governed.

MICRO: LOST POINT OF IDENTITY COMPARISON

What are the implications of European governance for the formulation and implementation of policies? What is the relevance of European governance for policy process and outcome at the micro level? Answers to the questions are urgent considering the steadily growing importance of European governance and networks in both a theoretical and empirical, as well as a normative sense (Jachtenfuchs, 1995, 1997; Diez, 1997; Jørgensen, 1997c; Kohler-Koch and Eising, 1999).

One reason behind the lack of micro-level approaches has been weaknesses in the theory and methods of many traditional studies of European integration and governance. Change on the micro level has in many parts been left in the dark owing to the preponderance of the reified 'old' and 'visible' structures ('the state', 'EU institutions') through which processes have been studied. These studies have not only been unable to reveal the deeper processes of European interaction but, more importantly, to distinguish them from other governance. There have been promising steps taken towards new so-called 'reflective approaches' to European governance. These are approaches that strengthen the focus on the perception, conceptualisation and practice of policy-making by people involved in European governance – the roots of an emerging new system of governance (Kohler-Koch, 1996; Jørgensen, 1997c). In order to take the study of the micro level further, there is now a need to elaborate conceptions and frameworks of analysis on the basis of which the nation-state and European governance can be clearly distinguished. The time dimension makes the contrasts appear more sharply.

Adam (1990) is right in pointing out that a focus on time helps us to identify new points of departure for social theory. The present book will show that a focus on time is 'no longer a luxury' (1990: 169).

Reflective approaches to European governance

EUROPEAN GOVERNANCE

As mentioned, European governance is seen below as a historically unique world view or practice of the legitimate management of political relationships and problem-solving institutions *beyond* (not above) the state. European governance actors are people embracing the world view or practically involved in this management.

There are many advantages of focusing on the understanding of the European Union and European policy-making as a system of governance. First, governance has generally been equated with the emergence of norm and rule-like systems and problem-solving devices (Rosenau and Czempiel, 1992), which makes it sufficiently broad for the transcending of the traditional borderline between domestic and European politics. This is of great importance in the investigation of a system in which the core of political life to an increasing extent has been situated *between* the national and the European levels (Kohler-Koch, 1997). The concept of 'multilevel' governance has put emphasis on the variety of 'degrees of transnational and transgovernmental *Politikverflechtung* rather than intergovernmental bargaining' (Risse-Kappen, 1996: 72). The great historical significance of today's European governance has even called for a new constitutional vocabulary, e.g. 'Federatio', 'Confederatio', 'Consortio', 'Condominio' (Schmitter, 1996). These are the underlying reasons why I do not search, for example, for a 'time logic of policy-making in the Union' (too closely associated with formal EU institutions) or an 'EU member-state logic' (restricted to the traditional delimitation of states).

Second, European governance also usefully reshapes our conception of comparative European politics. My method is to investigate the temporal dimension of European governance, with the help of empirical material that would traditionally be defined as 'national'. European governance has been shown to denote truly European policy-making ('the Euro-Polity', Schmitter, 1996, or the 'European policy process', Mörth, 1996). The concept has successfully guided empirical examination of such areas as 'the political economy of European welfare states', 'the European social policy regime', 'the competences of regional actors in the Union', 'EU social movements', 'European environmental governance', 'European social policy' (Cornett and Caporaso, 1992; Marks *et al.*, 1996; Kohler-Koch and Eising, 1999).[7] What recent research has clearly shown is how the patterns of participation of European actors (from national and European administrations, business and trade union organisations, etc.) in EU policy-making are fused into a European policy process (Wallace and Young, 1997). Thus, it is important to remember that the empirical material used in this work is first and foremost an expression of European governance rather than examples of national politics.

THEORETICAL BACKGROUND

Like many time researchers of today, I believe that the emerging perception of post-state time 'cannot be encompassed by classical theories based on a separation of past, present and future, linear causality and a positivist methodology' (Adam, 1995: 124). Calls for interpretative approaches to social time have been frequent (Fabian, 1983; Adam, 1990; Bourdieu, 1990; Nowotny, 1992). The theoretical downgrading of political time in studies of European governance has been explained by the very nature of a positivistic–structuralistic tradition – the origin of mainstream European integration theories – which philosophically has its foundations in concepts of space, extension and networks. In this spatially dominated discipline, the dimension of time has tended to be ignored (Ekengren, 1996a).

The time theory debate has been echoed in the discussions of international relations (IR) theory in the 1990s. The IR theory debate translated the positivistic –interpretative and explanation–understanding poles in social science into a theoretical dichotomy. Keohane (1989) coined the concepts of 'rationalistic' and 'reflective' theories of change of the international system. In the rationalistic perspective, the sovereign state is taken for granted as a premise in the investigations of the rational calculations and decisions of governments. The only dependent variable is the decision-making alternatives between which the actor chooses. Keohane calls the second view 'reflective' because, in contrast to the rationalistic view, it emphasises change in policy makers' thinking about their decision-making framework (e.g. norms of sovereignty, national identities and interest, international system characteristics) in which they evaluate alternative options. This kind of change might be due to participation in new practices – for example, in new institutions of world politics. Keohane suggested the study of these practices as a research task for reflective theory, which, according to him, was seriously weakened by its lack of a research programme (Keohane, 1989: 173).

To answer Keohane, this book's aim is to show how a presumed shift from ideas and practices of reified state time seems to emerge from actors' interpretations of complex interactions within European governance. These theoretical and empirical concerns in the study of time and IR are the origin of my own selection of theories and methods. My search for new approaches to time and European governance has been greatly inspired by recent discussions on post-positivistic theories of the international system (Smith, Booth and Zalewski, 1996) and European governance (Jørgensen, 1997c). The reflective approaches in the book are not chosen only for their particular strength in the study of social time, but also for their empirical potential and value in the study of European governance in general. The following section discusses the advantages of reflective approaches, but also their weaknesses, particularly with regard to their underemphasis of agency and their still relatively poor empirical record.

A NEW FOCUS

Besides Keohane, those who have set the parameters for the development of a reflective approach to international relations and European governance studies include Dessler, Wendt, Adler and P.M. Haas. In Dessler's terms, reflective approaches should be capable of identifying and classifying rules of various sorts (1989: 444). In Wendt's (1992) view, change must be understood as a process of identity and interest formation in which states constantly internalise new understandings of themselves and of other states. It is, according to Wendt, mainly through relations with other states that the individual state acquires new role identities and interests. Practice exists before the norm. To illustrate international change, Wendt depicts how Western Europe formed a collective European identity after the Second World War. This development was largely brought about through setting up collaborative institutions, that became associated with 'new intersubjective understandings and commitments' (Wendt, 1992: 417). Preliminary empirical research on these theoretical premises has given rise to conceptions such as socially constructed 'communities', based on collective normative knowledge (Ruggie, 1993; Neumann, 1994; Adler, 1997) or 'international politics' (Wendt, 1995). Jørgensen has shown how reflectivism embraces many different theories, which makes it more appropriate to talk about 'reflective approaches'. In contrast to Keohane, Jørgensen does not make a distinction between reflective and interpretative approaches. Instead, he convincingly shows how all reflective approaches have their philosophical roots in phenomenology and ethnomethodology, the linguistic tradition, hermeneutics, critical theory and the tradition of genealogy.[8] 'Reflectivism is, in short, a metatheoretical category and not a theory' (Jørgensen, 1997a: 4). Like Matlary, I believe that reflective theory has shown its greatest comparative advantages within the field of epistemology, despite the fact that it has come to include approaches (e.g. parts of constructivism and the discursive tradition) that also suggest new ontological outlooks (Matlary, 1997: 203–204).

Well-grounded empirical research inspired by reflective approaches grew steadily in the 1990s (Klein, 1990; Onuf, 1994; Young, 1994; Christiansen and Jørgensen, 1995; Matlary, 1995; Wæver, 1995; Wendt, 1995; Wind, 1996a, 1996b). However, there is still a rather wide gap between metatheoretical and theoretical contributions on the one hand and empirical research on the other. In large part this gap can be accounted for by the strong emphasis on theoretical development that has naturally come to characterise reflectivism in its early years when it challenged traditional 'rational' IR theory (Jørgensen, 1997c; Matlary, 1997). In other words, reflective approaches, and particularly their constructivist strand, have lacked middle-range theories able to address when, how and why social construction matters – theories that can clearly specify the actors and mechanisms that bring about change and how they vary from country to country, thereby avoiding 'empirical ad hocism' (Checkel, 1998: 325). The relatively low empirical value of reflective approaches in general is closely connected to the questions related to the relationship between agency and structure, in both theory and empirical research.

There is a tension between the broadly recognised and well-documented macrotransformations, conceptualised as world views, identities and epistemic communities that the reflective theories have convincingly shown, and a feeling that reflective studies are not empirically rich enough to count as valuable as, for example, neorealist contributions. The investigations have shown that policymakers are affected, but have failed to define the relationship between *agent* and *structure* with the sophistication required by a theory capable of generating practical empirical research strategies – that is, research able to answer the question of how decision-makers use rules and norms (Checkel, 1998; Krause, 1998):

Today we know little about the impact of EU institutions on member-states because we have few historical studies that trace how formal rules are practiced, how informal rules constrain new entrants, how the policy initiative of the Commission determines the agenda and influences how one views the policy problem, and so on. (Matlary, 1997: 212)

APPROACHING TIME

The reflective approaches used in this book are all grounded on philosophical realism and, as a consequence, the view that empirical research is meaningful. To be clear: an interpretative epistemological outlook on political events and structures, many of which are of course socially constructed, does not imply ontological constructivism. The notions of time, the practical sense of time and the human consciousness of time investigated in this book are non-material facts of reality. They are 'social facts', in contrast to 'brute' facts, 'which are true (or not) apart from any shared beliefs that they are true' (Ruggie, 1998: 13). The main research question concerns how we best might gain knowledge about these social phenomena. Reflective approaches hold that the best methods are those providing frameworks for an interpretation of how the subjects of study understand their own situation, for reflectivism, unlike positivism, does not believe that social and political life can be studied from the outside, from a neutral tower of observation, treating actions as decontextualised behaviours, but rather that it has to be understood 'from within' (see p. 20).

Reflective models were first used to examine changes in state interests and forms. However, this strength in rule identification is even more needed when norms beyond the state are in question (Jørgensen, 1997c). Here the task is to define change, not by describing something in relation to established state rules, but by delineating inductively whole new fields of study (Bourdieu, 1990; Wind, 1997). What is there beyond the state? As the empirical chapters 2–4 will show, reflective approaches embrace advanced methodological instruments to deal with the classical problems inherent in induction of making as few pre-assumptions as possible in empirical investigation without losing sight of what to look for. To classify the temporal rules of European governance calls for both very stringent but also inductively open methods of norm identification in everyday policy-making (Ekengren, 1996a, 1996b).

EXPLAINING AND UNDERSTANDING

The aim of my work is not to establish causality between brute facts of real institutions and a new social time. However, my approach does not exclude the existence of a relationship between this reality and human ideas and practice. The relationship is conceived of as human 'sense making'. This focus on human interpretation implies that ideas can be causes as well as practice in the complex mutual relationship between agency and structure sketched above. By striking a new balance between agency and structure in the study of European governance, the theories in this work also implies a particular view of the mixture of understanding and explanation components in social science research. Reflective approaches have always struggled with the question of to what degree their main mission of interpretation and understanding should also contain elements of explanation (Jørgensen, 1997a: 4–5; Matlary, 1997: 203–205; Ruggie, 1998: 1–39, 85–101).

When we say that an event was *caused* by another, we don't mean that we can observe such causality, as in natural science, but that we can establish the *likelihood* of one explanation over another. The background factors to the experienced tension can be found in the debate between IR researchers whose works are grounded on a scientific – realistic (in the philosophical sense) – positivistic view, and spokesmen of a hermeneutic approach. Smith (a scholar of the former tradition) argues that structures/rules 'remain, in a critical sense, external' (Hollis and Smith, 1990: 206) to the decision-makers, and that the task of the researcher is to explain how action, perceptions and beliefs are conditioned by structures:

> Thus, I do not think that I have a particular problem merely because I see structures in the social world and yet cannot prove, in a Positivist sense, their existence. Rather, my notion of structure is that positing their existence gives us the best explanation of social action … These structures may be as specific as the bureaucratic structure of a state, or as general as the structures of racism, patriarchy, and class. (Hollis and Smith, 1990: 207)

Hollis, on the other hand, stresses that the 'world' and the 'reality' the researchers and the observed actor are dealing with are social constructions: 'International relations are what the rules (such as they are) and the decisions of foreign policymakers (and others) create' (Hollis and Smith, 1990: 203). Consequently, the actors always have a great room of manoeuvre for their actions, and are not in any sense 'determined' by structure. Furthermore, their disagreements emanate from their view of the importance and the consequences of understanding the actor 'from within'. Smith believes that a focus on the insider's view 'overemphasises the realm of choice and underemphasises the realm of constraints' (Hollis and Smith, 1990: 206). 'My individuals come in as members of bureaucracies, dominated by their role and with little freedom of manoeuvre' (Hollis and Smith, 1990: 211). Hollis' short answer is: 'unlike you, I regard it as crucial that the actual players are bureaucrats, not bureaucracies' (1990: 213). The problem is in various forms formulated as a clear choice, for example: 'to understand the rules governing action is to understand action. To affirm it is to hold that rules (or institutions) make the actors; to deny it is to hold that actors make the rules' (1990: 215). The authors conclude that the two traditions are very hard to reconcile: 'The implications of this is that in all discussions of social life there are always and inevitably two stories to be told, one concentrating on Understanding, the other focusing on Explaining' (Hollis and Smith, 1990: 211).

Hollis and Smith were not alone in the far-reaching agency–structure debate that paved the way for much reflectivist research in the 1990s (Wendt, 1987; Carlsnaes, 1992, 1993; Ruggie, 1998: 199–255).

One of the most developed and influential models was Carlsnaes' (1992) synthesis of structural and agential factors in the understanding and explanation of foreign policy change: 'the policies of states are a consequence of, and can only be fully explained with reference to, a dynamic process in which both agents and structures causally condition each other over time' (Carlsnaes, 1992: 256).

I believe that the best way to give proof of the strengths and to contribute to remedying the weaknesses of reflective approaches is to let my empirical findings speak for themselves. By taking seriously the empirical insights that have evolved during decades within the narrative–interpretative, ethnomethodological and socio-semantic traditions, my studies will be an answer to the charge that reflective approaches have only metatheoretical value. It is in the modelling and carrying out of empirical research that the operationalisation of the relationship between macro and micro, agency and structure and understanding and explaining will take concrete shape. The findings will show the degree to which the dichotomies of explaining–understanding, agent–structure, objectivism–subjectivism, freedom–determinism and conscious/intentional–unconscious/unintentional action will be developed and transcended.

Notes

1 See, e.g., *International Political Science Review,* (1998), referred to in chapter 5, which breaks new ground for the study of 'time and democracy'.
2 For an overview, see Fraser (1968).
3 It was the Swedish geographer Hägerstrand who laid the foundation for systematic research of the relationship between social time and space in his investigations of geographical diffusion waves (Hägerstrand, 1968). He discovered general rules of how waves of innovations, communications and messages change in character as a function of the distance both from the time and the geographical point of origin.
4 In 'mainstream approaches' I include functionalism (Mitrany, 1966; Taylor, 1990), federalism (Pinder, 1991), neo-functionalism (Haas, 1958; Schmitter, 1969; Lindberg and Scheingold, 1970), intergovernmentalism/neoinstitutionalism (Keohane and Hoffmann, 1991; Moravcsik, 1998), transactionalism (Deutsch *et al.*, 1957), regime theory (Mayer, Rittberger and Zürn, 1993), the interdependence literature (Keohane and Nye, 1975), but also most recent attempts, such as combinations of 'all the classic schools' (Kelstrup, 1992) or conceptualisations like the Community's 'multiperspectival' (Ruggie, 1993) or 'polycentric' (von Bogdandy, 1993) character.
5 Ruggie's concept comes very close to some earlier attempts to provide a new conceptual basis for the analysis of change in global politics. Among these can be mentioned James Rosenau's (1990) depiction of a 'multicentric world'. It is here interesting to note that also in the most recent examinations of change in the international system in general, the spatial dimension is still very dominant. Rosenau has for example attempted to produce evidence of fundamental change by deliminating a new political space, 'the Frontier', 'in-between' international and domestic politics (1997).
6 For the more specific intergovernmentalist or neoinstitutionalist arguments in favour of a conception of the Union as based on a state-centric system see, for example, Keohane and Hoffmann (1991) and Moravcsik (1991).
7 During the last few years the notion of 'governance' has also been developed within traditional 'domestic' policy areas (labour market, education policy, environmental regulation,

etc.), in terms of public management of complex networks of many different participants (governmental organisations, political and social groups, European institutions). Here, the new forms of governance have, owing to the growing variety of forms of interaction between government and society, and between the social and the political, resulted in a slide from the hierarchical governance of government to more horizontal systems of regulation in which self-government plays a more important role (Kooiman, 1993).

8   Jørgensen takes as a point of departure Neufeld's (1993) distinction of the five philo-sophical traditions upon which reflectivism draws. The most prominent spokesmen of each tradition are Husserl and Schütz (phenomenology/ethnomethodology), Wittgenstein, Winch and Taylor (the linguistic tradition), Heidegger and Gadamer (the hermeneutic tradition), Marx and Habermas (critical theory) and Nietzsche and Foucault (the tradition of genealogy).

2

The oligopoly of the future
The changed status of political promise

From ex ante evaluation to scanning the future

At the end of 1988, the Social Democratic Under-Secretary of Foreign Trade responsible for relations with the European Community, Carl Johan Åberg, argued under the headline 'Who will decide in Sweden?', that EC membership would seriously reduce national autonomy. This was not the case in other international fora in which Sweden cooperated because all the international agreements concluded there had to be approved by the Swedish parliament. Moreover, the supranationality of the European Community had, according to the Under-Secretary, been strengthened owing to the Single European Act (SEA) of 1986 which, among other things, empowered the Council of Ministers to decide by qualified majority. This made it possible to decide against individual member countries. For Sweden, this was unacceptable, Åberg claimed: 'The Swedish constitution is so deeply rooted in our history that many of us find it hard to imagine giving up a part of our rights to decide about our own destiny' (Åberg, 1988: 137).

Sweden should not participate in binding international cooperation if there was a risk of having decisions 'laid down' for 'us' from 'above'. Sweden should choose the measures it found most beneficial, a freedom it would lose if it joined the Community's more binding form of cooperation. In a speech at a Social Democratic Party meeting the same year, Åberg underlined this point:

> There is no compulsion to harmonise taxes and currencies. It is the goods market we want to coordinate, not so much other things. It will be difficult to coordinate a free movement of labour. Furthermore, we cannot accept a free right of establishment. We must first *evaluate the effects before* we can accept the 'freedoms' of the EC. (quoted in Olsson and Svenning, 1988: 26) (italics added)

One year later, in December 1989, after the fall of the Berlin Wall, the Swedish Prime Minister, Ingvar Carlsson, argued *in favour* of closer cooperation with the European Community:

> cooperation does not mean submission to somebody. West European integration is not necessarily dictated by big finance and multinational giants. One of the purposes behind our search for closer cooperation with the EC is to reach a higher degree of coordination in the struggle against unemployment. Such a struggle is also part of the visions envisaged by the President of the EC Commission, and by many Social Democrats in the member countries. In fact, it is one of their highest wishes to have Sweden participate in this work by means of our experiences of a well-functioning policy of full employment. Why should we assume that this is not possible? (Carlsson, 1989b)

The views above clearly reveal a change in the perception of the principles that should guide Sweden's political future development. In Åberg's first quotation, the representative of the Swedish government described the political future, 'our destiny', as being the outcome of purely Swedish decisions. It is something that should be under control, and for this reason decisions must be taken only after their effect on the future has been evaluated. In Carlsson's quotation, the government's conception of the nation-state's future had changed into a considerably more open attitude towards coming time, and the Swedish ambition was no longer to 'control' the future, but *to promote certain goals in cooperation with others*. The change from an approach towards the future in which the effects of decisions should be evaluated in advance to a rhetorical question about European possibilities based on common visions is significant considering the centrality of labour market and employment policy for national autonomy. What had happened during the year that separates the two views of the Social Democratic government with regard to the meaning of the political future?

This chapter studies the way politics is related to the future in European governance and how it matters for politics and policy-making. Future outcomes obviously carry more conclusive weight for Åberg than for Carlsson in motivating action. As in this book as a whole, political and institutional change is seen not as the cause of a new political consciousness but as the context from which hypotheses can be drawn about the *motivations* behind the new conceptions actors in European governance are presumed to hold. Even though institutional incentives and motivations for a new view of the future might seem very strong, it is important to remember that the actors *could* historically have developed a thinking in a different direction than what was actually the case.

Exploring the political future

The understanding of the meaning of a political 'future' was much debated during the 1990s. In 1989, Fukuyama declared 'the end of history', alluding to

today's experience of a time in which traditional ideological cleavages have with-
ered away owing to the emerging world-wide consensus about what the future
should bring. Many sociologists and geographers have concluded that 'the future'
has become an abstract phenomenon outside people's individual and local control (Giddens, 1990). A prominent place among these studies has been given to
the origin of our apprehension of the future, to 'the discovery of the future' in the
eighteenth century (Lewin, 1990), how the meaning of this future was created
(Koselleck, 1985) and incorporated into the modern state and political system
(Gross, 1985).

One of the most developed and influential methods for the exploration of
the consciousness of the future is the *semantics of historical time* elaborated by
Koselleck within the field of conceptual history or *Begriffsgeschichte*. Here, a
consciousness of historical time is interpreted from historical concepts and the
narrative structure of written history. For empirical research it is a great merit
of the semantics of historical time that it provides us with simple but acute interpretative tools for the deduction of a time content; instruments capable of producing an answer to the question: in exactly what way do different perceptions
of time differ in meaning? Another advantage of Koselleck's approach is that it
includes a programme for situating a specific time consciousness in a broader
historical context. It was the nation-state's institutionalised monopoly of the
control of the political past and future which, together with the 'temporalisation' of the way politics were formulated, created the particularity of modern
nation-states (Koselleck, 1985: 3-20). In this chapter I shall build on Koselleck's
programme, and on the closely related *socio-historical semantic school*, which
both base their recreation of human consciousness on methods of textual analysis of written historical sources.

The purpose of Koselleck's methods is to examine shifts in the meaning of
certain key concepts and the creation of new ones during selected historical
periods.[1] His main interest has been to investigate certain 'key shifts' in the early
modern period, particularly in the French and German languages. Since the
time of the French Revolution, there has, according to Koselleck, been a development towards an increased inclusion of future oriented conceptions and what
he calls 'movement' in discourses about society, for example the concept of
progress and a new ideological vocabulary created with the suffix '-ism'. Koselleck calls this development the 'temporalisation of political language'. In order
to investigate temporal consciousness on the basis of written material, Koselleck
interprets the texts from the viewpoint of two anthropological categories,
namely 'experience' and 'expectation'. He attributes the temporalisation to an
increase in the weight given to expectation at the cost of experience in the internal structure of concepts (see discussion of method on p. 30). The concept of
progress implicitly downplays the importance of earlier experience and puts
emphasis on the openness of coming time, and the newness expected from it. A
good example of a shift of temporal meaning over the centuries is the word
'republic'. Before the Enlightenment, the term connoted the clearly demarcated

field of historical rules of governance, while it subsequently came to refer to everything expected from a future non-despotic constitution. Accordingly, the extent to which some particular concept is oriented towards the past, present, and future may vary throughout history. The creation of words with the suffix -'ism' indicates movement and the legitimation of political decisions by making 'the future' more open for construction, and hence 'revolutionary'. The new political concepts not only expressed change, but also guided the transformation of society in certain directions. The concepts possess a certain autonomous power to create a new consciousness. Koselleck thus interprets historical change to be partly the result of a conceptual struggle, particularly regarding the right to define the future (Koselleck, 1989: 33; cf. Stråth, 1990; Trägårdh, 1990).

The dimension of expectation is of such great importance in defining the future, because concepts do not only register historical–political change, they occasionally promote new political arrangements as well (Koselleck, 1989: xxv). Another branch of the analysis of historical texts and discourse is lexicography. In contrast to conceptual history, this school focuses on *everyday language*, from which conclusions about 'the mentality' of the period are drawn. It is interested in language as a whole, as a system of signs and as an expression of a culture. It has been inspired by structural linguistics, which attaches great importance to the independent social status of language (Schöttler, 1989: 40). *Socio-historical semantics* has played the role of a bridge between *Begriffsgeschichte* and the linguistically oriented discourse analysis. The questions it poses are the same as those of the social and conceptual historian, while its models of empirical research have been borrowed from the lexicographic tradition. Socio-historical semantics was developed as a critique of the historical study of isolated concepts, whose historical meaning, the former claimed, can be understood only in a larger linguistic context (Reichardt, 1985: 83).[2]

Thus, socio-historical semantics focuses on the *everyday language*, which is held to reflect an historical period's collective consciousness. The methods borrowed from semantics are semiotics, symbolics and the linguistic mapping of dichotomies such as 'contradictory' and 'associated' words. Socio-historical semantics has borrowed these methods without falling in the ontological traps that have come to be associated with the tradition of discourse theory, for example 'the death of the author' in the study of texts (Schöttler, 1989: 52-53). The purpose of the linguistic loan has instead been to produce structured *encyclopaedia* of the socio-political vocabulary of the time, reflecting peoples' collective consciousness (Gumbrecht, Lüsebrink and Reichhardt, 1983; Reichardt, 1985; Schöttler, 1989).

According to socio-historical semantics, the empirical material should be selected on the grounds of its *representativeness* of the period studied, and its ability to provide material for the construction of *discursive homogeneity*. The former criterion is fulfilled by identifying the historical actors and groups, that may be considered to be involved in 'normal' linguistic praxis and change, and the latter is fulfilled by systematic delimitation and separation of synchronic linguistic fields of praxis or wholes. In the following, I shall combine Koselleck's methods of temporal anthropology and the socio-historical semantic construction of representative historical languages. The approach will be applied mainly to the case of the Swedish language of European governance.

A research model for the future

The case of Swedish

I have selected material mainly from one language used in European governance because I believe that the explorative nature of my research has more to gain from a probing examination of a single well-delimited case than from a broader comparative analysis. A study of several cases, which are chosen for the sake of generalization, pre-supposes that there is a given and recognised object of empirical analysis so that the main efforts can be devoted to collecting as much evidence as possible for, or against, this or that generalization. My project is at an earlier stage at which the object of research is as yet assumed, and its aim is to ascertain whether the presumption of a distinct meaning of the future associated with European governance is correct. In order to carry out the socio-historical semantic approach with a satisfactory amount of empirical evidence, the study needs to concentrate on a surveyable empirical material, which the single-language approach can provide, not least in the construction of coherent linguistic wholes.

There are other reasons for choosing Swedish for my case study. Sweden is one of the new members of the European Union, a fact which provides unique opportunities for the empirical investigation of the validity of the assumed difference between nation-states and European governance. First, the comparison of the two languages is facilitated by the fact that Swedish became a language of European governance at a relatively recent date. It has not been difficult to find 'national' and European governance texts of a similar character and covering the same political subject area. This eliminates many problems of comparability and makes it possible to put emphasis on my main task of a *comparison* of meanings. Second, the historical context for the emergence of the Swedish language of European governance can also be easily delimited. I believe it makes sense to talk about the intensification of Sweden's political involvement in European governance from the mid-1980s (e.g. the establishment of the Dynamic Economic Space between the European Community and the European Free Trade Association (EFTA) in 1984 that took cooperation beyond free trade) up to 1995 when the full EU membership was achieved, as a period. During this period Swedish politicians and officials were gradually incorporated into a fundamentally new managerial and institutional setting for decision-making. This process of transformation constitutes a highly relevant context for the motivation of a new consciousness of the future. Third, good command of the language on which the encyclopaedia is based is particularly important in the interpretative realm of the semantics of historical time, where a word's right value should be determined. Hence, being a native Swede, my choice of Swedish is appropriate.

Do Swedish patterns really express a European governance consciousness? Is not the Swedish encyclopaedia of European governance so unique that it would be more appropriate to talk about it in terms of Swedish governance? In relation to the broad lines of development with which I shall sketch the historical context, Sweden (and Swedish) is a normal case. Even though Sweden is a late-comer to European governance, the country's institutional as well as ideological (debates on autonomy and EU membership, etc.) paths must for my purposes be considered to be very similar to that of other states (cf. Denmark, Great Britain, France in the 1950s or at the time of the referendum on the Maastricht Treaty in 1992). However, when discussing the representativeness of the Swedish version, or 'dialect', of a European governance language, elements of a *comparative outlook* are needed. In order to prove that the Swedish linguistic version is not an exception in the family of European governance languages, I shall for the sake of comparison include excerpts of other national dialects (English, French and Italian) in my structural analysis. In order to ascertain whether or not the meaning of the future in European governance is not like one of the other international contexts, I shall contrast it to traditional diplomacy and the Council of Europe. The criteria on which the texts have been selected are two: they must be representative of the *political consciousness* of the period, and *linguistically homogeneous*. Linguistic uniformity is in my case achieved by the creation of synchronic fields of linguistic practice in national and European governance, respectively.

The *historical context* behind the motivations of the production of the chosen European governance texts was the process leading up to Swedish membership of the Union in 1995. It included new institutional arrangements (European Economic Area (EEA), European Economic space (EES), etc.) and a debate on Swedish autonomy concerning the institutional form of the country's relationship first with the Community and, later on, as a full Swedish member. The purpose of my account is not to rewrite or problematise the history of Swedish–Union relations or to present a contribution to the theoretical discussion of autonomy. The description is based on the main organisational developments and mainstream arguments, and held at a level of abstraction that I have judged appropriate for generating plausible hypotheses about why a new consciousness has been created. Other conceptual ways of describing the period could of course have been chosen (for the most recent see Jacobsson, 1997; J. Gustavsson, 1998). My goal is that the background below will give a plausible description of the erosion of the institutional and ideological conditions for the national time consciousness, conditions that were established in the sixteenth century when the nation-state replaced religion and the church as the main controller of the future (Koselleck, 1985: 3–20).

Languages of experience and expectation

I will mainly use the synchronic perspective where meaning is defined in an analysis of the word's relation to other parts of the language at a given moment. It is here that the difference of emphasis with Koselleck's diachronic investigation of various terms' evolution over time is most clearly seen. The next question concerns what, in analytical terms, should be counted as a complete, comprehensive everyday language. On how many words and expressions should the synchronic analysis be based – or, in other words, how extensive should my encyclopedia of a European governance language be? In some lexicographic models, the ambition has been to include, for example, *all* nouns found in the investigated texts, with the help of quantitative and statistical methods. The socio-historical semantic school argues that the claim of completeness must be defined in relation to the diachronic questions to be answered. Reichardt limits his analysis of changes in the French political language between 1680 and 1820 to around 500 so-called 'basic concepts' (e.g. 'philosophy', 'terrorism', 'fanatic', 'civilté').

The development of these is examined both diachronically and synchronically. In practice, this means that the structural features are not penetrated as deeply as in lexicography (Reichardt, 1985: 79). Within socio-historical semantics it is admitted that it is not possible to determine the exact reasons behind some particular historical change, whether they are historical or constituted by linguistic contradictions. The methodological consequence of this approach is the need of an argument in terms of reasonable motives for my selection of texts, what should be counted for as linguistic change (what level of detail in the history of the terms), and their relation to the historical context (Reichardt, 1985: 39). My structural analysis is based on the hypothesis that the consciousness of the future held by politicians and civil servants *outside* European governance differs from that held by those who participate in European governance.

My hypothesis calls for the putting together of both a *national* and a *European encyclopaedia of governance* from the empirical material. The former functions as the necessary diachronic point of reference, in contrast to which the contours of the time content in European governance can better be distinguished. The national encyclopaedia is of course less extensive than the European one. The aim is to reveal structural differences in the form of linguistic shifts of meaning, new concepts, metaphors and semantic constructions (Gumbrecht, Lüsebrink and Reichhardt, 1983: 192). To create synchronic languages for comparison, excerpts from French, British and Italian languages of European governance (in equivalent empirical material) are presented. Since the selected languages differ greatly in the length of time and the extent to which they have been used in European governance, to find common patterns of time consciousness among them would considerably strengthen my case. On the presumption that there is a significant difference between what could be called the *political* and the *administrative* language,[3] I make a division between the two. The analytical advantage of this division is that each of the two languages is more homogeneous when treated separately than when drawn together in one encyclopaedia. Consequently, I shall search for a consciousness of the future within two discourses; the political–ideological and the bureaucratic–administrative. The basic homogeneity helps to reveal change, diachronic as well as synchronic, more distinctly.

Furthermore, the division makes possible interesting and fruitful comparisons. Is the difference between the sense of time in national and European governance greater in the political or the bureaucratic discourse? How should the difference between the two discourses be characterised: to what extent are the great expectations of the future, that characterise nation-state time, kept within the *political* discourse of European governance, but not in its administrative discourse? Or do the two languages follow identical paths with regard to temporal content? This double analysis makes my argument more thorough and convincing. Together, the political and administrative languages mirror in a comprehensible fashion the political consciousness of the period, which is to say the predominant mentality of the political elite at the time. Time is to be recognised in the encyclopaedia with the help of the anthropological categories used by Koselleck:

> Both these categories are excellently suited for discussing historical time, for past and future are joined together in the presence of both experience and expectation. These categories are also suited for discovering historical time in empirical research, since through their content, they guide the concrete agents of social and political movement. The relation between experience and expectation is not solely a relation along a chronological line. Rather, the space of expectation and experience is somehow 'fused' in the present status. Thus, we possess all three dimensions of time in these two categories. Through the medium of certain experiences and certain expectations, concrete history is thus produced … Both temporal extensions are dependent on each other in very different ways. In experience, historical knowledge is stored that cannot be transformed seamlessly into expectation. You cannot deduce immediately from your experience to expectation. If that were possible, history would always repeat itself. Just as with memory and hope, the two dimensions are different in status. (Koselleck, 1985: 28–29)

It is with these categories in mind that I interpret the meaning of the future on the basis of expressions, metaphors and words used in the everyday languages. It is important to note that 'the future' is not to be found exclusively or even primarily in concepts necessarily connected with explicit temporal references, such as 'timetable'. All politics is generated from particular experiences and particular expectations. All time encyclopaedias have for the sake of presentation been organised into the following four categories of political time:[4] concepts and expressions referring to (1) political action; (2) longer historical trends (what I have labelled 'processes' and 'projects'); (3) qualities (competences) of political actors; (4) the correct moment for action ('timing').

Sources

The historical category is reproduced with the help of secondary sources about the institutional developments of the Swedish relationship with the Community

and a traditional content analysis of official statements, debate articles, etc. concerning Swedish national autonomy in the context European governance.

The *political language* of the day is constructed from the political programmes of the seven parties represented in the Swedish Parliament: the Christian Democrats (Kd),[5] the Environmental Party (Mp),[6] the Centre Party (C),[7]
The Conservative Party (M),[8] The Social Democratic Party (S),[9] the Left Wing
Party (V)[10] and the Liberal Party (Fp).[11] The ideological bent of the programmes and the particular political positions of the various parties with
regard to the European Union are of little importance, since it is the everyday
political discourse in which all parties share that I am interested in. The material is chosen because of its high degree of linguistic homogeneity. The texts are
examples of the way political action is formulated in general, independently of
any particular party political outlook. The programmes are chosen because
they are highly representative of the political consciousness of the institutional
situations under investigation. They are created by the people who one could
justifiably claim to be the central producers of the Swedish political language.
The language of the programmes includes virtually the whole political vocabulary of the period 1985-95. In order to distinguish the political language of the
nation-state from that of European governance, one set of materials deals with
purely national politics, while the other set concerns the parties' policies
towards the Community/Union. The obvious purpose of this division is to
construct two synchronic semantic fields, delimited by textures of connected
words, expressions and subjects. The result is the appearance of two different
languages, two mental maps: the language of politics in nation-states and in
European governance, respectively.

To compile the encyclopaedia of administration a selection of Swedish
public commission reports is used. As with the political material, one selection
of reports discusses reforms of the Swedish public administration as a response
to a perceived need of a general improvement in *efficiency* (produced 1979–82),[12]
while another group concerns, on the one hand, the consequences of Sweden's
closer cooperation with the Community for the Swedish *administration*
(1989–93) and, on the other, Swedish experience of EU *membership* (1995–96).[13]
All the Swedish reports were to a large extent based on interviews and question-
naires that were completed by Swedish civil servants of the central state apparatus. They cover a broad spectrum of the administration, and include all kinds of
questions, from personnel questions to ethics and structures of internal communication.[14] The mainly French material used for comparison is also made up
of public reports carried out by the French ministries.[15]

The evolving oligopoly of the political future

National protectionism for monopoly of the future

MODEL RESPONSE

The Swedish 'model', created by the Social Democratic Party (SAP), which has held power for nearly the whole period since 1932, was long seen as an example for the world. The model was based on an economy that is very open and highly dependent on trade and on a high level of taxation that enables the government to carry out policies of extensive income redistribution and to maintain a large public sector. A high degree of national economic and political autonomy was a pre-requisite of the model. The Party's labour market policy was seen as particularly remarkable. To combat unemployment was for the SAP perhaps the most important task facing a government. Rapid structural rationalisation of the economy has been combined with an active and efficient state-led transfer of labour into new growth sectors. Unemployment was never allowed to increase. Various kinds of international cooperation or coordination that put constraints on these policies have been seen as a threat to the model and to Swedish independence.

Sweden's policy *vis-á-vis* the European Community has always had the character of a response to the organisation's internal development; for example to its further steps in economic integration. The Swedish debates have reflected a fear of economic discrimination rather than peace-building idealism or supra-nationalism. The question has been how to keep strong economic links with the Community without being a member of the organisation. Membership was ruled out at an early stage as incompatible with Sweden's policy of neutrality. In a famous speech held at the congress of the metalworkers' union in 1961, the Social Democratic Prime Minister Tage Erlander spelled out the reason why Sweden could not join the European Economic Community (EEC). It was in the Prime Minister's view not acceptable that a majority of the member countries could decide policies applicable for the whole organisation 'against the will of many other member-states'. That decisions were taken by majority vote was according to Erlander a fact in the fields of economic, tax, and labour market policies as well as concerning regulations for capital movements, custom rates, social reforms and working and employment conditions. The national government had a right only to express its wishes and make proposals to 'something called the Commission', which formulated the final policy. The Prime Minister ended his speech with the words:

> It is not surprising if we are hesitant towards an international agreement which can considerably limit our ability to conduct a policy which has been a guideline, not only for a majority of the Swedish people, but also for parties in other countries. (Erlander, 1961)

The speech came to have a programmatic function for the Social Democratic policy *vis-á-vis* the Community for almost three decades.

POLITICAL RESTRAINTS

The most important reason for the intensified debate in Sweden about the European Community in the 1980s was the organisation's decision to speed up the process of economic integration (Commission, 1985; Cecchini, 1988). When the Community started to talk about a turning point in European integration towards 1992, the Swedish government decided to pursue a policy of *parallel harmonisation* with the Community's internal market (Proposition 1987/88: 66, 1987: 25), a step which gave rise to a new round of the autonomy debate. What was more harmful to Swedish sovereignty: staying outside while passively adapting to the Commission's White Paper or being a member of the Community with all its commitments, but also with a say in the decision-making?

Considerations of sovereignty as well as of autonomy[16] have always played a crucial role in Sweden's decision to stay outside the European Community until the 1990s. Faith in the Swedish nation-state was strong after the Second World War, and it soon became strengthened even further. The people had seen that a line of policy based on national sovereignty had kept it untouched by the war. In the following decades, the same nation-state proved to be superior to all other states in creating the welfare society. The loyalty Swedes held to the Swedish authorities as promoters of the 'Good State' explains much of the strength of the policies aimed at protecting national sovereignty and autonomy.

The free trade agreement of 1972 remained throughout the 1980s the only legal treaty regulating cooperation between Sweden and the European Community. The joint Luxembourg declaration of 1984 and the following EC–EFTA ministerial meetings were exactly in line with Swedish aims: to try to keep the economic links as close as possible without being too bound by formal agreements. However, the government began to divert more and more energy to its 'European policy' and asserted that a deepened relationship with the Community was one of the 'central objectives' of its foreign policy. The EES became the catchword for Swedish policy towards the Community soon after 1984. The arrangement meant an extension of the Community's internal market benefits to the EFTA countries through their parallel harmonisation with the implementing of the 300 proposals in the Commission's 'White Paper' for the completion of the internal market.

The emerging oligopoly

'NOT FOR THE MOMENT'

In 1987, the Social Democratic government still considered membership of the Community incompatible with the policy of neutrality (Proposition 1987/88: 66: 25). However, this governmental proposition slightly redefined the traditional line by adding that membership was *for the moment* not an option. Implicitly, this passage opened up the possibility of an accession in the future – the first time such a step had been officially suggested. The Swedish readiness to negotiate a lasting, closer, and wider relationship with the Community was underlined more frequently and clearly by the Swedish Ministers. Sweden wanted to pursue deepened cooperation in all sectors except in the field of security and foreign policy. However, 'there are also limits to the extent Sweden can submit itself to supranational decisions in the field of economic policy' (Proposition 1987/88:66: 26).

As so many times before, the Social Democratic government feared a loss of autonomy in the economic–political field. For Communists and Environmentalists, the domestic effects of giving up autonomy entailed weakening in the political goals promoted by the two parties (Hermansson, 1987: 153–169; Gahrton, 1988: 10).

A question often posed for the Social Democratic party and the labour movement concerned the extent to which people were ready to compromise the future of the Swedish model ('the People's home') with European conditions. For many, 'time must not be turned back' (Gidlund, 1988: 100–101). A harmonisation of Swedish tax levels with EC levels could be a setback for the model. It was stressed in this context that for the moment Sweden had no unemployment, and this was in sharp contrast to many of the Community's member-states. However, a new question was opened up by Social Democratic debaters: would a Europeanisation of the labour market *automatically* imply increased difficulties for Sweden to hold down the rate of unemployment (Gidlund, 1988: 101)?

SHIFTING VIEWS

One of the most significant shifts in the view on economic–political autonomy was formulated by the Chairman of the powerful Metal Workers' Confederation,[17] Leif Blomberg. Whatever one thought about the European Community, it was, according to Blomberg, in the long run inevitable for Sweden to participate in European economic integration if it was not to lose the economic foundation of its welfare and employment policies. The question was instead: 'Is the condition for Swedish enjoyment of the economic fruits of the integration that we have to give up autonomy over how these resources will be used?' (Blomberg, 1989: 5). To this rhetorical question Blomberg answered implicitly in the affirmative when he argued against 'an unrealistic Swedish isolationism'. Instead he emphasised that a long-term *strategy* for Europe was necessary in order to secure Swedish welfare. The strategy should aim at a 'welfare say' in the European integration process by means of the support of forces in Europe working for the social dimension of integration (the other Nordic countries, transnational trade union confederations, etc.). Sweden and the trade unions could in this way regain power in order to influence the *direction* of the use of economic gains. This would compensate for the losses of national autonomy. Social Democratic parlamentarians began to question the government's strategy of being 'both outside and within':

> The alternative to a far-reaching, passive, Swedish adaption policy could under certain circumstances be an adhesion to the EC with neutrality reservations and an active policy pushing for our political trade union values and goals. Such an active EC policy could be part of a strategy of strengthening the left-wing forces within the

EC. If Sweden, Norway and Austria entered the Community, the possibilities for EC's 'social dimension' would be strengthened. (Olsson and Pettersson, 1987: 180)

Without calling for Swedish membership, two authors connected with the trade unions opened up a new European future for Sweden and the Swedish labour movement. After having described the strength and progressiveness of social democratic forces within the Community, they put their faith in the European Parliament's future role as an instrument for a more united European left. There was no longer any national road to socialism:

> We would not support EC membership, if it meant that other governments took decisions about Swedish policy. On the other hand we would advocate restrictions on sovereignty if it meant that representatives of the European people, to which the Swedes belong, take joint decisions for the future of Europe. (Olsson and Svenning, 1988: 254–255)

The chances for a strong European labour movement were described by trade union spokesmen as not 'pitch black' with the exception of the British section. In France, Spain, Greece and West Germany the labour parties and trade unions had shown considerable strength and could constitute reliable partners in a *common 'left force'*. According to the Swedish Confederation of Trade Unions (LO), centralisation towards Brussels was not all bad; it was worth giving up national sovereignty if this resulted in fruitful cooperation. The work carried on within the European Trade Union Conference (ETUC) was mentioned as the most important example of 'benevolent Europeanisation' (Larsson, 1988: 7-9). It was concluded that the renaissance of European integration initiated by capital and industrial interests in fact facilitated the trade unions' social and economic demands, and improved conditions for their ideological renewal (Svenning, 1988: 7).

THE EUROPEAN OPTION

In September 1989, Prime Minister Ingvar Carlsson quoted Erlander's classical speech of 1961. However, he did not refer to the most well-known section, namely where the autonomy argument is turned against EEC membership. Instead he emphasised another section, initiating the following quotation from the speech:

> A country that wants to participate in international cooperation has to be ready to modify its national autonomy to a certain extent. On many occasions Sweden has contributed to, and accepted such restrictions. But this does not mean that we in any form and to whatever extent are prepared to give up sovereignty. In each particular case a careful evaluation of advantages and disadvantages must be made.

> These were Tage Erlander's words in 1961. And they are still valid. This is what the up-coming negotiations with the EC are about; what can we give and what can we take. When these negotiations are ready we will make an evaluation. Only then will

we know what is of greatest use to us – to participate in an extended cooperation or to refrain from it. (Carlsson, 1989a: 11)

When discussing each policy area, the Prime Minister formulated the problem as a tension: 'how should we combine our strong wish to cooperate with the rest of Europe with our endeavours to preserve as much national domestic autonomy as possible?' According to Carlsson, the future looked bright for extended cooperation, because his feeling was that the goals of the Swedish/ Social Democratic model were shared by an increasing number of European countries (Carlsson, 1989a: 15). In December 1989, after the fall of the Berlin Wall, Carlsson continued what can be called the 'Swedish inversion' of the autonomy argument. In an answer to a critique of the party's policy of cooperation with the EC for being detrimental to environmental standards, Carlsson stated:

> Why not turn the argument the other way around. We all know that our environmental situation to an increasing degree depends on the environmental policies of other countries. Therefore, we need more, much more international environmental cooperation. No country can alone manage the environmental problems, no country has in this field anything to gain from protectionism … Cooperation does not mean submission to somebody. West European integration is not necessarily dictated by big finance and multinational giants. One of the purposes behind our search for closer cooperation with the EC is to reach a higher degree of coordination in the struggle against unemployment. Such a struggle is also part of the visions envisaged by the President of the EC Commission, and by many Social Democrats in the member countries. In fact, it is one of their highest wishes to have Sweden participate in this work on the ground of our experiences of a well-functioning policy of full employment. Why should we assume that this is not possible? (Carlsson, 1989b)

The question now became how to evaluate and improve the conditions for these European possibilities. The logic of conditional argumentation became increasingly used: 'Sweden cannot be a member *if* the political union is realised … *Should* the motives for our policy of neutrality disappear – a common European security system – yes then we are in a new situation … Were the EC to develop a system of more coordination, Sweden could not' (Carlsson, 1990) (italics added).

In July 1991, the Social Democratic government applied for Swedish membership of the European Community to the president of the EC Council of Ministers. The Swedish people decided in a referendum in the autumn of 1994 that Sweden should join what was then the European Union. Sweden has been a member since 1 January 1995.

Strategies for future European possibilities

In the transformation of the institutional and conceptual framework during the 1980s and early 1990s, a qualitatively new view of the political future was created by leading Swedish politicians. The new language was characterised by a weakened trust in the Swedish state's monopoly of control over the political future – a belief that had been held since the sixteenth century! However, the substitutes for this nation-state-controlled future were only vaguely expressed: 'work together in Europe for the same goal.' The Swedish future was depicted by the politicians in terms of possibilities, found together with others. Furthermore, it was formulated in terms of cooperation and consensus, but also of conflict and divergent interests. In this new situation a *strategy* was needed as a tool in the struggle for a future which, in comparison with the past, was more unknown owing to the greater number of co-players. This was what was entailed in making the future 'European'. Many of the controversies in the debate were caused by uncertainty whether this conception of coming time was the starting point of a process leading to a more controlled future at the European level, or to a constantly undefined, unsettled and uncontrollable coming time. Nearly all debaters admitted that there was no straightforward answer to whether a closer relation to the Community or membership of the Union would make Sweden better or worse off. Could a possible increase in overall autonomy compensate for a loss of sovereign rights? The result of the 'equation' differed among the debaters and political parties because the European future was so uncertain. Here is a clue to a new meaning of the future in European governance. For many it was not membership of the Community as such that mattered: the important thing was to gain influence *in Europe to take part in a European future.* The possibility of influencing this new future became more important than the traditional control of the whole sequence of events in the decision-making process, from policy initiative to implementation, which was what the preservation of national autonomy in practice meant in a time perspective. It was this traditional outlook that was expressed by the Under-Secretary of Foreign Trade when he declared that 'we must first evaluate the effects before we can accept the "freedoms" of the EC'.

The background to these politico-institutional changes was the growing economic and political impact of the Community on Sweden. Not being a member was too costly for Sweden in economic terms. The inversion of the autonomy argument expressed a realisation that the nation-state's ability to secure the welfare of its people by its own political efforts – through promises and implementation of future reforms – had been eroded. For the welfare state, giving up the means to decide over traditional welfare policies was tantamount to losing its monopoly of control over the future. The price, in the form of a loss of traditional national autonomy, had to be paid. Consequently, a new direction in Social Democratic policy and influence was called for. The policy of 'Social Democracy in one country' was outdated. Far more than in earlier periods, it was now argued that the Community institutions should be used as tools to a Social Democratic Europe. Progress could no longer be guaranteed by the nation-state alone. And it was now said that 'progress' was a future goal Swedes had in common with other Europeans.

The semantics of European futures

Against the historical background of the previous section, some hypotheses about the production of the texts expressing European governance that I have selected can now be formulated. The aim of the political programmes I have chosen was to formulate policies for a situation faced by a new member-state. My first reading of the public reports shows that their purpose was to suggest proposals to streamline the administration and adapt it to the new institutional and ideological conditions. The proposals were presented with the aim of enhancing national strategic thinking and action, as a means to better performance in the Community on the grounds of the inverted view of autonomy that had shown that a central state apparatus for purely domestic public administration was outdated. The analysis had shown that the conception of the political future had changed from something that could be rationally prognosticised and planned, to something for which a strategy was needed. The question was now: what consequences did the new institutional and conceptual framework have for the construction of a new political and administrative language, that presumably contained a new semantic balance of the past, present and future? The structural analysis will deepen our understanding of this new conception of political time, for all political actions and administrative reforms are produced within the medium of particular experiences and particular expectations:

> Experience and expectation are two categories appropriate for the treatment of historical time because of the way they embody past and future. The categories are also suitable for detecting historical time in the domain of empirical research since, when substantially augmented, they provide guidance to concrete agencies in the course of social and political movement. (Koselleck, 1985: 270–271)

The future in international politics

DIPLOMACY

Cohen (1981) divides the language of diplomacy into 'grammar' and 'vocabulary'.[18] He lists the following principles of grammar: 'rules are to be kept', 'all agreements are of limited validity', 'within a given rule system, all rules are discredited when one rule is flouted', 'reciprocity is a necessary condition of the stability of rules of the game between powers of equal status', 'any departure from previous patterns of behavior may be seen as a precedent for future action', 'the meaning of a signal is its function in the political process', 'no signal is redundant in the information it contains' (Cohen, 1981: 22-30). This grammar seems to contain very little experience. The rule that 'any departure from previous patterns ... may be seen as a precedent for future action', shows that the expectation horizon is drawn out only from the most recent event and is not dependent on any longer tradition of actions. The language is able to collect only the experience of the last action of the states in question. The experience of the international system, expressed in diplomatic language, is one of a short memory. The historical hypothesis might be: it is not possible to collect experiences of a longer past because different states do not agree on what might be counted as a 'common past', let alone a common experience of it. The general character of the vocabulary has been described by Cohen in the following terms:

> Conscious of the very close attention paid by diplomatic observers to actions and articulations of all kinds and of the paramount importance of being able to say no more and no less than is intended, the diplomatic profession has evolved, over many years, a very subtle and variegated stock of words, phrases, euphemisms, gestures and manoeuvres, each item having its own weight and shade of meaning. (Cohen, 1981: 31)

From this 'non-redundance' other specific characteristics may be derived: a legal terminology, a vocabulary of 'constructive ambiguity' designed to leave future options open, 'the loaded omission' (the use of no words at all to signal a critique or an unpleasant message), and diplomatic understatements separating tone from content (e.g. 'agreement in principle' = postponement, 'concern' and 'surprise' = strong disagreement, 'an unfriendly act' = threat of war). This vocabulary is to be found at a level of abstraction so high that it sometimes creates meaning without any words at all! This lack of concreteness in the diplomatic vocabulary makes it difficult to formulate more extensive spaces of experience or expectation horizons. In fact, when it comes to commitments for the future, the vocabulary of direct reciprocity and vagueness gives it the character, not primarily of a bearer of experiential meaning, but of a provider of ritual exactness, making possible smooth communication in situational *moments*. The diplomatic language thus contains a vocabulary which is traditional in form but incapable of creating any longer experience horizons. This has not resulted in an open future in the progress oriented modern sense, but in a rhetoric minimising engagements of coming time, turning the semantic weight of the 'subtle and variegated stock of words, phrases, euphemisms, gestures and manoeuvres' towards the present.

COUNCIL OF EUROPE

The language of the Council of Europe (CoE) was put together on the basis of the documentation of negotiations within the Committee of Ministers of the Council (Ekengren, 1994). The everyday language is characterised by the traditional fields of competence of the organisation: the support of human rights (HR) and the institutions of constitutional and democratic states. Furthermore, it is coloured by the decision-making principles of the Council, of which the most important is the rule of unanimity in all decisions of importance. These two determinants have resulted in a very formal negotiation language built on legal terms and expressions of compromise. The strict rules of conduct are there to help contain and manage conflict situations. Owing to the atmosphere and politics of consensus, and the sensitive area of human rights (formal criticism for violating HR is in today's Europe considered a serious setback for a country), compromises agreed to by all member-states are most often found. The rule of unanimity often results in decisions which express the smallest common denominator of member-states' stances. The outcome is a language built on references to the overriding interests of human rights, 'European values' (democracy, individual freedom, freedom of speech) and on a vocabulary largely made up of technical and legal terms.

The temporal connotations of CoE language is characterised by both its diplomatic heritage and a vocabulary of institutionalised multilateral relationships. Together with special legal concepts, the former puts limits on the extent to which a linguistically led transformation of the future can take place. The parsimony of the judicial language of the HR machinery aims at de-politicising the language and judifying the collection of common experiences. This 'time of precedents' is inherently non-visionary; what is expected of the future are simply new precedents without which history in the CoE would always repeat itself – a future thus created that does not include movement. Even though the future is perceived in strongly progressive and value-laden terms, it does not harbour the kind of expectations of change characteristic of the languages of the modern nation-state. Instead of a future that is progressively controlled through political action, the medium of CoE experiences and expectations creates a time in which the future realisation of European values is passively awaited. In what ways do the semantics of European governance differ from these languages of comparison?

The future in European governance action: political language

NATION-STATE ACTION

In the national context, party politics is constructed as proposals to be effectuated in the future:

> Setting priorities in the distribution of public resources is a political task. This fact is an important reason for publicly financed programmes for social security. These shall be guaranteed in law and agreements.[19]

> We have made many reforms in education. There are more to come.[20]

> I [John Major] believe that we should ensure that the tax and benefit system helps people. That is why I plan – as a long-term goal – to cut and then abolish inheritance tax.[21]

Political promises are loaded with a self-evident expectation that there are no restrictions on their future immediate fulfilment – as soon as the party eventually comes into government, that is. The results of policy are national laws, agreements and rights. The sequence of political action creates a strong movement towards the future: ideological or political standpoint – promise of future implementation – law. The rhythm that gives meaning and form to this sequence is seen as an irreversible succession from the present to coming time.

That is, policies go through clearly defined phases and it is this fact which makes it possible to hold such temporal expectations as scheduling. Such construction is clearly analogous to the concepts of movement and anticipation that characterise modern political terminology. Political action is directed towards a clear and concrete end in a linear coming time:

> Advertisement for alcohol and tobacco *will be* prohibited.[22] (Italics added).

> Our priorities as regards employment are:– to radically reduce the working week (to 32 hours straight away and to 28 hours by the start of the next century) by passing an outline law.[23]

There is a clear interplay between a before and after guiding political action in the present: 'Things are not right today, but will be soon.'

The space of experience is created by a legalistic vocabulary that codifies the past in laws. Legislation is the final product of progressive policies and constitutes the firm ground, the easily distinguishable benchmarks, on which the linear future can be continuously built. The legislative process, and the law it produces, are the most concrete expressions of national progress. The self-confident expectations inherent in the formulation of national policies have their experiential basis in the national legislative process, and reflect the notion that the nation controls, and should control, its own future.

Three themes dominate the language of political action in European governance: action as *attitude, promotion* and *strategy*.

ATTITUDE

Political action in European governance is conceived as a durable position, a general attitude, a constant in the policy-making process. As with plans and timing (see pp. 48 and 59), this attitude implies a very loose temporal ordering of the different parts of political action. One can characterise the European language of political action as being more similar to an *ideological* vocabulary than to that of operational policy. The party stance is often a resolution to stand firm for or against some aspect of the EU process, rather than a plan for concrete action – 'The Congress has decided that the Environmental Party should strive for the abolition of the Treaty of the Coal and Steel Community'; 'The Environmental Party will act to counteract the attempts to transform Europol into an operational police force such as the FBI'. A particular family of metaphors is developed as a consequence of the fact that action is mainly about attitudes:

> In what way should the Environmental Party act within the EU, of which Sweden is now as a matter fact a member – as a watch-dog, a co-player or both?[24]

> The Environmental Party believes that Sweden should maintain the supremacy of Swedish constitutional law over EU law.[25]

Political time in the nation-state is structured on *cause* (pledge or action) and *effect* (accomplished policy). In European governance, the promised effects of political action are highly conditioned: 'if EU development Y, then we will implement our policy X' (cf. national policy: 'We will implement X in the future'). Policies are not only conditioned by external developments, but also by the anticipation of the direct will of the voters. This factor is often formulated as questions such as in the cases above: 'The EU membership does not automatically solve Sweden's problem. However, it considerably improves our possibilities to create a better society for current and coming generations.'[26]

By means of a new usage, a shift is made from a national future of great self-reliance to *possible futures* of Europe, or rather a broader variety of means to ideologically defined goals for future policy. In this structure, the expectation content of the everyday political language is weakened. Also, here, the experience content is different in European governance.

The vocabulary of political action in European governance is there to express an action that happens at the same time as something else: a 'development', a 'direction of travel', a 'power', are always inserted in these contexts. These external processes are not fixed in time in a concrete situation of decision-making, but function as abstract time–space dimensions to which action can relate. Consider the difference between how party positions are defended in national politics and in European governance.

National politics:

Such has been the success of the Government's economic policies that Labour has been forced to switch from direct attacks on the Conservatives' record on unemployment to scare-mongering about job insecurity … Labour deliberately confuses job insecurity with the flexible, lightly regulated labour market which the Conservative Government has built … A flexible labour market means that more jobs can be created. And, rather than leading to more job insecurity, this extra flexibility has boosted our competitiveness, strengthening our bid to ensure Britain remains the enterprise centre of Europe.[27]

European governance:

to safeguard the UK's hard won opt-out from the job destroying Social Chapter and to oppose attempts to give more powers to the European Parliament and the Commission … Britain's lower levels of unemployment show that Britons are more likely to be in work than their European counterparts. At just 8.6 per cent of the workforce, unemployment is well below the EU average. In Germany, the figure is 8.6 per cent, and in France, 11.6 per cent (Eurostat, December 1995). Britain has a higher proportion of the working age population in work than any other major EU country – 68 per cent compared with 65 per cent in Germany, 59 per cent in France and just 45 per cent in Spain.[28]

Political claims are in the context of European governance formulated as an attitude whose trustworthiness is mainly strengthened with 'independent' facts of a general comparative nature (as in the second quotation above), not with earlier fulfilled promises. The shift might seem negligible, but in fact it shows that the basis of political argument is in a *process of change*. In national politics, particular experiences (e.g. unemployment records) are presented as direct effects of earlier governmental policies and expectations ('rather than leading to more job insecurity, this extra flexibility has boosted our competitiveness'). The expectation content of future policies – further progress – is consequently very high. Since the deregulative measures already taken have beneficial effects, there is no reason to suppose they will not continue to do in the future. In contrast to European governance, the expectation follows 'logically' from experience.

The language of attitude tones down the expectation that the future has something qualitatively new to bring. What accounts for this difference is the fact that political causes and their effects are presented as if they took place simultaneously, in contrast to the sequential, linear order of national political language. There is a shift *from time oriented fulfilments to task oriented attitudes* as the central feature of politics.

PROMOTION

In European governance, plans of action contain few symbolic benchmarks, which constitute the main vehicle for forward movement in the modern semantics. There is a future tense, but its link to the present is weaker than in national semantics. The temporal logic between pledge and codification is diluted, because everything is subject to negotiation. A clear dividing line between the present and the future does not exist: 'The aim of the Christian Democrats is to promote the use of the principle of subsidiarity as a guide.' The future appears in a dimmer light: there is no end point, no way to confirm the success of ideology or policy, in terms of which political promises can be made. There are no benchmarks for further action. Consequently there is neither a need to create timetables of political action – including, for example dates of implementation – nor a possibility of doing so: 'The Christian Democrats wish to work for Swedish action within the EU in favour of more educational programmes.'[29] Forward movement is lost since formulations of future goals and work have the same temporal content as promised political action in the present. Expressing current political action in such terms as 'to work for' and 'to act in favour of' does not contain assurances or timetables of any future tranformation or implementation (cf. national legislation). Instead, what is pledged is the same kind of action over time, without intervals that are built into the modern language of national politics. The result is that the future and the present closely resemble each other in European governance. The *action* is the same as the *result*.

The terms of promotion are self-referential: 'to work for' is politically self-sufficient now as well as in the future, thereby leaving the linear political logic of promise fulfilment that characterised national domestic politics. What it was that led to this or that outcome is difficult to determine when politicians constantly 'work for' the same goal. In European governance, the link between policy ('opt-out from the job destroying Social Chapter') and outcome ('Britain's lower levels of unemployment show that Britons are more likely to be in work than their European counterparts') is diffuse and abstract. Unlike domestic politics, in which particular goals can be accounted for in terms of a certain degree of political input, capital or effort, there is no direct link, no proportional relation between political cause and effect. Thus, the subtle changes of the action terms in European governance reflect the erosion of linear temporality, and give way to a non-linear causality, in which the present action and future efforts and effects are mutually exchangeable. The underlying logic is that experience and expectation are more alike in European governance than in national politics. There is very little qualitative difference between, on the one hand, the collection of experiences described in terms of 'EU's health regulations are only minimum standards',[30] and on the other, expected 'improved possibilities for preventive health measures'.[31] Since both experiences and expectations in European governance are less clear-cut in content, alternative pasts (owing to the existence of a great variation of national traditions, rules and laws) and futures (e.g. progress under certain circumstances) are made possible. There is simply no direction for national parties' health policy in the Community: towards improved or impoverished standards? The European future is a force that is in full effect in the present. 'To promote' in the European networks effectively erases the boundary between the present and the future. The future is already here in that the politician promotes certain values today as well as tomorrow and the day after tomorrow. The European future is already realised in the present.

STRATEGY

As shown, the nature of political action in European governance is strongly conditioned by the apprehension of the future. The attitude with which politics is conducted is a new one that implies a wait-and-see strategy. Owing to the new temporal implictations of action, *strategy replaces planning*. I see this making action conditional on coming events as a compensation for the short horizon of experience within European governance, and as a substitute for the domestic linear and causal-like transition from the present to the future. Every one of these newly constructed notions of conditional action contains an implicit transition period, during which it can be ascertained whether or not the particular condition will emerge. Experience is, so to speak, *awaited in the present*. Since present action occurs before anticipated experience, the 'past' becomes identical with the semantic forms in which the future is anticipated. Present action is not so much loaded with expected experiences, as with ideologically desirable ones.

'Strategy' makes the best of the politically unattractive preoccupation with the protection of present achievements rather than with future progress:

> The tendency has been unequivocal. The EU has gradually increased its area of activities. This can be seen as a step towards a federal state, since the constitution of such a state always contains regulations concerning who decides what. Ordinary international organisations usually simply describe what they themselves do. Even so, a precise division of competence can be useful. Best of all would be if this

resulted in a radical reduction of EU power and an increase in national, and particularly regional and local [powers].[32]

This type of statement, which restricts the number of alternative futures, is made semantically possible by the ambiguity of experience in European governance. In the example above, the contested space of experience makes it possible for the language to express preference for two divergent paths of development simultaneously. The temporal coefficient of this semantic move is not mainly that of change, but of shaping possible change into acceptable forms by closing down alternative interpretations. That is why so many actions in European governance are preceded by interpretations closing or limiting the openness of the future. Compare political action's references to ideological '-isms' in modernity for the purpose of widening the horizon of expectation.

Semantically, strategy bears the seed of the horizon of expectation, because the way coming situations are experienced strongly demarcates the frontiers of what could possibly be expected from the future, beyond which the unthinkable reigns. In other words, the *prognostic* potential of the everyday language of political programmes and promises is losing ground in European governance. It is for this reason that the language of European governance does not generate experience to the same extent as the political language of modern nation-states. Luhmann (1976) talks about 'an open future as a present future which has room for several mutually exclusive future presents … We can think of degrees of openness and call "futurization" increasing and "defuturization" decreasing openness of a present future' (1976: 140–141).[33] As noted earlier, the more open the interpretation of the past, the less firm is the ground on which to base prognosis and thus political promises. The replacement of prognosis by the ideologically nurtured presupposing of a certain development and strategy is just an expression of the greater uncertainty of the field of political action. The generality of strategy is needed in order to encompass experiences that are ambiguous and difficult to interpret. The political language has become more abstract in order to make comprehensible European governance, which is far more complex than national government. This dissociates the conditions of everyday action from experience to an even higher degree than in the modern language described by Koselleck. Experiences can to an even lesser extent be transformed into expectations. 'European possibilities' does not only mean that there exist several futures, but it also connotes a more vague meaning of 'the future' generally. 'Strategy' makes political action corresponding to this abstract future.

The future in European governance action: administrative language

NATION-STATE ACTION

Action in the Swedish administration of the 1980s can be summarised as a continuation of planning under more flexible forms. Planning activities had for many years been defective. Now it was time for the Cabinet to recapture its precedence in planning matters from the bureaucracy. In other words, the monopoly of the control of the future should be restored to the highest level. However, the prediction and planning ambition was the same; the time horizon is '10–20 years or more' (SOU, 1983: 39: 15). The declared aim of the reforms was to base the government's planning on regular and formalised revaluations at points in time 'decided in advance'. Through these checkpoints it was thought that better planning, more in harmony with 'developments', would be achieved. We could say that the suggestions were aimed at making progress more dependent on the experiences of earlier policies and planning than it had been. The language of the national administration revealed that expectations of the future had been too great. A more thoughtful approach was needed for future progress, it was argued.

COMMUNITY TIMETABLES

The planning vocabulary has disappeared from the language of European governance. Instead, the *Community timetables* have replaced planning as the main preoccupation of the national administration. Explicit references to time are salient features of the material examined to an extent not even approached in the reports of the early 1980s. The same emphasis on time was found in the French material investigated. In fact, in the proposals for adapting the civil service to the requirements of EC decision-making, terms with explicit temporal connotations were used on almost every page. The vocabulary included expressions such as 'EC timetables', 'the time frameworks of national preparations', 'the EC's successive time phases',[34] 'time-consuming', 'respite', 'time period', 'set term'; these referred to the EC's decision-making procedures and their consequences for domestic administrative procedures and praxis. With these were built up verbal structures aiming at creating an image of an administration submerged into a completely new time framework of action:

> The form and timeframes for national planning will be determined by the nature of the issue and EC timeframes.[35]

> One factor that can not be overemphasised is the quickness needed for the preparation of decision.[36]

> The Timetable is not the same within all areas.[37]

Much of the everyday language was based on the underlying premises of 'the immediate need' of a 'fundamental reformation' of the Swedish administration and decision-making procedures in order 'to keep up' in 'the hurry' created by EC timetables.

CONTINUITY, COORDINATION AND ANTICIPATION

'Continuity' of action in European governance is the means to meeting the challenge posed by the new speed of decision-making: 'among the conditions for a successful Swedish performance should be emphasised the importance of continuity'.[38] This continuity in the form of long-term mandates should provide civil servants with a framework, a 'room for manoeuvre', within which they could act quickly, without the need of being in constant contact with their superiors. Owing to the need to keep up with 'the increased pace', it was proposed that the information conveyed verbally (e.g. over the phone) should gain in importance at the cost of written reports which, if needed, could be sent at a later stage 'for the records'. Hence, it was with explicit temporal terms that officials' means of communication were specified.

Another catchword in the administrative langue is 'coordination'. The time-based terminology defined the forces pressing for uniform national strategy in the EC negotiations: the rapid decision-making process in the Community required a very advanced system for central coordination and control in order to enhance the pace of handling issues, and to ensure that national representatives could exercise influence: 'Managing EC membership effectively depends on strengthening capacities to handle preparatory work and especially to upgrade coordination'.[39] 'Coordination is expensive and difficult. It typically requires a substantial investment of top management time'.[40] 'Unless coordination among ministries is redesigned, a great deal of time and effort will be wasted in demarcation disputes'.[41] A third term was 'anticipation': a central task for the sections of the national administration involved in European governance was to anticipate legislative development:

> a thorough knowledge of the legislation in other Member-States is indispensable for efficient preparation of Community negotiations. Such knowledge would make it possible to anticipate the positions defended by the various Member-States during negotiations on a text in Brussels, and would consequently help to make preparations for the discussion more effective. This would help us to make a better-informed guess about the inevitable compromise and a more accurate assessment of how it would affect our interests.[42]

What, then, are the horizons of experience and expectation of 'continuity', 'coordination' and 'anticipation'? In the semantic sub-field of administrative action are collected experiences from present time (legislation in other EU member-states). The language registers experiences without having a prognostic potential. The three concepts served to generate action in the immediate situation with a relatively low ambition with regard to anticipating its consequences in the longer term. Their meaning was shaped in order to gain national advantages in the market-like competition between administrations, and consequently weighted towards up-coming presents in the form of negotiation situations. The aim of 'continuity' was to preserve the predictability felt to be lost. The coming time that was of importance was restricted to the time span within which it was possible to estimate administrative efficiency in terms of maximising national interest in the drafting of the next-coming EU law. In this management of action, the national administration should be organised to cut as large a piece as possible out of the EU cake. The purpose of the European governance vocabulary was

to optimise influence for the moment. The consequence was that it did not contribute to the meaning of the goal and direction of the process as a whole.

I now discuss the future in projects and processes. Under this heading I
interpret the themes in European governance that express longer trends and
predictions.

The future in projects and processes: political language

NATION-STATE LONG-TERM POLICY

> The vision of the Environmental Party is long-term sustainable, democratic soci-
> eties, that function within the limits set by nature locally and globally.[43]

> At the election, people will face a choice. A choice of two futures. They can choose
> a future where prices and mortgage rates are firmly under control. They can choose
> a future that looks rosy, with the best economic conditions this country has seen
> for a century, created by millions of hard-working people and the government,
> together. And they can choose a future where British interests will be fought for in
> Europe. Or they can risk a future with an untried, inexperienced, unrealistic alter-
> native. We will win that election, because on all three counts it is too risky to trust
> Labour with Britain's future.[44]

The expectations and plans for the future are drawn in a language that is
deliberately used to dismiss alternative interpretations of past experiences, so
that there can be no doubt about which future to choose. The future follows
almost logically from these parameters of experience. Semantically, the future is
filled with self-confident progress and a strong forward movement that is built
into the constructions by means of pledges, for whose fulfilment very few
restrictions are expected. This is the language of the national policies as a vehicle of progress. In the nation-state, long-term political ambitions are temporally
ordered as straight lines. The formulations are heavy with expectation and
strongly allude to the desire that the hitherto experienced state of affairs should
not continue.

PROJECTS

The experiences from which expectations of the future are drawn are in European governance most often declared to be found within the institutions of the
Union. Based on such experience, long-term action cannot achieve the same
degree of reliability, ambition and self-confidence as that found in the language
of national prognosis – the mother of expectation. Here, 'our project' is left
more open with regard to substance:

> Our European project will be implemented through the European institutions,
> which are based on the principle of shared responsibility, as a vehicle for coopera-
> tion on joint projects sovereignly adopted by each country.[45]

Just trust us; it is *our project* in European governance. The difference in temporal
content is striking: 'the project' talked about is more one of form than substance.

The European governance language is experientially mainly built on the very institutions of future decision-making. Institutional questions step in to provide material from which experience in European governance is made. The dynamics of the future is conjured up mainly by institutional themes.

However, it is first and foremost the significant lack of actual experience that characterises the European governance language of 'projects'. The term says very little about the origin of the phenomena it is supposed to connote. The European governance 'project' does not take its point of departure in tradition, but in the present. The aim of referring to European politics in terms of project is to steer voters onto de-politicized paths.[46] The non-ideological vocabulary of European governance makes it possible to win popular support without making political commitments of any great substance. The future is drained of expectations and made empty. Projects have little claim on anticipating the future. The heavy emphasis on projects has the effect of holding the question of concrete experience at bay, for these terms are even more estranged from people's everyday experiences than the modern concepts of movement (Koselleck, 1989: 303).

The concepts of projects defer the burden of proof to the future to an even greater extent than the ideological language of movement. They make the project immune against future criteria of desirability, thereby making it almost impossible to reject it in the present on the ground that it can, or will, not be fulfilled in the future. However, some of Koselleck's general conclusions are still valid: the more abstract the concepts, the more political use can be made of them. They can bear all possible interests, experiences and expectations. The European project is self-referential: the project is a project is a project ... with its 'raison d'être' drawn from broadly recognised values and experiences of very high universal applicability:

> For a Europe founded on values: the European Union should *get back on course* ... Today, European's most pressing concerns are unemployment, insecurity, poverty and the future of the welfare state. The European project should take these concerns as its point of departure (emphasis in original).[47]

The new usage implies a new emphasis on the *forms* of political action. The new meaning of the future is a result of the fact that the tension between experience and expectation in European governance languages is weaker. The temporalisation process prevails owing to the fact that the pure forms of European political processes and decision-making are expected to develop in an accelerating tempo. The 'project' is in European governance made an *empty vehicle for political movement*:

> Our objectives for the IGC are: to entrench subsidiarity within the EU. To make Europe work better – we want it to be decentralised, deregulated and competitive ... to protect Britain's veto by opposing extension of Qualified Majority Voting [QMV] – the process by which decisions can be taken without the consent of all Member-States.[48]

Longer trends of the project are not shaped in the form of value-loaded prognoses. Instead, the key words used are 'visions' or 'perspectives' (to be promoted)
in the absence of more distinct futures. The limited amount of experience in
European governance, even though compensated for by interpretations of its
'principles' and 'values', provides a weaker base on which to build expectations.
There is much regret that the future is not taking the same meaning as in traditional politics:

> Socialists declare themselves, on the contrary, in favour of an ambitious and bal-
> anced construction project for Europe. The European cause can only gain ground
> in public opinion if the political issues are clear and if the identifiable political forces
> propose clearly formulated futures.[49]

The self-generating EU project provides its own historical legitimation. If
the project was fully completed, it would no longer serve as a tool for the generation of action in a self-referential way. Contrary to the normal meaning of a
project, the European project is something that goes on without end. Without
clear sequences over time, the difference between the destiny and the origin of
European governance is blurred. To do nothing means to lend support to the
on-going process.

PROCESSES

The expectations born out of the limited space of experiences are often perceived
in a vocabulary of 'processes'. These can be strengthened, or by themselves be the
subject of action:

> The obsessed attention given to the Maastricht criterion regarding public finances
> has resulted in the neglect of other important challenges for the European unifica-
> tion process. First and foremost, we need to relaunch the construction of political
> Europe, and review the Maastricht Treaty with the view to strengthen the Union's
> political profile and its democratisation. The progressive increase of the Union's
> competences should not imply more power to the bureaucracy but the development
> of democracy. The unification process takes the shape of steps which do not only
> comprise the Monetary Union, but also the other political, economic and cultural
> integration processes prescribed in the Maastricht Treaty.[50]

The key words are given a processualised form, e.g. democratisation. Instead
of one singular political trajectory with a well-identified goal, there are several
on-going processes in relation to which a favourable or critical attitude or standpoint is formulated. The processes overlap and their contents are open for interpretation. 'Process', which is mainly negatively defined, is an expression, as well
as a linguistic dynamo, of a more insecure open future than in the modern
national context.

In fact, almost all politics in European governance is grounded on the conviction that there is a 'EU process' going on. This process is thought of as an
independent force which one can reject or approve of and join. It tends to be a
process without subjects. Some writers have described the modern historical

consciousness as dominated by the view that human actors are only objects in history (cf. Arendt, 1976, 1978). In our semantic perspective, the strong 'processualisation' of language in European governance makes it easy for actors to conjure up the feeling of inexorable, rapidly approaching events and developments, which cannot be retarded. Politicians portray events in a manner that makes their own particular party programme appear as the most obvious and best method to manage (not control) the process. The difference in the confidence of controlled progressive change in modern language is significant. The movement of a *neutral, highly abstract, value-free* process is clearly not the same as the progressive movement created by modern language. In the former, the main drive of politics is process management, in the latter Utopia. As Nassehi (1994) puts it, in the modern semantics of time 'time itself contains the Utopian energies which resolve the difference between promise and fulfilment' (1994: 50).

In the language of European governance, the future is losing its Utopian content. The basic image is that it is no longer possible to manipulate 'destiny' by means of human prediction, planning and implemenation. To what extent are we in the semantics of European governance witnessing a revival of the notion of the power of fate that was so strong in pre-modern politics and society (cf. Giddens 1990: 30; Jacobsson and Øygarden, 1996)? My empirical material indicates that modernity's replacement of the view of fate as Fortuna, which had for so long dominated people's minds, is reversed in European governance. Fate is today the process of European integration which you, at least as an individual person, party or country, cannot do much about. When modernity's particular tools of manipulation cease to make sense, when their power of interpretation is weakened, the future can no longer legitimate the present. Language has unloaded its expectations. When the future can no longer legitimate the present, some other justification of it has to be searched for elsewhere. The past has once again to be discovered, or rather constructed, as shown in my empirical examples. However, it seems as if this drive backwards is not strong enough to arrest belief in the notion of 'development'. What is left is a language for the creation and management of inevitable moments of insecurity making up the process. Fate as 'European process' resembles the ways in which 'misfortune' is socially constructed by policy-makers generally as a means to avoid accusations for mismanagement and policy fiascoes (Bovens and 't Hart, 1998: 73-92). The particular strength of 'the European process' for purposes such as these derives from the fact that it is so widely recognised to be beyond the control of national politicians.

The subjectification of the very process of European governance is sometimes so strongly pronounced that the most political action can attain is delay:

> Denmark's strategy of exception has most probably only resulted in a delay of some years in Denmark's adaptation to the Union. In the same way, Sweden's refusal to be a full member of the WEU and EMU would just mean a retardation in time.[51]

Thus, the language of European governance gives a new status to omission of political action. You are obliged to act, regardless whether you like the process of European integration or not. The responsibility held by the politicians engaged in European governance is consequently ambiguous: on the one hand, they formulate policies under the conviction that they are responsible for the actions they take in participating in the process, yet on the other, they are relieved of such responsibility owing to the self-generation of the future included in the notion of process:

> A serious problem is that the EU's road towards being a superpower is proceeding step by step. Those who do not blindly put a check on everything are running the risk of contributing to something that facilitates the development of a super state.[52]

The blunt vocabulary used for connecting or disconnecting the EU past with the future, such as 'blindly put a check on', bears witness to the low content of experience on which present action is based. The temporal semantics of 'stop or go' conjures up short horizons of both the past and the future. Expectations on the future are derived directly from previous experience. The processualisation of language is meant to embrace the future within notions whose main aim is not to open up a new future, but to continue to create movement, which is still obviously desirable, even with a very limited control of future political outcomes. By the means of processualisation, the loss of a progress content is minimised. The future opened up is a future of possible progress, a future of new conditions, portrayed as a more real future yet to emerge: 'It [the single currency] paves the way for a higher European ambition, that of a European Union that is capable of developing a societal model.'[53]

In the modern language described by Koselleck there is a tension between the instrumental use of the concepts, e.g. to mobilize people for the future, and their potential meaning. 'The central challenge had always been to change existing conditions, that is, initially to redefine them; but this was possible only by an anticipation of a future lacking actual experience' (Koselleck, 1983: 305). In European governance, there is a similar tension between instrument and meaning, but in this case the fact that experience is lacking is not used to justify leaving wide open the question of what 'navigational instruments' need to be created to guide us towards future progress. Because, historical legitimation is considered important, experiences are instead *sought for and constructed by anticipating the EU's future*: 'when we do act, we anticipate that our experience *at that time* will be ...' Consequently political stances are to a large extent historically self-legitimated. History appears as makable also in Koselleck's modern world, and the purpose of placing it under human authority is to emphasise the future's openness for innovation. In contrast, the construction of the past in European governance aims at providing a privileged interpretation in order to *narrow* the range of possible future directions. History is there to give the language of the present the capacity to be as precise as possible in order to shorten the horizon of the future, to stand against the sweeping winds of EU processes, to make politics less visionary.

European 'processes' contains certain qualitative benchmarks as suggested by the term 'European construction'. This expresses the fact that Europe and a European polity is being built piecemeal, step by step, as a house is constructed. The conception of a stepwise construction is closely related to the short horizon of expectation, and reflects the limited space of experience through which present action can be mediated:

> To rescue the process of building Europe, the Socialists must present evidence about social conditions ... the next two foundation-stones in the building of Europe must, in order not to jeopardise the whole building, be society- and citizen-oriented.[54]

The house-building metaphor is brilliant: the European house cannot be built at once, given the experiential content of piecemeal construction, and the unknown final future appearance of the house. In European governance, a diagnosis of the building site can be made more or less in common with European partners, not the architectural plan. In contrast, the history of the welfare state is not told as the erection of a 'building' through adding annexes and additional storeys. It was built as a whole on the basis of a plan. The Swedish 'People's Home' was created with parental love. A home is never erected.

Coming time approaches stepwise but without the end points in the construction of national time oriented fulfilments: rules are continuously laid to rules, like 'Treaty revisions', but their nature is mainly one of links in the depoliticized chain of process. Rather than being tools in a time of optimising progress, they open up 'potentials' and create possibilities of new definitions. The characteristics are also most visible in dissatisfaction with the 'piecemeal' political logic:

> The time has come for the project adopted by the Member-States to abandon *the logic of piecemeal institutional measures*, even at the risk of a problematic debate. We Socialists are prepared for such a debate.[55] (emphasis in original)

The notion of process and movement is often injected in a hidden way. Compared to the revolutionary modern language, built up of semantic constructions representing and engendering a process of permanent change and progress (Koselleck, 1983), the vocabulary of political plans and actions used in European governance indicates a process of permanent change but leaves out the question of progress. Like Progress in modern time, Process in European governance is weighted towards the future. The difference between the two is one of total weight.

The future in projects and processes: administrative language

The time of the Swedish administration in the 1980s was built up with distinct and well-defined time spans within which detailed prognoses were formulated. It has often been noted that there exists a 'surveyable' future. Continued 'expansion' (progress) seems to be given by nature. The 1960s is the Golden Age to be copied. The idea that the future is loaded with the expectation of good things and progress shines through the language as whole. The texts of administrative reforms try to tailor a new language for an identical balance between experience and expectation under the banner of 'reconsideration'. 'Political cycles' that cannot be controlled must be 'broken', rules must be adapted to the 'development of society', and 'social progress'.[56] The language reflects an ambition to seize power over the future, at the cost of a less progressive tone. Despite these changes, it differs significantly from the European governance language with regard to temporal loading.

The European governance texts put emphasis on the uncertainty with regard to the possibility of designing longer time perspectives and predicting historical trends. The terminology was vague and expressed a striking insecurity with regard to the validity of prognoses: the length of the time spans of forecasts of EC developments was typically 'long-term' or 'a ten-year perspective', and doubts were raised as to the value of any kind of prediction whatsoever. The reasons given for this scepticism were formulated: 'the biggest difficulty is that we have had to compare processes with each other, not states of affairs', 'realities change, prognoses go wrong'.[57] The Europeification of central administration is described in terms that suggest constant movement, and a flow of events. In the absence of a more precise language of prognosis, many truisms are stated, such as 'the greatest consequences will be discovered in a long-term perspective'. Most often, the prognostic attempts are legitimatized only with very personal, individual assessments, apparently without any basis in an analysis of experience. The civil servant or the politician give the impression that they expect their often laconic statements about a possible coming time to be accepted on their own authority: 'Our judgement is that this development is not very probable.' Another technique of giving a statement the appearance of a prognosis is, as in the political sphere, to make it strongly conditioned on developments and consequently on future action as well: the construction 'developments can … if' was probably one of the most frequently used forward-looking notions. A large part of the future oriented semantic field suggested an implicit underlying conditionality just by its very tone – 'There are signs of', 'expressions of long term goal are'.

The word 'sight' (long and short) was frequently used as the temporal basis of diagnosis and prognosis. Even though the vocabulary was characterised by very vague expressions regarding predictions within specific areas, the language was more clear-cut when it came to defining the overall direction of European integration. This was formulated in terms of an 'unavoidable' 'historical development', giving the impression of an almost inevitable and irreversible process. The spirit of the texts engendered the feeling that Swedish officials had no alternative than to follow the 'European development' and to be 'flexible' and 'adaptable'. On the other hand, the need for better planning was stressed as a measure to counter-balance the growing rate of change in European governance. Here a strong tension is built into the language: the problem is to combine more flexibility and adaptation with long-term control over events.

And what was meant by the oft-cited 'legal Europe' ('l'Europe de demain sera avant tout juridique'), used as a catchword for longer trends? Here, it seems as if the space of experience is erected through a knowledge of EU rules, and that the national horizon of expectation can be established and extended only by an ability to elaborate, interpret and apply these very regulations.

The administrative discourse reveals that establishing the formal conditions for policy-making requires much more time and attention at the cost of forward-looking operative action and initiative. These legal conditions were in national semantics already settled, and to a large extent a non-issue in much of the bureaucratic language. The visionary atmosphere created by a language of expectations of planned progress did not have to be as contaminated with formulations of complex technicalities concerning methods of implementation as in the discourse of European governance. In sum, like the political language of processes, the administrative language of European governance is characterised by constructions trying to hold back and cope with an accelerating development increasingly felt as out of control. The language of coping is given the tone of positive expectation ('we need to influence the EU in a direction we believe in'), but inevitably comprises a changed balance between experience and expectations, and consequently a decreased pace in modernity's temporalisation process. The struggle for favourable conditions, and a better national position in the multilateral game, shrinks the semantical space left for experiences and horizons of expectation. This part of the European governance encyclopaedia is mainly weighted towards the present situation, towards a political now, in which one has to take part actively and offensively.

The future in competencies: the political language
Very few examples were found within this category.

The future in competencies: the administrative language
> European competence is something that constantly changes and develops. Developments need to be followed continuously and the knowledge of the EC has to be brought up to date constantly.[58]

EUROPEAN COMPETENCE

One significant difference between the national and the European encyclopaedia was the appearance in the latter of newly created semantic fields and words for qualities and competencies that were needed for Swedish civil servants dealing with the Community. One such field concerned *'European competence'*. The concept was used in all kinds of contexts, and functioned as a label for the new kind of civil service required by European cooperation. The words most often associated with European competence were 'quickness', 'flexibility', 'strategy' and 'informality' (in the French material: 'compétitivité', 'rapidité', 'efficacité'). The historical challenges that this competence was explicitly aimed to meet were the inescapable underlying forces of 'European integration', 'the development of information technology', etc. At a more practical level, such competence would assure an 'efficient national handling of EC issues' and the 'assertion of Swedish influence' in EC institutions:

> European competence is largely a question of the ability to handle change, that is, to be able to acquire, to readjust, to think in new directions and to meet and deal with new, unknown situations.[59]

'European competence' was associated in the texts with many other expressions, the main one being 'European reflex' ('europa-reflex', 'le réflexe communautaire', 'le réflexe européen'). Together they constituted the basic semantic core around which other qualities, institutional reform proposals and causes of change were twined:

> Competence is not only knowledge. It is about attitudes towards a task, and about engagement, willingness and capacity to reach goals. Even though knowledge is an important part of European competence, it is not enough. It is crucial to be able to use this knowledge in practice, to be able to evaluate, to think strategically, to make priorities, to organise, to communicate, to take the correct decisions and much more.[60]

> The public administration therefore needs to
> * acquire a European reflex
> * switch from a defensive to an offensive approach
> * coordinate all public agencies better than before.[61]

> acquérir le réflexe communautaire, passer de la défensive á l'offensive, et pour cela mieux coordonner l'ensemble des partenaires intéressés.[62]

The uniqueness of this type of competence is emphasised by the fact that a completely new expression is coined by linking 'European' to 'competence' in order to depict it. Moreover, the meaning of the word 'competence' is changed from something that mainly registers a couple of concrete skills to a broader concept evoking a coming time which demands of civil servants a fundamentally new way of being and behaving. The symbolic strength of the concept (and its associated terms), together with its central position *vis-à-vis* other semantic fields, legitimize a whole range of 'necessary' adjustments and adaptations of attitudes and qualities of actors.

The concept of European competence has little to do with experience in traditional administrative work – that is, it is not just descriptive. On the contrary, its uniqueness is brought forward by contrasting it with such traditional virtues of the civil service as 'formality', 'long-term preparation', 'reflection', 'accuracy', 'expertise', which are less flatteringly described in such terms as 'passive knowledge', 'excessive rule obedience', 'slow information transmission', 'defensive methods', 'concentration of the EC work and expertise to a too limited number of people'.[63] Thus, the concept functions as a borderline, a watershed, distinguishing the present and future from the past of a domestic way of handling issues. In downplaying tradition, the concept is more oriented towards the future than the past. However, 'European competence' also implies little with respect to expectation. In the European context, although the future does exist, it seems to be largely unknown and consequently unforeseeable, but something you should be 'prepared' to meet in as 'flexible' manner as possible. In sum, experience is degraded to 'awareness', 'a feeling', and expectation to 'reflex'. The content of earlier experiences and of expectations of the future does not 'fill up' the concept of European competence. Much room is left for the *present*. European competence/réflexe is about how better to handle, on an ad hoc basis, the present situation and the immediate future, about which not much can be known in advance. It mainly defines the skills and the preparedness needed to meet and to manage unexpected developments within the Union. All texts express an adaptation to an inexorable development, the temporal consequences of which are explicitly spelled out. What is required to meet this challenge is 'European competence'.

Furthermore, the concept of European competence implies a synchronic broadening of competence as regards officials' general education (with an emphasis on language, other member-states' EU organisation and EC law and its application), at the expense of a diachronic knowledge of national circumstances. In the French material, this new emphasis is expressed as a critique of the current education of prospective state civil servants.

EUROPEAN EDUCATION

The quality of the national officials should be raised by education in the name of national efficiency and influence in European governance. However, the desirable European reflexes, which should 'penetrate' every ministry and be internalised by every official, could be fully acquired, the texts claim, only through practical experience within the institutions of the Community or other member-states. This unconscious feeling for what should be done in European matters corresponds in domestic politics to the 'national reflexes' that have taken decades (centuries!) to develop. This view of the achievement of the 'feeling' makes a posting in Brussels a good enough experience to be counted as European competence. Emphasising the personal experience implies a de-emphasis on knowledge of a 'documented' past: the officials' personal experience is put in focus because this seems to be the best way to learn about European governance in the absence of a commonly recognised and documented administrative past that can be drawn from. That being the case, the ground for common expectations is weak. The administrative adaptation that is suggested to be accomplished through the technique of encouraging officials to gain personal experience of European governance outside their national context is curiously individualized:

> Would it not be very interesting and useful for a future local government official to spend a few months as a trainee in one of the Commission departments that manage the structural funds or in one of the German Länder?[64]

The 'super generalist', the official with broad competence in many fields, is held to be the ideal. She or he should have skills that enable them to cope with any unforeseen problems in a quick, efficient and flexible manner and in several languages – that is, with the skills traditionally associated with the diplomatic profession. The call for these skills seems to be a function of the rapidity of EU decision-making and the concomitant narrowing of attention to the present required to handle complex situations in constant flux. The role of the special- ist is toned down. To what extent does specialisation have a place in European governance?

EUROPEAN COMMUNICATIONS

Interesting shades of meaning with respect to the future can be discovered in the texts of the administrative reforms produced in Sweden after it entered the Union. Weaknesses in the proficiency with which Swedish civil servants conduct EU-related negotiation and adminstrative routines are highlighted. What is called for are the skills for 'analysing issues in a European perspective – back- ground, political and cultural contexts' (Statskontoret, 1996: 7), and 'effective negotiations'. Another concern was communication between higher (min- istries) and lower authorities, between Stockholm and Brussels. Among the recommendations put forward to improve information diffusion were the 'rules' that all types and channels of communication (instructions from minis- terial to authority level, as well as reports from Brussels to Stockholm) should be documented in written form and produced in time to meet strictly defined deadlines. This was particularly important with respect to EU questions recur- rently discussed over a longer period of time, since officials should always be able to trace the origin of the current negotiation, and the evolution of the opin- ion of other member-states, over time. Therefore, oral instructions and reports should be prohibited. (Statskontoret, 1996: 7: 29). A more open attitude towards direct contacts with other member-state administrations was needed (*Statskon- toret, 1996: 7*: 48; SOU, 1996: 6: 33-72; SOU, 1995: 132: 79-85).

In sum, the everyday language of these later texts tried to compensate for the lost value of national experience by various counter-measures. The experi- ential content had to increase – the call for 'documentation in written form' was made to check the tendency towards purely oral communication because it ran the risk of losing 'the longer perspective' and 'the past'. Civil servants must find a way to collect their new administrative experience in European governance in written form. This puts a strong emphasis on the transmission and storage of information, at the same time as civil servants' attitudes are coloured by experi- ences of a more recent past that is broader and more complex because it changes at a faster pace than before. Consequently, the written language of the past in European governance tends to be of a more synchronic character than the cor- responding language of the national civil service.

The future in timing: political language

There is also a difference between national and European governance with regard to a 'good' and 'bad' time for political action. In the national programmes, the timing of action is of less importance because the implicit automatic starting point for the fulfilment of political party promises is the point in time when the party comes into governmental power. All policy is formulated as if it could be put into action immediately. In European governance, the question of what is considered as a 'good' or 'bad' time to take concrete action is made more open. Here, the institutional factors that explain this openness are easily discernible: it is simply not possible for politicians to specify timing preferences when they do not each have autonomous control of the trigger for joint EU actions. Politicians are less restricted in their timing of action, because temporal expectations are not as settled they are in national politics, where competing preferences are more articulated. Given this background, it is difficult to assess when time is 'ripe' for political action; more specified programmes of action cannot be demanded from political parties, because nobody knows what could be a reasonable time for their implementation in the European process.

The lack of openly declared intentions about when action will be taken, at least in the long run, might make timing a subject of informal negotiation, leading to the establishment of hidden, sector-specific mini-schemes covering shorter periods of time (cf. Glaser and Strauss, 1971: 45). The political language is formulated with the purpose of postponing clear commitments for the future, commitments that would make people organise themselves accordingly on an ad hoc basis. This hesitation creates a semantic dynamic that reinforces insecurity about the future: the political language of European governance has a tendency to be very short on facts and plans with regard to coming time. In this way, it not only expresses an insecure future, but also makes it.

The future in timing: administrative language

It is difficult to find any discourse on timing in national semantics. The reason could be that this particular temporal dimension is of less relevance in a national setting where administrative procedures have long been established, and where the time for implementing a decision is part of the decision itself. The lack of a language of timing is a result of there being no significant advantages to gain from timing. A moment is said to be 'ripe' for action in European governance when the action anticipates and forestalls the moves and actions of other EC participants. According to my encyclopaedia, 'anticipation' is needed owing to the 'faster pace' of the EC decision-making process. In the EC context, Swedish officials should try to present their ideas and initiatives 'as early as possible in this process'. Or as it is put in an oft-used metaphor, 'one has to jump on the train as early as possible' in order to be allowed to participate in drawing up its 'route' and 'timetable'. 'Too late' and 'in time' are the main parameters for localizing civil servants in time:

> A serious problem is that the national parliamentary consideration generally begins at a stage when it is too late to influence the form and content of Community law.[65]

> The drawback of this decision-making procedure is, according to the Danes, that ministries usually come to fix political guidelines too early.[66]

> If Sweden is to be able to influence the EC it will be important to safeguard and promote Sweden's interests at an early stage of the decision-making process … well before the decision is made … Sweden will be able to influence.[67]

> influence is exercised all the more effectively since it is *upstream from the procedure*.[68] (emphasis in original)

A semantic consequence of this opening up of a whole vocabulary of 'late–early' considerations was a strong emphasis on the informal parts of decision-making. In the studied texts, little space was devoted to descriptions of formal decision-making procedures.

The language of administrative timing created semantic fields spelling out how to 'market' ideas. In European governance economic and commercial metaphors were in general used much more frequently than in the national language, which gave the language a special temporal connotation. In notions such as to market ideas, the future is inherently conceived of in the short term (invest today for returns tomorrow), and can hardly be filled with any great expectations.[69] It was in the process better 'to forestall', than 'to be forestalled'. Although a remarkably large amount of space is given to the vocabulary of 'anticipation' and 'forestalling', the bias towards the future is not the same as in the time of modern states where control of the future meant progress. Instead, control of the future becomes semantically central for technical reasons of national influence. With good timing, the national stance is given better conditions to affect the outcome: 'the sooner the idea is known by others, the easier it is to rally support behind it and to build coalitions with like-minded partners.'

And if this does not work, 'the future', or rather steps into the future ahead of others, can be used as a leverage on partners who supposedly do not want to be left in 'the past':

> In case such proposals are not accepted, it will be necessary for us to go on ahead by ourselves in order to influence the other member-states by our example.[70]

Finally, this part of the language of European governance is also characterised by its neutrality as regards the content of the anticipated future. The timing of future action is fully contained in the present, and reduced to a technical question. The very fact that the language of timing in European governance is given proportionally greater space than in the national discourse results in a technocratisation of the meaning of time. In languages of timing, there is little allusion to good or bad substance of policies. Instead, the art and effort of formulation are devoted to expressions of neutral moments for ripe actions, to 'le moment venue'.[71]

From prognosticised progress to coping with alternative futures

Comparison of the languages of the nation-state and European governance reveals remarkable differences. The fact that the linguistic patterns found in the Swedish texts correspond to those found in the equivalent French, English and Italian material constitutes strong evidence for the correctness of distinguishing between 'the future' in the nation-state and in European governance. My mapping of the everyday language of politics shows that experiences in the European context were collected in a new way. Owing to the fact that so many of the experiences were new and very different from national ones, there was great scope for the creation of a new language to describe them. The aim of the new concepts and semantic constructions was not only to register change, but also to *generate politically desirable expectations* and future actions. They did so by the means of a specific temporal meaning, expressed through a qualitatively new relationship between experiences and expectations. The view of the future in European governance was given its general characteristics by the phenomenon of the 'extension of the present' into the future. The semantic consequence of overloading the present with considerations of an immediate nature is that the planning of the future, which has to take place in the present, is crowded out. The future 'shrinks'.[72]

In contrast to the progressiveness of modern states, the future is perceived to be more uncertain, insecure and unpredictable. The differences to state time are detectable in a shift from a nation-state's language of self-confident 'progress' to European governance's vigilant warnings of 'preparedness'. We are taken from nation-state progress to European governance preparedness through a shortened time horizon of the future.

Political promise as effort instead of objective

This chapter has presented clear evidence of a difference between the connotation of the future in the political life of the nation-states and European governance. The trade union leader, Mr Blomberg, could hardly have imagined that he, in expressing his concern about Swedish influence in Europe, paved the way for the incorporation of Swedes into a new apprehension of the future beyond the state. It seems appropriate to describe the process as if the new historical context sparked off the creation of a new consciousness of the future among Swedish politicians and government officials. In fact, it is only in the light of the structural analysis that the full significance of the nation-state's 'loss of monopoly' of the political future can be understood. The structural analysis shows that the participation in the European future advocated in the autonomy debate did not mean that this future was equivalent to, and an unproblematic substitute for, the national future. The European future that Prime Minister Carlsson talked about was no longer synonymous with progress. It could mean progress, but its more adequate connotations are *possibilities* or *conditions for progress*.

The logic of European futures

The new view on autonomy held by leading political figures generated a fundamental shift of attitude towards the political future. The autonomy debate's concepts of 'coordination', 'participation', 'a welfare say', 'active policy' and 'common decisions for the European future', generated linguistic structures built on expressions such as 'promote', 'sight', 'break', 'instigator', 'administrative competition'. The debate's shift of emphasis from preserving autonomy to exercising national influence was the origin of a whole semantic field made up of 'flexibility', 'rapidity', 'preparedness', 'strategy', 'anticipation' of a 'future difficult to predict'. Furthermore, the lack of explicit reference in political programmes and governmental reports to times good for action did not mean that timing had become less important. On the contrary, since no schemes of policy implementation were specified beforehand, the politicians' control over the future was replaced by a greater freedom with regard to timing of action, which might make it harder for the electorate to exert democratic accountability (cf. chapter 5). The difference in temporal implications between the language of European governance and nation-states helps to explain tensions and contradictions in the autonomy arguments. Many of these were a result of debaters' ambitions to clothe a new relation between Sweden and the Community in a language rich in the implications of national time. As innocent a formula as 'to work for', was in fact an expression of the *changed status of political promise*.

The new form of promise no longer included timetables or any specified implementation. On the one hand, Carlsson strongly wanted to keep open the possibility of evaluating the results *before* taking a decision – in order to see if they would mean progress or not: 'When these negotiations are ready we … make an evaluation. By then we will know what is of greatest use to us – to participate in an extended cooperation or to refrain from it' (Carlsson, 1989a: 11). On the other hand, the Prime Minister's statements expressed an understanding of the fact that autonomous Swedish control of the future was in fact lost. This was particularly clear when he turned towards an uncertain future with rhetorical questions about the *possibilities* of EC cooperation: 'In fact, it is one of their highest wishes to have Sweden participate in this work … Why should we assume that this is not possible?' (Carlsson, 1989b). The functional–structural comparison reveals that closer Swedish cooperation with the Community was not only a question of a 'higher degree of co-ordination', as formulated by Carlsson – it affected the temporal content of political action, that is, the very logic of politics.

Towards a post-modern future?

In the logic of European governance, the political future changes from being equivalent to progress, which can be rationally prognosticised and planned, to unforeseeable 'presents' for which a *strategy* is needed. At a deeper level, the aim of the semantic fields was to counter-balance a future perceived as more difficult to predict owing to uncertainties of the outcomes of the EC institutions. The smaller the space of experience, the vague and more abstract is the language. The vocabulary of European governance is clearly not an expression of the temporalisation that Koselleck talks about. Rather it gives the impression that there are great difficulties with both leaning on past experiences *and* relying on predictions and expectations of the future. The present has gained ground in the consciousness of those involved in European governance. The best expression of this was perhaps the concept of 'preparedness', which alluded to the fact that experiences were of little use for the present and the future. In the languages examined the view was expressed that the future had become more uncertain, insecure and unpredictable. The texts contained fewer clear expectations about future possibilities and progress in comparison to those of the modern nation-state. The concepts' strong orientation towards the present compensates for the lost movement of the language of modernity. European governance is slowing down (putting an end to?) the process of temporalisation by means of a semantic temporal structure where the dimensions of experience and expectation have both shrunk, leaving more room for the present. My results lend support to Luhmann's view that the temporalisation process is limited to a certain historical period. However, even if the analysed texts were very vague regarding predictions of more specific trends, they expressed a more firm view regarding the overall direction of European governance. This was perceived to be an unavoidable and irreversible historical development. Officials gave the impression that they had no other alternative than to follow European developments in whatever unpredictable direction they might take, and therefore had to be flexible and adaptable: 'we need to follow suit in European processes and try to make the best of it.' The quality of the future could be described as mainly neutral. At a more implicit level, we have a presentiment of a more unreliable, ominous and sometimes unhappy future. The description of how to market ideas and how to time their introduction constituted a considerable part of the temporal vocabulary. It was better to forestall others in this process, than to be forestalled.

It is fruitful to contrast my results with Koselleck's own prediction of what will follow the modern era's temporalisation of the political language which, to repeat, is built on the view that 'the lesser the experiential substance, the greater the expectations joined to it'. Koselleck anticipates that the trend of optimising progress ('Neuzeit') may be broken when the process of technological transformation slows down and the corresponding political designs are realised. Then 'the old expectations worked themselves out on the basis of the new experiences … Thus it could happen that an old relation once again came into force; the greater the experience, the more cautious one is, but also the more open the future' (1985: 288). My study points in another direction: semantically the downplaying of progress in European governance cannot be attributed to an increasing weight of experience. Instead, the insecurity of the future is the result of a political language that has lost expectations *as well as* experiential substance in utterances of present action. In the minds of actors involved in European governance, the nation-state has lost not only its monopoly of the control over the future, but the sense of the existence of a politically relevant future horizon. It remains to be seen to what extent this loss constitutes the end of the period which started with the replacement of religion and the church by politics and the nation-state as the main controllers of the future. It is, for example, still too early to draw any conclusions regarding whether the investigated future in European governance will eventually turn *modern* or will remain *post-modern*!

Let us now turn to the dominant and all-embracing present that seems to be evolving in the wake of the shrinking future.

Notes

1   Other examples of influential research within the tradition of the analysis of historical texts are Skinner (1988); Farr (1989); Garcia (1990).

2   Closely related is Quentin Skinner's attempt to solve the problem of the 'cause' and meaning of a certain historical text. The meaning of a text can in Skinner's view be understood in the light of imagining alternative texts that could have been produced at the same time as the text studied. 'It follows that the essential aim, in any attempt to understand the utterances themselves, must be to recover this complex intention on the part of the author. And it follows from this that the appropriate methodology for the history of ideas must be concerned, first of all, to delineate the whole range of communications which could have been conventionally performed on the given occasion by the utterance of the given utterance, and, next, to trace the relations between the given utterance and this wider linguistic context as a means of decoding the actual intention of the given writer' (Skinner, 1988: 63–64).

3   See Edelman (1988), who makes the same distinctions although for very different reasons.

4   Adapted from Sjöblom (1987: 255–267).

5   In Swedish: Kristdemokratiska samhällspartiet (Kds). Since 1996 Kristdemokraterna (Kd).

6   Miljöpartiet.

7   Centerpartiet.

8   Moderata samlingspartiet.

9   Socialdemokratiska arbetarpartiet.

10 Vänsterpartiet.

11 Folkpartiet liberalerna.

12 There is no space here for a thorough description of the historical context in which the need for the reports expressing a national language arose. The official reasoning for commissioning these publications was summarised as the perceived need to enhance the planning and steering capacity of the Swedish administration.

13 Reports commissioned by the Swedish government are of two kinds: *Statens offentliga utredningar (SOU)* and *Departementsserien (Ds)* – depending on whether the minister authorises an expert outside the administration or within it to head the study. Most often, reports are the collective product of a group of politicians and civil servants. Thus, it is more correct to say that the texts are expressions of the administration in a broader sense rather than of a purely civil servant consciousness. The initiative to commission a report can emanate from various actors, interest organisations, etc. The selection of reports dealing with European governance includes nearly all the official reports that were produced within the subject area of the relations and adaptation of the Swedish administration to the Community or Union. Consequently, they must be considered highly representative of the consciousness of the time.

14   The reports are 'Förnyelse genom omprövning' (SOU 1979: 61), 'Förslag till utbildning för högre chefer i statsförvaltningen' (Ds 1980: 2), 'Politisk styrning – administrativ självständighet' (SOU 1983: 39), 'Statsförvaltningen och EG' (SOU 1993: 80), 'Statsförvaltningens Europakompetens – Om behovet av kompetensutveckling hos myndigheterna inför integrationen' (Ds 1992: 96), 'Statsförvaltningens internationalisering – En vitbok om konsekvenser för den statliga sektorn i Sverige' (Ds 1993: 44) and 'Sverige och den västeuropeiska integrationen – sammanfattning av konsekvensutredningarna (Swedish Foreign Ministry, 1994)', 'Utvidgning och samspel – Förhållandet småstat-stormakt: svenskt identitetsbyte' (SOU 1995: 132), 'Ett år med EU-Svenska statstjänstemäns erfarenheter av arbetet i EU' (SOU 1996: 6), 'EU-medlemskapets effekter på svensk statsförvaltning' (Statskontoret: 1996: 7) and 'L'adaptation de l'administration française à l'Europe' (de Clausade, 1991). For a summary of the reports see Ekengren (1995).

15   The main reason for commissioning them is declared to be the increased pace of the completion of the EC's internal market programme and the new challenges this posed for the French administration.

16   For a thorough discussion of sovereignty and autonomy see Dunér (1977).

17   *Metallarbetarförbundet.*

18   For other similar linguistic wholes see e.g. Connoly (1974), Geis (1987) and Jansson (1991). Lars-Göran Stenelo (1980) has mapped out the language, or as he puts it, 'the conceptual framework' of foreign policy predictions. Klein (1990) has examined how the Soviet threat was discursively constructed in the West. Useful for the construction of 'international languages' is also a tradition within IR theory concerning information processing in decision-making within the central state apparatus (e.g. Steinbruner, 1974). These analyses have emphasised the importance of speed, intelligence and 'mediatised' images' (Der Derian, 1992) for the generation of 'the world in their minds' (Vertzberger, 1990).

19   Swedish Christian Democrats (Kds) (1993: 29).

20   John Major, British Conservative Party, 'A Nation of Opportunity', Speech to the Social Market Foundation, Church House, Westminster (1992: 2).

21   Major, 'A Nation' (1992: 5).

22   Swedish Christian Democrats (Kds) (1993: 36).

23   The French Green Party: 'On Employment' (Les Verts français: 'sur L'emploi'), on the Internet (January 1997). (All the relevant web addresses are listed at the end of the Bibliography, p. 176.)

24   Swedish Environmental Party (Miljöpartiet) (1994: 2).

25   Swedish Environmental Party (1994: 9).

26   Swedish Christian Democrats (1995: 3).

27   British Conservative Party: 'Talking Politics', Building A Europe of Nation-States: Our Vision, on the Internet (1997).

28   British Conservative Party, 'Talking Politics'.

29   Swedish Christian Democrats (1995: 12).

30   Swedish Christian Democrats (1995: 8).

31   Swedish Christian Democrats (1995: 8).

32   Swedish Environmental Party (1994: 9).

33   For this reference I am grateful to Kerstin Jacobsson, who uses it in her excellent paper 'Den historiska fantasin. Om erövrandet av det förflutna och konstruktionen av framtiden. Eller: vår bästa tid är nu', unpublished paper (1996).

34   SOU (1993: 80: 24).

35   SOU (1993: 80: 20–21).

36   SOU (1993: 80: 157).

37   SOU (1993: 80: 176).

38   SOU (1993: 80: 184).
39   Ds (1993: 44: bilaga 1: 6).
40   Ds (1993: 44: 19).
41   Ds (1993: 44: 24).
42   de Clausade (1991: 29).
43   Swedish Environmental Party (1994: 2).
44   Prime Minister John Major's 'New Year's Message', at the Conservative Association Chain (29 December 1996). On the Internet (4 January 1997) (Conservative Party: 'Press Room': CPC Lectures).
45   French Communist Party: 'The Communist Party Project', 29th Congress of the French Communist Party. On the Internet (January 1997).
46   Cf. Jacobsson (1995: 2).
47   French Socialist Party, 'Policy Text on Globalization. A Project for France in Europe, Facing up to Globalization: II.1.3'. On the Internet (4 March 1996).
48   British Conservative Party: 'Talking Politics: Building A Europe of Nation-States: Our Vision'. On the Internet (10 February 1997).
49   French Socialist Party, 'Policy Text. A Project for France in Europe, Facing up to Globalization: II. 5 – For a Political Europe', On the Internet (4 March 1996).
50   Italian Conservative Party (Forza Italia), 'Programme 1996, Section 92: The European Union'. On the Internet (5 January 1997).
51   Swedish Environmental Party (1995: 12).
52   Swedish Environmental Party (1995: 7).
53   French Socialist Party, 'Policy Text on Globalization. A Project for France in Europe, Facing up to Globalization'. On the Internet (4 March 1996).
54   French Socialist Party, 'Policy Text. A Project for France in Europe, Facing up to Globalization: II. 5. For a Political Europe'. On the Internet (4 March 1996).
55   French Socialist Party, 'Policy Text. A Project for France in Europe, Facing up to Globalization: II.1.3'. On the Internet (4 March 1996).
56   Ds (1980: 2); SOU (1979: 61, 1983: 39, 1993: 80).
57   Swedish Foreign Ministry (1994: Part 6: 2).
58   Ds (1992: 96: 21).
59   Ds (1992: 96: 21).
60   Ds (1992: 96: 21).
61   Ds (1992: 96: 36).
62   de Clausade (1991: 15).
63   SOU (1993: 80: 170).
64   de Clausade (1991: 57).
65   SOU (1993: 80: 49).
66   SOU (1993: 80: 100).
67   SOU (1993: 80: 183).
68   de Clausade (1991: 23).
69   This economic turn has also been found in analyses of politics in general, according to which the time horizon of economic actors has spread to the political sphere concurrently with the growing deregulative trend in Western welfare states during recent decades (e.g. Maier, 1987). Thus, European governance may constitute an additional arena of this marketisation of politics.
70   Swedish Foreign Ministry (1994: 3: 22).
71   de Clausade (1991: 24): 'Lastly, this broader consultation, which could be organised by the "European cell" in each ministry …, and reformulation of the main ambiguities in the text would allow the SGCI (Secrétariat Général du Comité Interministériel pour les questions de coopération économique européenne), whose role is to ensure that France's position is coherent, to perform its task as efficiently as possible when the time comes.'
72   The concept is borrowed from Nowotny (1992: 508).

3

Back to the present
New conditions for political action

From a nation-state of simultaneous events to EU deadlines

> The idea of a sociological organism moving calendrically through homogeneous, empty time is a precise analogue of the idea of the nation, which also is conceived as a solid community moving steadily down (or up) history. An American will never meet, or even know the names of more than a handful of his 240,000,000-odd fellow-Americans. He has no idea of what they are up to at any one time. But he has complete confidence in their steady, anonymous, simultaneous activity. (Anderson, 1983: 31)

The feeling of a national present has been prevalent at all levels of the political life. The image of a national 'now', where national simultaneous activities are taking place, has constituted the basis for national politics and a national political culture.

In the nation-state government, coordination was carried out through the means of a confidence among political parties and actors that no action would be taken before all concerned had been consulted – or ideally, before it could be agreed to, a pattern that could be achieved by means of a mutual tacit under-standing of each other's priorities. The system of a national present of action – the moment when tacitly coordinated actions were pursued – created the image of national simultaneity.

Also in central government, coordination was carried out through the means of a confidence among ministries and agencies that no action would be taken before it could be agreed to by other ministries concerned. Most of the coordination between ministries so that they could act collectively on behalf of the Cabinet as a whole was 'passive and tacit coordination' (Larsson, 1986: 165; Bulmer, 1986; George, 1992). This passive coordination did not imply that relations between the ministries were in any case close and coherent and that active measures were then unnecessary. On the contrary, the ministries were distinctively separated from each other. National governmental consent and coordinated action were achieved through a mutual confidence among the national ministries about what their respective responsibilities were and what position they held on various issues. The consent was built on a confidence that simultaneous activity for consistent national action was taking place.

The idea of a national political present had the form of a mutual confidence that proposals were not put forward *until* they were known to be acceptable to all ministries and to have been discussed with other relevant interests. There was a confidence in tacit adaptation for consistent national action, a confidence that nobody would go ahead *before* having heard and incorporated the views of concerned parties into their own proposal. The process implied a tacit 'national interval' made up of the time necessary for ministries to anticipate and adapt to the opinions of the other ministries. The result was a common 'clock' taken for granted within central government. At the moment one of the ministries presented a proposal, the other ministries knew that everybody could then agree to it, even without having played an active role in its elaboration. It was this interval that made possible the feeling of community based on temporal 'coincidence' of general agreement throughout the central bureaucracy.

In this way, politicians and officials awaited each other in a natural 'national sequence', which made them appear to acting as a 'sociological organism', as a 'we'. The system of tacit coordination was an expression of the idea that national government as a whole would not take action until it acted as a single whole. The basis for this conception was a confidence in the steady, anonymous, simultaneous, tacit coordination among colleagues.

In European governance, the confidence in colleagues' activity is not the same.

> [At] the EU-secretariat, whose role it is to co-ordinate the whole thing and make sure that there is a realistic Swedish position and that there actually is a homogeneous Swedish position on all questions. Many of the issues and questions which arise in the EU context affect more than one ministry and then the position has to be co-ordinated. We are in a new situation in so far as we do not control the timetable anymore. The timetable for making decisions is controlled by the [EU] chairmanship so that means that we cannot do what we did before, namely to wait until every differing view has been settled. We have to be ready in time when a proposal comes up in the Council of Ministers, Coreper or whatever. (Swedish EU Co-ordination Secretariat)[1]

Nothing reveals the erosion of the confidence in national simultaneous activity better than the difference between the expressions 'make sure ... there is a homogeneous position', and the 'tacit and passive' coordination of national governance. Outside European governance, certain questions of course could also affect more than one ministry, but in that case the 'tacit' coordination between ministries was seen as the 'active' one (Larsson, 1986). In the case of European governance, 'active' coordination seems to be highly explicit and formalised. While homogeneity and simultaneity in national politics and policy-making are tacitly taken for granted, they have become an issue in European governance, something that has to be 'made sure'.

What happens to policy-making in the active upholding of the image of a present for political action, compared to the passive one of the nation-state? Are we in the active coordination for meeting EU deadlines and following EU timetables seeing the emergence of a European consciousness of the present? The task of this chapter is to ascertain the existence of a feeling of a distinct present in European governance and analyse its implications for policy-making.

The idea of the political present

The present in perspective

The idea of the present, and the closely connected simultaneity, has historically played an important role in the creation of political and cultural identities and communities (McLuhan, 1964/1973; Benjamin, 1973; Kern, 1983; Adam, 1995: 107–148). It was the introduction of a singular national calendar which helped to create the image of a national 'we-ness', a national time frame, which gave citizens a feeling that their daily activity was taking place simultaneously (Anderson, 1983). The nation-state became the main defender of this unique national 'now' that, in Anderson's view, was a condition for the development of a national consciousness and an imagined national community (for Anderson, all communities where the inhabitants do not know each other personally are imagined). However, the main *creator* of this social now was the first 'national' literature. Anderson describes how the first national novels in particular created the fiction of a common national present. He characterises this time as a 'homogeneous, empty time, in which simultaneity is, as it were, transverse, cross-time, marked not by prefiguring and fulfilment, but by temporal coincidence, and measured by clock and calendar' (Anderson, 1983: 24). The image of being together in time, of national simultaneity, was diffused not only by means of a national literature, but also by a national press. The national press provided and represented a national collective calendar, a national time for the imagined national collectivity to live in. The thinking of a 'nation' was confirmed by the fact that simultaneous, in the sense of on 'the same day', 'national' events were gathered on the front page of the newspaper. Thus, here the ground for the imagined national connection was the *calendric simultaneity*:

> The date at the top of the newspaper, the single most important emblem on it, provides the essential connection – the steady onward clocking of homogeneous, empty time. (Anderson, 1983: 37)

Anderson speculates about the technological conditions of national simultaneity. One of them was the fast development and spread of clocks and calendars that supported the image of a single standardised time towards which everybody on an individual basis could relate their actions. The effect was a present that was taken for granted.

The formative period of the *global* extension of one 'present' and the feeling of simultaneity was 1880–1918. Between these years were developed the techniques that made possible the 'ability to experience many distant events at the same time' (Kern, 1983: 67). For example, by 1912 the wireless telegraph linked land stations and ships at sea in an 'instantaneous, worldwide network', and at 10 o'clock on the morning of 1 July 1913, the Eiffel Tower sent the first time signal transmitted around the world. From that moment, 'succession gave way to simultaneity' in world affairs. In Kern's terms, it was the 'drama of simultaneity', owing to the diplomats' inability to cope with the instantaneous transmission of telegrams between Europe's capitals, that caused the July crisis which led to the First World War (Kern, 1983: 259–286). A whole new culture of time and space was in the making in people's minds.

International presents

What is fundamentally new in today's international system is:

> Not just the passing of time itself but the rate of change in some variable unit of time. That implies the use of a concept of social time … An increase in the amount of change per unit of time represents an acceleration of social time. When Henry Adams referred to the Law of Acceleration, he meant that the density of events per unit of time was increasing in a predictable way. When observers reflect that 'time is speeding up', that is what they have in mind. (Scott, 1982: 48)

In fact, today's rate of change in the international system, described as 'simultaneous processes of aggregation and disaggregation', has been taken as evidence of an epochal change of the international system (Rosenau, 1997: 23). Ruggie (1989) has conceptualised the result of the links and networks created between people in terms of 'non-territorial regions', such as 'the globe itself'. Every human being, every group of people, is at every moment existing in several 'presents', 'nows', each of which is responding to their respective:

> space/time complexes in which they are embedded. Simply put, the globe is one such 'present'. And it has changed radically since the time when it first made sense to speak of a global factor in world politics. (Ruggie, 1989: 31)

Rosenau (1997) has specified the international present when examining the same responses in different parts of the world within the same time frame: e.g. 'the 1988 outbreak of peace.' He rules out the possibility of coincidental simultaneity, and concludes that only *systemic simultaneity*, in the form of combinations of systemic variables such as the 'lowering of superpower tensions', can explain how it is possible for peace to break out at the same time on a global scale (1997: 428–429). An example of today's simultaneity idea is the analysis of the importance of 'coinciding' events and timing in the literature on international mediation (e.g. Kleiboer and 't Hart, 1995).

The international negotiator simultaneously draws on temporal aspects of two fields of action – e.g. a certain stage in the national preparation of negotiation and the international 'calendar'. The optimal moment is the one when the most advantages can be gained at the two 'sides' of the time framework. The instantaneous sending and receiving of information is now possible because international actors are in constant contact through communications networks and new specialised functions in the civil service, such as the 'linking pins' with the specific task of selecting and transmitting information (Jönsson, 1990). New communications technologies have been of great importance in the interplay between domestic and international fields of action. The two can today to an increasing degree be linked together in time and space by the actor thanks to the greater availability of information from both fields.[2] International organisations constitute new media of time–space distanciation, bringing foreign policy actors together in time and space in a more regularised and systematic way. They provide opportunities of *co-presences*,[3] which facilitate the communication and interpretations of meanings. The organisations also constitute important media fora for the interplay between domestic and international or European timetables of action (Ekengren, 1996a). New patterns of time–space routinisation are emerging within the framework of this interplay (Giddens, 1990).

A European present?

What, then, are the implications for the perceptions of the present and simultaneity that follow from the interconnectedness in European governance? If national activities were, as Anderson (1983) suggests, experienced as simultaneous by the national community, were 'non-national' activities perceived as *not taking place at the same time* in people's imagination, but 'before' or 'after'? If this is the case, a challenge to the idea of a national present can be defined as something that blurs the distinction, the sequence, between an international or European 'before' or 'after' and a national 'now'. The search for changes in this direction is central in distinguishing a European conception of simultaneity. Signs of this kind of erosion within European governance have already been touched upon. Recent research has shown that precisely the feeling of simultaneous national *and* European policy-making activities is the main factor behind the erosion of the apprehended distinction between the 'national' and the 'European', and consequently evidence of European governance (Mörth, 1996):

> In practice, the domestic venture on information technology took place in parallel with an increasing Europeanisation of this policy. The policy-making took the form of partly parallel strategies and not of one initial phase of domestic measures which later passed into European cooperation. (Mörth, 1996: 190)

This pattern of parallel national and European policy-making is today found in a growing number of policy areas. The idea of a distinction between a national 'now' and a European 'before/then' seems to be losing ground in sectors such as telecommunications, environment, energy, immigration, communications (Andersen and Eliassen, 1993; Wallace and Wallace, 1996).

To catch the elusive present

The poetry of the present

Through the method of close reading, Anderson depicts the poetic techniques behind the first national novels that created and brought forward the idea of a national simultaneity. He uses the example of the first Filipino literature:

> And in the phrase 'a house on Analoague Street' which 'we shall describe in such way that it may still be recognised', the would-be recognisers are we – Filipino – readers. The causal progression of this house from the 'interior' time of the novel to the 'exterior' time of the (Manila) reader's everyday life gives a hypnotic confirmation of the solidity of a single community, embracing characters, author and readers, moving onward through calendrical time. (Anderson, 1983: 27)

Here Anderson points out that the poetic ground for the image of simultaneity is the use of a 'we' that unproblematically takes part in a time 'they', the Filipinos, have in common. 'We' as well as 'our':

> 'our young man' … means a young man who belongs to the collective body of readers of Indonesian, and thus implicitly an embryonic Indonesian 'imagined community'. (Anderson, 1983: 32)

Anderson convincingly shows how the poetic creation of the fiction of national simultaneity lies at the very core of the imagined political community of the nation:

> The horizon is clearly bounded: it is that of colonial Mexico. Nothing assures us of this sociological solidity more than the succession of plurals. For they conjure up a social space full of *comparable* prisons, none in itself of any unique importance, but all representative (in their simultaneous, separate existence) of the oppressiveness of *this* colony. (Anderson, 1983: 30)

Anderson underlines that in order to explain how the notion of simultaneity could play such a crucial historical role, we must understand that the meaning of 'simultaneity' was fundamentally new. It meant *coincidence* in time of *independent events*, which was very different from the medieval notion of simultaneity as the coincidence of the past and the future in the present. Thus, not only was the national connection to simultaneity new, but also 'simultaneity' in itself. For in the engendering of the new image of simultaneity new narrative techniques were invented, e.g. the word 'meanwhile' (Anderson, 1983: 24).

Although Anderson himself does not provide a more elaborate definition of the ontological status, his understanding of the present as being just imagined, an idea, represents a *narrative* view of time. A particular perception of time comes into existence at the very moment it is narrated. In Anderson's case, national simultaneity appears as a bi-product of the particular way in which national novels were written. Thus, it had its origin in the very technique of story telling.

The essence of the present

Paul Ricoeur (1984–88) has presented a narrative, 'poetic' solution to the character of time. According to Ricoeur, human beings cannot reach time either as a cosmological phenomenon, or a phenomenological one. Time does not exist for humans until someone tells a story about it. To tell a story about time is to order lived-through temporal experiences – the only human phenomena with a temporal dimension – into a narrative 'whole'. These conclusions are grounded on, on the one hand, Augustine's definitions of time (in his Confessions) and, on the other, Aristotle's theory of the reproduction, 'imitations', of human experience by means of story-telling (Poetics). The basic problem of time is that in philosophical terms it has no being – can have no being – yet we treat and talk about it as if it did. The problem is how we can experience something that does not exist: 'How can time exist if the past is no longer, if the future is not yet, and if the present is not always?' 'How can we measure that which does not exist?' (Ricoeur, 1984: 7–8) In contrast to Augustine's phenomenological view that time exists in the form of human expectation (prediction) and memory (history), Ricoeur argues that these entities have to be articulated before we can say that there is time. It is only 'the poetic art of emplotment' which can give an answer (Ricoeur, 1984: 52–87). Ricoeur's argument is simply that time and the present cannot in itself be directly observed, that it is properly invisible.[4] The plot is only an 'imitation' of reality of certain past events and therefore, in contrast to a 'copy', a creative 'inventive' act. Ricoeur draws a parallel with the artisan who 'invents' things, 'as if'. However, the inventive character of the 'imitation' is, according to Ricoeur, only one dimension of emplotment. Another is how the plot is related to time (Ricoeur, 1984: 52).

The story makes cosmological time human in the sense that it reproduces temporal experience. Narrative brings human order to our elusive experiences of time. What we as researchers can do is to analyse this mediation by means of emplotment between the 'practical field' and the refiguration of temporal experience in the form of narrated, 'constructed', time: 'we are following therefore the destiny of a prefigured time that becomes a refigured time through the mediation of a configured time' (Ricoeur, 1984: 54).

Ricoeur's ontology is basically Kantian: although we use and talk about time as a category, time in itself is invisible. Visible time is the time mounted in the narration – in the story, not in consciousness (in the form of pre-narrative, 'pre-linguistic' memories, expectations). The epistemological consequence of 'Ricoeur's time' is that speculation about a 'real' time beyond the story and the text is of little interest. Time and the present is mounted in 'the poem' of the teller, which consequently requires a 'literary' interpretation of the empirical material: what are the specific narrative techniques behind the story, compared to other ones?

Reading a European present

In the following, I shall use Anderson's idea of simultaneity as a product of a common calendar and a particular narrative technique as a point of departure.

What is the calendar of European governance and how is simultaneity told in European governance? My objective is to look for a possible change in the perception of the idea of simultaneous national activities within a well-delimited case study of European governance. It is the ideas, the 'poetic roots', of the present in European governance that are in focus.

In this work, the challenged fiction of national simultaneous activity and a presumed emerging feeling of a European present are examined through the study of interview material collected within the administration of European governance. In order to display a difference between the fiction of national and European simultaneity, I compare national ministries' coordination for collective action on behalf of the Cabinet as a whole, *outside*, respectively, as *a participant* in European governance. My assumption is that the differences with regard to people's interpretations of coordination in the two situations will reveal the degree of civil servants' confidence in national and European colleagues' simultaneous activity.

What can be counted more precisely as belonging to the poetry of simultaneity can be decided only in a close, 'literary' reading of the answers. To what do 'I', 'we' and 'our' (implying a boundary to others) refer to? 'National', 'European' or other colleagues? What activity is seen as taking place at the same time: 'ours' or 'theirs'? Or only 'mine'? By means of what common codes and conventions does a civil servant 'group of simultaneous activity' constitute itself? How are micro-level interaction and macro-level institutions imaginatively connected? Can any new fictional techniques be discerned (analogous to the creation of the image of parallel stories)? Does the telling of 'simultaneous activity' in European governance differ from the coincidental one of national states?

Perceptions of the present and simultaneity in European governance are sought in interpretations of European governance given by British, Swedish and Danish civil servants. Their views were collected in interviews between 1994 and 1996.[5] The material presented is dominated by answers of foreign ministry officials. I focus my study on this ministry because, being the largest ministry in all three countries, and having a central position in relation to other ministries, and in the coordination of national activities related to the Union, I believe that its officials give representative accounts of coordination in European governance. Other ministries are, of course, of great interest in the search for a new sense of simultaneity, but I believe my restriction in this work is justified. To guarantee that simultaneous activities of the central government are coordinated has always been an important responsibility for the foreign ministry. The basis of this coordination rests on long-established coordination routines of the ministries. One example of these is the rule that the foreign ministry can rely upon the specialised ministries not acting *vis-à-vis* the external world before a common national view has been agreed upon. Possible challenges to these routines and the most developed expressions of a sense of simultaneity in European governance are very likely to be found among the officials whose role has been to guarantee consistency and thereby create confidence in national homogeneous activity.

The idea of a national 'organism', constituting a framework of simultaneous activity, is very clearly exposed in the concrete working methods of particular ministries. Foreign ministries constitute a good example. The traditional proce-dure within foreign ministries is to prepare for particular international events (e.g. forthcoming meetings in multilateral organisations) or for a quick response to world events; there is a clear distinction between the phase of national prepa-ration and the phase of external action or reaction. Thus, the foreign ministry's basic working method has traditionally been based on the understanding that the national preparations are not simultaneous with the international event towards which they are aimed.[6]

The European governance calendar

> A timetable may seemingly consist of a description of events or activities given inde-pendently of it. But all timetables are essentially *time–space organising devices*. A timetable does not just describe how events or activities are fixed in relation to one another, it is the medium of their very co-ordination. Timetabling organises the day of the individual just as it co-ordinates the activities of potentially large numbers of individuals. (Giddens, 1987: 160) [emphasis in original]

> Each government has to work to the deadlines imposed by the Community timetable, at the same time taking into account of the pressures which stem from its domestic environment. (Wallace, 1973: 17) … Each government has had to accept a comparable burden on ministerial and official time as the number of Council sessions and committee meetings has steadily increased. (Wallace, 1973: 84)

Indicators of a common calendar

The European governance calendar is here represented by EU meeting schedules and timetables, of which there are many indicators. Official EU data indicate very clearly the extent of calendric coordination of civil servants engaged in European governance. Wessels (1990) has collected figures for the total frequency of meet-ings held in 1985 within the European Commission, Coreper, the Council, the European Council and the implementation committees (see table 1).

During the 1990s the Council of Ministers on average met over 60 times a year (Wallace, 1990: 216–221). In 1994 over 90 meetings were held. Since the establishment of the EEC in 1957, the Council had on 22 April 1997 met exactly 2000 times.[7] Committees like the Committee of Permanent Representatives (Coreper), the Special Committee on Agriculture and the Article 113 Commit-tee meet weekly. All in all, around 200 committees and working groups consti-tuted by national officials examine the Commission's proposals and prepare the deliberations of Coreper and the ministerial meetings, over an expanding range of policy fields (Wallace, 1990). The total time allotted for all Council meetings (i.e. all policy fields) was about 120 days in 1988. However, there is a great vari-ety between the various policy sectors; the foreign ministers, for example, meet

Table 1 Meeting frequency in some EC organs 1985

General number of translated sessions	7,747
Number of governmental experts in expert groups at the Commission	15,652
Number of meetings session days	3364 (1984)
Average intensity of interactions (working days per year)	6
Number of 'Councils' (number of sessions)	16 (70)
Implementation committees:	
Number of civil servants (higher professional level without language sector) [translation and interpretation]	2,521
Number of civil servants of West German Ministries (higher professional level)	4,292
Percentage share of the total number of the West German ministerial units handling EC related issues (%)	25

Source: Wessels (1990: 233–234).

once a month, while the ministers responsible for health questions meet more seldom. It is often said that some ministers see their EC partners as often as they see their national cabinet colleagues. In addition, up to 900 national civil servants participate at sessions of the European Council. All together, approximately 16,000 meetings of Commission and Council organs, committees and working groups took place in 1994.[8] In 1987, 550 expert groups of 'independent experts', of which around 70–80 per cent came from national administrations, prepared the Commission's proposals to the Council. To this one should add the national officials' participation in the implementation and administration of EC regulations and law in over 250 implementation committees under the Commission, and within the national administrations themselves (Wessels, 1990: 236–237). There is a tendency for the number of meetings to increase and thus the extent of national civil servants' involvement and time spent. Considering the fact that the ultimate reason for all meetings is the proposals from the European Commission, one indicator of this trend is the increasing number of proposals; between 1975 and 1986 it increased from 339 to 608 (Wallace, 1990: 221). In 1986 the implementation of over 300 directives began to complete the Internal Market programme. By September 1994, 268 of these had been adopted by the Council and between 181 (Greece) and 220 (Denmark) had been implemented at the national level.[9] In recent years, however, the annual number of Commission proposals for legislation has stabilized and in some years even decreased.[10]

All Swedish ministries had at the beginning of 1996, after one year of EU membership, participated in the work of the Council and within the Commission's implementation committees (the Ministry of Agriculture participated in over 100 implementation committees, thirty expert committees and ten

Council working groups; the equivalent figures for the Ministry of Social Affairs were ten, twenty-three and eight; for the Foreign Ministry: 'more than five', zero and 'a great number'). Nine out of thirteen ministries had been represented in the Commission expert committees. Twelve had at some point during the year been dealing with the implementation of EU law, and eleven had participated in the preparation of 'EU questions'. Ten out of thirteen had had EU-related tasks falling outside the five categories mentioned above, such as information about the Union, preparation of the Intergovernmental Conference (IGC), preparation of EU positions in the United Nations (UN), investigations concerning cases before the European Court of Justice (ECJ), etc. The approximate shares of the ministries' EU-related work in relation to the total working hours were as follows: one ministry devoted 5–9 per cent to EU-related work, three 10–19 per cent, seven 20–39 per cent, and two out of thirteen more than 60 per cent. All ministries stated that their workload had increased owing to cooperation in the Union and that the number of personnel needed to be increased. None of the ministries declared in 1996 that they had sufficient resources for the accurate management of EU-related tasks. Resources were needed for participating in EU negotiations, elaborating instructions and guidelines for negotiators, analysing EU issues, etc. All the ministries have adopted strict rules for the form in which their staff are to report from EU meetings and the time limits within which it should be done.[11]

It is interesting to note that the ministries believed that it is much more important to increase their resources and to improve the communications (particularly by electronic means) between themselves and other public authorities than to try to increase the amount of time allotted to the preparation of the government position on EU questions. This priority is an expression of the fact that as the deadlines for handling EU-related issues, originating from EU decision-making demands, can hardly be changed, the civil service must adapt by increasing its capacity to meet them. From the perspective of national administration the timetabling of European governance seems to be inexorable.

During 1993 the British ministers participated in the European Council and the Council of Ministers concerning the following sectoral policies: institutional, economic, budgetary, monetary, Internal Market, external relations, trade, aid, agriculture, fishery, transport, energy, regional, industrial, environmental, social and research and development (R&D). British ministers participated in about sixty-five EC meetings during 1993. Many of the meetings had the character of a following up of earlier decisions – i.e. they were to a large extent only a ministerial confirmation of a continuous collaboration between civil servants in various working groups of the Council's and Commission's implementation committees. The Council decisions very often establish a framework for the day-to-day supervision and administration of some matter by the national civil servants and often imply deadlines.[12]

On 22–23 March, the Environment Council agreed a decision which establishes a monitoring mechanism for emissions of carbon dioxide and other greenhouse gas emissions within the Community. This will require all member-states to prepare and update regularly national programmes to limit these emissions.[13]

Or in an even more direct way:

Member-states are required to enact the measures necessary to comply with the directive by 1 July 1994 and apply them with effect from 1 January 1995.[14]

The [Eco-management] scheme has to be implemented in all member-states by 13 April 1995. The Government has recently issued a consultation paper setting out its preferred options for establishing a competent body to operate the scheme in the United Kingdom and for accrediting the independent verifiers.[15]

Another indicator of the extent to which the agenda of European meetings influences civil servants of European governance is their participation in working group meetings in Brussels. Groups of officials of the Foreign and Commonwealth Office (FCO) presently make approximately 110 visits to Brussels per year.[16] During 1994 there were on average sixteen working group meetings of national foreign ministry officials from the twelve member-states each month within the Union's Common Foreign and Security Policy (CFSP).[17]

The effects on the parliamentary side also indicate the level of impact of the Common European Calendar. A total of 732 EC documents and 143 explanatory memoranda by government departments were discussed in the British parliament during 1993. Of the EC documents, 428 were defined in the House of Commons Select Committee as 'not legally and/or politically important'. As concerns the rest (304), 68 were taken up for debate in the following forms: five plenary debates (10, 16 and 31 March; 9 and 13 December) and forty-four Standing Committee debates (13, 20 and 27) (2 debates) January; 3 (2), 10 (2), 17 and 24 February; 3, 17, 24 (2) and 31 (2) March; 28 April; 5 (2), 12 (2), 19 (2), 25 and 26 (2) May; 9 (2), 23 and 30 (2) June; 7 (2), 14 (2), and 21 (2) July; 27 (2) October; 2 and 30 November; 1 (2), 8, and 15 (2) December. In the House of Lords, EC issues were discussed on twenty-one occasions during 1993.

Adapting to a European calendar

There are, of course, differences between individuals, departments and ministries with regard to the consciousness of the European Calendar. However, it would seem that the influence of EU timetables is even greater than the official quantitative data indicate. Interviews conducted with national foreign ministry officials reveal that the Calendar influences *indirectly* many of those officials in the ministries not directly responsible for EU questions. The fulfilment of EC obligations is most often given priority at every level of administration, and thus subordinates other issues by placing EC deadlines above national ones in importance. The extension of the European impact on national ministries is large:

> Every section of the Foreign and Commonwealth Office, whatever policy area it is concerned with, now has to address the EU dimension, and consider what would be the views of EU partners. They are now enmeshed in the process of CFSP which was not the case in earlier times. It is becoming much more of an all embracing network.[18]

In addition to the EU meeting schedules, there are other devices for the standardisation of a common administrative clock for European governance. One of these is the regularisation of information exchanges among EU colleagues (cf. the role of the telegraph in the establishment of a standardised American time in the nineteenth century (Carey, 1988)). The regular information diffusion between actors involved in European governance strengthens the sense of a common present. The CFSP and its special Correspondence Européenne (Coreu) telegram system between the foreign ministries of the fifteen member-states can serve as an example:

> Certainly the fact of sharing information creates confidence, if everyday you see Coreus coming in from different countries, and 80 per cent of the Coreus with what you would entirely agree with, it is a constant reaffirmation that there is a certain European approach which really does have something in common. It strengthens realisation of what is common between us, and then we can narrow down the areas of difficulty and focus on those. Not necessarily overcome them but at least we have a better chance to see what is common and what is not.[19]

Although the various fields of EU cooperation differ from each other, the CFSP sector reveals interesting devices for the provision of a European governance Calendar that to a large extent can be generalised to European governance as a whole. These include the direct contact between colleagues via telecommunications, and the large volume and rapid pace of information they exchange in an informal manner. The Coreu system is constituted by direct telefax lines between the fifteen foreign ministries, through which the common foreign policy concerns of the day, or rather of the hour, are instantaneously transmitted, creating a feeling of constant connection between CFSP colleagues. Owing to the fact that the Coreu makes possible the instant transmission of a constantly updated common agenda of foreign policy issues, it leaves little room for a purely national foreign policy calendar. Following the CFSP Calendar and agenda has to be given priority in everyday work. The Coreu system makes possible an exchange of information 'with extraordinary rapidity', as one official of the European Commission has put it (Nuttall, 1992: 23). The size of the information flows is impressive; the number of telexes increased from 4000 to 12,000 between the creation of the Coreu in 1973 and 1992 (Tonra, 1997). In 1994 the figure rose to 12,699 (Luif, 1995: 47). This amounts to 200–300 messages per week. Through this system, national officials are constantly reminded of the CFSP dimension in their foreign policy-making. A telex sent by one of the fifteen administrations can result in reactions and possible actions in the other fourteen within a couple of hours. There is a tendency for the information transmissioned through Coreu to accelerate in pace and expand in scope. Officials at each national foreign ministry now have access to reports about the world from four-teen other ministries, and participate in regular meetings of the more than fifty working groups within the CFSP (Tonra, 1997).

The CFSP Calendar's clocking of EU foreign policy can be seen in the new *routines* that are common to all in European governance. One of these has been labelled the 'consultation reflex', which exists both at the ministerial level and between the embassies of the fifteen in 'third' countries. The most important result of this reflex is a higher degree of predictability among the foreign ministries regarding both the thinking and action of EU partners (Pijpers, Regelsberger and Wessels, 1988). Thus, the consequence of the Coreu system is not just a question of new priorities with regard to time allocation; it also results in a new European 'time praxis' for the everyday work in the form of new admin-istrative routines and new rhythms of decision-making at the national level. For example, the timing considerations in this 'telex diplomacy' point to the fact that there are common moments of decisions – common presents – within which civil servants can play with time:

> If we want to influence the handling of a certain subject we should get our Coreu in first, we should get it in before other countries if we possibly can. Of course, that places certain demands on the machinery here at home, because you must have enough manpower and expertise in order to define your policy very quickly. (Foreign and Commonwealth Office, London)[20]

The basis for this strengthened feeling of a need for timing is that foreign policy makers know that they all receive identical messages over Coreu *at the same moment* as other European colleagues.

Common agendas confirm the thinking of a present in European gover-nance. The significance of a common agenda is that it constitutes a list of simul-taneous concerns for the various actors. The great importance of the acceptance of a growing EU agenda *as such* has been observed by many. Nuttall (1992) has pointed out the crucial role of an agreed CFSP agenda for the existence and functioning of EU foreign policy cooperation. The fact that the agenda for a par-ticular EU meeting is transmitted instantaneously to member-states creates a new qualitative input to images of simultaneity: the organisation of people in time and space is based not only on common timetables, but on a common order of concerns, priorities and substantive matters. Might it perhaps be fruit-ful to search for a new, *issue oriented* sense of simultaneity, rather than a direct analogy to the sense of simultaneity as the coincidence of independent activities in time that Anderson (1983) has pointed to as part of national identity? In order to answer this kind of question, we need to understand the broader stories by which the present is made to make sense in European governance.

The fiction of a European present

> Fiction seeps quietly and continuously into reality, creating that remarkable confidence of community in anonymity which is the hallmark of modern nations. (Anderson, 1983: 36)

> Certainly the fact of sharing information creates confidence … it is a constant reaffirmation that there is a certain European approach which really does have something in common. It strengthens realisation of what is common between us. (British Foreign Office)

The squeezed national present

BLURRED BORDERS

The division of labour between the departments and ministries of a national government is felt to be not as clear-cut as it was:

> The world was very nicely divided before entering into the EU. Not anymore because all questions affect each other so we have seen many cases where the desk officer for a certain country at the political, but also here at the trade department, are involved in making instructions. But it is a bit impractical. (Swedish EU Co-ordination Secretariat)[21]

EU timetables have created the risk of overlapping work owing to the fact that national ministries are not aware of each other's work to the same extent as before. On a deeper level, European governance blurs the borders between traditional 'tacit' divisions of political subject areas:

> There is a bit of everything but internal policy and external foreign policy mix now to a large extent and yes I would say that our foreign policy in a traditional sense of the word is much more interrelated with internal policy. This general trend is being very much enhanced, in the case of Sweden, by our entering into the EU. The inter-relation has become much more apparent as soon as we entered. (Swedish EU Coordination Secretariat)[22]

The division of labour between national ministries can no longer be taken for granted; it has to be continuously supervised by means of centralised 'coordination' and the spontaneous growth of new normative guidelines:

> Sometimes we are making policies, which means that we write what we think the policy should be on a tentative ground and then see if others agree. Sometimes we are contributing to policy that is representing the FCO's interest in the policy that somebody else is making. It might be the DTI [Department of Trade and Industry]: … Let's take a case when the DTI is making a policy and there are four departments within the foreign office that have an interest. What we would normally do is – assuming this a European matter – the EUD [European Union Department] of the FCO would first of all talk to the other departments in the foreign office. What do you think about it? Can we agree on a foreign office view that represents all of us? And usually we are able to do that, and then it would normally be the EUD that

would write to the DTI to say this is the FCO view on this policy on which you have the lead, and by doing that we try to influence them. It is very rare in the UK system, that a policy is to be made in any ministry against the active disagreement of any ministry. So the DTI has an interest in listening to what we say and to try to build our interest into their policy, and that is happening all the time. So that is what is happening when another ministry is leading. When the FCO is leading there are two possible cases: either it is a subject where some other department in the foreign office has the most important interest and then they would usually consult us to build the European Community interest into their policy. For example if there was a whole, say, review of UK relations with any country, for example India, going forward, that review would have to take account of the European aspect and the South Asian department that led the review will consult us for our opinion on the European aspects of UK relations with India. If the main subject was the EU's relationship with India, and we were trying to define what the UK attitude towards EU negotiations with India was, that would be my department that would take the lead and make sure that the South Asian department or any other department who had an interest in India contributed. (European Union Department (EUD), Foreign and Commonwealth Office)[23]

And that means that the heads of the units will have a strong, a relatively strong role and they will also at that level co-ordinate between sorts of different ministers' competence and I think that this is a result of membership. (Swedish EU Secretariat)[24]

I think it is generally understood that when the Community is acting then the European Union Department leads. And where the CFSP is acting then the geographical departments take the lead and coordinate their practice and procedures through the CFSP unit. I think that is a useful guideline that we all follow and the mistakes we make are very few, partly because of the coordination mechanisms that operate all the time. (EUD, FCO)[25]

These 'stories' reveal that the synchronisation of national actions is by no means taken for granted and that new techniques of active coordination are being developed. The very fact that great attention is given to the question of which ministry or department should play a leading role is itself an indication of a change in outlook from one that expresses general confidence that the activities of the rest of national government are being conducted simultaneously to one that shows clear awareness of a temporal sequence of action with one ministry or department leading and another following.

The conventional modes of coordination that have upheld the degree of national uniformity needed for the confidence in a common homogeneous action are eroded. The erosion is most clearly revealed in the deliberate attempts to keep traditional procedures, and in the anxiety of losing also the instrument for these very attempts:

People working at all levels in the foreign ministry will have much more frequent contact with colleagues in the other Euro ministries [British ministries involved in EU decision-making]. And I'm sure this is a good thing. But it will make policy process much more open and therefore much more flexible. And it is difficult to see where the formal mechanisms for agreeing British policy will fit into that. I suspect that it means that, and this is already happening, British policy will be informed already by these long-term informal contacts. That will have to be taken into account when decided what we in Britain should do. (Policy Planning Staff, FCO)[26]

On European Community work a great deal of time is taken up by talking with other ministries. There are very few Community subjects that only affect the Foreign Office. The DTI [Department of Trade and Industry] is almost always affected and the Ministry of Agriculture, the Treasury usually has a view. So a lot of my life is to talk to ministries that are not the Foreign Office. (EUD, FCO)[27]

The new situation has arisen from the fact that 'we do not control the timetable anymore' (see quotation on p. 68). It is therefore clear that the underlying factors challenging national procedures include not only harmonising the substance of issues, but also 'when'-questions. Questions about timetables are made explicit because they lie outside national control. In the Union, different national departments and ministries of the same member-state follow different timetables for decision-making, and consequently need to formulate positions in relation to these 'external' deadlines. The temporal Europeanisation of national government is uneven. Confidence in national homogeneous actions of all ministries requires active, explicit coordination to be maintained.

The fact that a national official who participates in the CFSP or other EU networks with a recurring cycle of meetings is constantly aware of what her colleagues in the other EU countries are doing and can communicate with them instantaneously gives rise to comparative uncertainty about the activities of colleagues in her own civil service:

As far as working in the European Union Department [is concerned], the main effect of the CFSP has been that we have to be much more careful that the work that we do does not start to trespass on areas of interest to the CFSP because if you are working all the time with European Union work it is very easy to take an interest in everything that is going on and to find that the work you are doing within the EC treaty has certainly taken on interests that really go outside the treaty and has more to do with foreign and security policy. That shows the necessity really for all the departments interested in the field to keep in very close contact with each other and tell each other what they are doing. (EUD, FCO)[28]

I for example have daily contact with the CFSP unit, by telephone, and we are placed quite close together so it is easy to just walk down and talk with somebody about a subject. And of course if we happened to have made a mistake, if the European Union Department has written about something that should be for the CFSP unit then it is not too embarrassing to issue a correction saying the views I put forward are subject to ratification of the CFSP unit whose concern this problem is. (EUD, FCO)[29]

But does this constitute a fundamental difference from the problems of national coordination? There is one major difference, namely that there is no time 'to wait until every differing view has been settled' (see quotation on p. 68) before national action is taken. This is the main reason why an active 'EU Secretariat' is needed. There is simply not enough time, no natural national interval, to achieve a general consensus among all the units concerned on all details of policy. The result is that the sequence of governmental actions previously taken for granted is now interrupted in the name of coordination. The present is not empty any longer; instead it is 'filled' with considerations. Fraser has argued that 'the width of the social present is determined by the time necessary to make people take concerted action' (quoted in Adam, 1995: 113). In European governance, the national present is, if not disappearing, seriously squeezed between demands for quick action by overlapping European timetables.

OVERLAPPING TIMETABLES
> *Which problems do you face when coordinating Sweden's policies?*
> Firstly, I mentioned the timetable of course. One cannot just leave things about, one has to know at an early stage what is going on. One has to put in comments from other ministries and from other parts of the Ministry of Foreign Affairs. (European Correspondent in CFSP, Swedish Foreign Ministry)[30]

The fact that things cannot be 'left about' is not only owing to limited time for national preparation, but also loss of confidence in the national *linear sequence* of coordination. The key component in the emplotment of simultaneity is the experience of *parallell* national activities in *separate* EU fora. The question is how to synchronise national actions when there is no time between the conclusion of negotiations in different CFSP organs and committees:

> It is clear that there is a Swedish policy in Vienna that is pursued in the weekly EU consultation meeting, sometimes several times a week. And then there are EU consultations between the capitals, and the CFSP meetings within the OSCE [Organisation for Security and Cooperation in Europe], which have to be coordinated with other CFSP meetings of other forms. Both COSEC, the [CFSP] working group for security policy, and some of the regional groups COEST [CFSP Committee for Eastern Europe and Central Asia] etc., have to be coordinated. In the case of Chechenia, the coordination was rather complex; EU has supported the OSCE activities in the region with parallel *démarches* through the Moscow ambassadors and various other means of bringing pressure to bear on the process, which has increased the time demands. It is no longer sufficient to work out a position in one forum, but to present positions in several fora at the same time and to coordinate them. (OSCE Department, Swedish Foreign Ministry)[31]

Since national diplomats sit on different CFSP working groups, they permanently work according to different timetables, that is the schedule of meetings for the working group. The complexity of various timetables, each of which is closely followed only by the official participating in the particular working group, undermines the experience of a common national foreign policy calendar for all diplomats. Their feeling of the ordering of national handling into an *initial* fixing of a national position, followed by a *presentation* of it to the outside world, is therefore eroded.

The breaking up of the national linear sequence is visible in the changed conditions for prediction in European governance. New styles of anticipation are created since national planning parallels CFSP deliberations. This simultaneity is made possible by the instant transmission of information between the two fields. The division of ministerial activities between various EU working groups gives rise to a new technique of prediction of European and international events:

> Due to the time constraints, an increasing number of issues have to be decided at lower ministerial levels. Within each area we hold internal 'loose threads' meetings where we try to predict various up-coming issues in one context. Thereafter, the official has to try to act in this 'spirit'. (Swedish OSCE Department)[32]

To uphold the image of a 'national' sequence, a new style of prediction is required. With new tools, such as the 'loose threads' meetings, national diplomats are trying to knit together parallel national activities in various CFSP organs into a fabric preserving the possibility of synchronised, homogeneous 'Swedish initiatives' and 'actions' in all fora. They are supposed to act in a constantly updated 'spirit' of a national organism. The background is that the initiation of a policy within CFSP is to a very high degree disconnected from the final CFSP policy outcome owing to the complex multilateral decision-making process. Succession of policy-making *within* the framework of a national present is in European governance replaced by simultaneity and instantaneousness:

> With all of these contacts happening much more quickly, and at so many different levels, and in so many different places – going back to timing again – the idea of there being a British policy, which then is reflected by every British diplomat that you talk to, that is not going to be true anymore. It is not true now. The information flows far too quickly for that. And in terms of talking about centralised control from a centre [from London] of what goes on in posts overseas we are well behind the game most of the time. The guidance will be issued after the event. There is much more autonomy for posts overseas. We would generally say who will react, who will interact with European Community departments and host governments and other governments, as they see fit, and only ask for help when they need it. (Policy Planning Staff, FCO)[33]

The multitude of simultaneous activities in European governance seems to have the paradoxical effect of recreating the kind of autonomy diplomat's enjoyed before the time of the telegraph, when they had to bear a great responsibility of their own (Kern, 1983: 274).

Owing to the number of fora and working groups and the extent of simultaneous meetings, government positions are in a *constant* formation process. The confidence in consistent action of the national ministries was to a large extent built on the imagination of one fixed national calendar, where policy actions and meetings could be sequenced over time and adequately represented by a national agenda. European governance erodes this idea of a singular national timetable. The feeling of simultaneous activities in European governance is undermining the exclusiveness of the national calendar. The number of CFSP working group timetables, together with the fact that national positions are frequently revised in various fora, create the need for *constant* and very active national coordination. The language of coordination does not contain the notion that national action is pursued autonomously, tacitly and simultaneously by the parts of central government, because it is built on the antithesis of the notion, namely the idea of active management for coherence in policy content and in time. People involved in European governance closely relate certain aspects of their imitation of their temporal experience with their account of coordination in central government. In this narration 'simultaneous activity' seems to play another role than the one Anderson associated with the feeling of national community and identity.

Stories of a European 'now'

EUROPEAN DEADLINES

As already mentioned, one central component is that timetables are made much more explicit in European governance than in national coordination. One of the most important characteristics of these timetables is the fiction of deadlines, which provides the basis for the feeling of a very marked and distinct European present:

> Certainly working to European timetables imposes far more deadlines than we used to work under. You have to have a view in two days time for a meeting that is taking place then. So perhaps I would have to admit that the pace of decision-making has increased. (EUD, FCO)[34]

> The first and foremost, I think, and the most important difference [to traditional foreign policy-making] is the deadlines: the fact that you constantly are confronted with deadlines within CFSP over which you have no control. You are much more externally directed, the external demand for decision at a certain point of time put pressure on you to get to a decision, even if you do not feel quite ready for it. The time pressure has become much greater. (European Correspondent, CFSP, Swedish Foreign Ministry)[35]

> The result of the time aspect is that positions have to be elaborated much more quickly than before and more 'to the point'. You have to specify the position and often in a situation when you did not expect to do that. Before we decided independently when to bring up a certain question. (West European Division, Swedish Foreign Ministry)[36]

As with the establishment of a national present, it is new communication technology that seems to make possible the European present. CFSP decisions are often discussed and taken collectively by the fifteen over the Coreu system. The difference from the incremental growth of a national calendric present is that the European present is imposed from the very moment you are involved in European governance. The deadlines are the tool that makes this system function, and the most visible representation of its existence. For the EU member-state, the national present is being gradually 'crowded out' by the European one in the accounts of the working day of its officials:

> The regularity of recurrent questions results in a completely new way of working. There is a time-binding effect which forces the individual officer to continuously follow each question and make preparations for meetings. (West European Division, Swedish Foreign Ministry).[37]

> The presidency still holds the most important role. It is for them to call meetings, to suggest the agenda for meetings, and lead the meeting and try to lead the partners to agreement at the right time. It is the presidency that usually urges that something should be solved in a week rather than a month. The presidency is in a position to give guidance and to put pressure on other states to meet a certain timetable. (Security Policy Department, FCO)[38]

The fact that the common CFSP present is thus imposed and enforced by the sanction of the necessity to participate at the date set for decision alters the character of the traditional ministerial present. The deadline stories of European governance are spread throughout the national bureaucracy, forming a discourse of a complex system of temporally disciplining norms and rules:

> The EU Secretariat is a contact point for the chancery of the Swedish Parliamentary EU committee. One of our circulars, one of our rules does concern the information, the flow of information basically to the EU Committee. We have issued rules that say that they [ministries] have to produce … to every important proposal being made by the Commission an informative memorandum, channelled in particular to the Committee. Also, about two weeks before the Council of Ministers meetings, an annotated agenda should be sent out, and general comments should be sent, by concerned ministries to the EU Committee. (Swedish EU Secretariat)[39]

> We have issued a rule that says that all of the reports from all meetings should be issued within 24 hours from the end of the meeting in order to sort of speed up the preparation of the conclusions … so we get a lot of faxes. We send a lot of instructions, it is basically an open line. (Swedish EU Secretariat)[40]

In the poetry of deadlines, new metaphors are used to describe the general organisation and sequencing of everyday work. Illuminating examples were found in an interview with a Danish diplomat, who was earlier engaged in the CFSP process.[41] Significantly, and without any direct questions related to time, he mainly used several temporal metaphors in order to describe his general impression of work within the CFSP. The dealings and planning of the officials was characterised as taking place in relation to a 'yardstick' (in the interview he used the Swedish word for yardstick: 'tumstock'), where the day(s) (1–2) of the foreign ministerial meetings felt like the 'meter marks' of the 'yardstick' towards which all endeavours were pointing, i.e. in the form of an intensification of contacts with national and other member-state colleagues, longer working days, etc. When the two days of ministerial meetings began 'almost all work of substance had been done'. He described these days as 'the pouring out in public of three months of hard work'. The ministerial meeting, the meter mark, constituted the culmination of each period in the temporal sequence and bracketed his personal experience of European governance into intervals. In his imitation of time praxis, the diplomat used the 'yardstick' as a configuration of the deadline structure.

EUROPEAN RHYTHMS

The stories reveal that formal meetings play a decisive role in the organisation of informal interaction and contacts of national officials involved in CFSP. However, they are not sufficient to capture the temporal experience; a flora of informal expressions has sprung up, such as 'the rhythm' and 'the tempo':

> The ministerial meetings are the broad parameters of the CFSP policy and objectives. And also the European Council to some extent. However, it is foreign ministers within the CFSP who sets the broad agenda. The individual desk officer will be closely involved and in contact with his counterparts in other foreign ministries. The political directors are coordinators and the European corespondent; they are sort of channels through which all forms of communications are sent. I am sure there are a lot of informal contacts directly between foreign ministries. (Research Unit, FCO)[42]

> The rhythm of political committee meetings are certainly quite important. It is a target for the work of the more specialised groups. But they would not have to go on to ministers because the political directors would see that they are fine and I think there is a rational amount of delegation in the system and therefore different working groups can work at their own speed according to the demands of the subject, and I think there is great scope for adopting the tempo that is needed for the particular challenge. (Security Policy Department, FCO)[43]

To what extent is the diminishing importance of formal temporal structures significant for European governance? Or is institutionalised time just not yet in phase with the subjective experience of political actors? In any case, judging from the innovative and original organising of time, a new emplotment seems to be needed in order to capture adequately the temporal experiences of the CFSP. A comparison of civil servants' refiguration of national temporal routines, in which objectified, formalised and regularised categories are normally used to a much larger extent, with the categories created by the officials involved in the management of relationships in CFSP, shows that the latter seem to mediate the experience of a flow, or continuum, of ad hoc contacts rather than distinct events. The narratives also give the impression that the small-scale temporal structures are largely regulated independently of the overarching ones: 'the ministerial meetings are only the broad parameters.' However, the micro temporalities are still told as being subordinated to objectivised and institutionalised ones. Conceptions like the 'rhythm of political meetings' and 'the tempo of the working groups' mediate between the interviewed officials' inner time, the interactional temporal structure at the micro level and ultimately official timetables. The strong emphasis on speed, rhythm, etc. in the plotting of sequence, clearly points towards a temporal experience of a different nature from the national one. Whereas the national 'now' was most appropriately described as a fiction of calendrical present, the European one might at this stage be called a *decisional present* owing to its narrative origin in the stories of coordinated decision-making.

EUROPEAN SPEED

An important ingredient that helps engender the feeling of a common present is a new way of talking about *pace* in European governance. EU and CFSP work is experienced as being more intense and more rapid than other matters dealt with in the civil service:

> The pace of decision-making has increased considerably. The fact that you cannot predict the moment when you are supposed to take a decision, forces us to establish internal ministerial structures that enable us to be *prepared* for decision. That has implied rather big changes with regard to our way of working ... a new preparation process, a series of internal coordination meetings. (European Correspondent, CFSP, Swedish Foreign Ministry)[44]

> People who work on EU jobs in the foreign office tend to be under pressure; they work long hours, and very intensively, they work at a very fast pace. They would tend to say there is a great pressure on resources. And there is always pressure to increase the amount of resources devoted to EU questions to keep up with the deadlines, the pace of communication. The volume of work on EU questions generally, not just CFSP, has intensified over the years. (Research Unit, FCO)[45]

> I think, what we [in the CFSP] have now is a rather extreme capacity for very fast reaction to a crisis where our interests are quite simple and can be very quickly defined and the message we want to give to the world is also quite simple. We have now the possibility to get our position agreed in hours rather than days, without people necessarily having to meet. So I think the use of the Coreu system is extremely important. (Security Policy Department, FCO)[46]

> The [CFSP] decision-making procedures are characterised by positioning with 'lightning rapidity' so that you end up with the group of countries you want to belong to in the subsequent process. Timing is of crucial importance. The responsible unit has to react quickly. The individual desk officer's power is increasing. You have to gain momentum in order to gain influence, because it is better to forestall the events, than to be forestalled by them. Bilateral contacts are of increasing importance because of the need to try to anticipate initiatives. You have to be at your office, available, all the time in case an initiative comes in through the Coreu. Otherwise you miss the chance. Coreu makes it possible constantly to keep up with every question. It is more important in the CFSP to know the other's views and to formulate a position of your own in relation to these, than to make more independent in-depth analysis of the issue. The way of working is different from before [i.e. outside the CFSP]. The flow of information in the form of initiatives of the member-states, increases the tempo of the decision making for the involved desk officer; there is always a need to judge *all* the initiatives so as to avoid the possibility that questions just 'roll on' too far to be reversed towards more desirable outcomes for you. If not you risk being dragged into a EU decision that you in the end have to attach yourself to as a CFSP member. It is difficult to put forward a simple 'no' to

an initiative; instead you have to 'jump on the train and try to drive it'. (Swedish Embassy, London)[47]

The experience of a high-speed system is the experience of many contacts within a limited time. The feeling of speed is generated by a new relationship between the number of contacts and meetings and the available time. The emphasis put in the stories on the high pace of work seems to be an effect of the experience that the pressure of time and stress emanate from outside; 'there is a time out there which you cannot do anything about, you just have to adjust to it and try to meet the deadlines it imposes on us.' And, similar to the results of the previous section, there is no time to await for others to solve the issues. The very fact that time is described as being beyond control to a higher degree than before also implies a sense of rapid-speed time. There are very few formal, predictable procedures referred to in the answers above; most of the temporal coordination seems to be negotiated intersubjectively on an ad hoc basis:

> So there is a sequence: sometimes of course it starts with the CFSP working group, and then has to go higher up to be given the blessing of committees that are higher up. And in that sense you have to take account of timetables. If you want something, i.e. you want to get it approved by a high level committee before a certain day, you have to work backwards. (OSCE Division, FCO)[48]

> It is clear, that the faster things go in the EU, the less thoroughly they are dealt with by officials. Of course, positions are fixed long before and are only up-dated … But the speed has increased enormously … It is more of the same, that is what it is all about. (Russian Division, Swedish Foreign Ministry)[49]

> To participate actively in the preparations of the various meetings means [being] actively on the Coreu net. That activity is a prerequisite for gaining support for your standpoints. Of course you can make a contribution to the discussion in Brussels, send instructions to COREPER etc. But in order to get a good start, to be ahead of the field in the discussion of a new issue, you need to transmit a message over Coreu. (Russian Division, Swedish Foreign Ministry)[50]

Objectified and permanent temporal structures are of little importance in the regulation of speed in everyday CFSP practice. This creates the feeling of a very flexible, fluid and open policy process in time. The division of everyday praxis into sequences of distinct 'events' and intervals is becoming more difficult in a 'fluid' speedy situation, in which clear-cut temporal brackets are not easily defined. The kind of sequence which reluctantly is emplotted has an end ('high-level committee meetings') but no specific beginning; 'you have to work backwards' in the process.

The increasing *direct* communication between actors of European governance is in itself an indication of speed in decision-making; information arrives at the foreign ministries directly without being slowed down by the processing of embassies. Judging from these narratives, the plot-makers seem to experience a change in pace to a large extent as an outcome of new information channels, new flows of information. It is this experience that calls for a new refiguration of time.

TIMING

In the creation of a common present in European governance, which passes by with extraordinary rapidity and which one must be alert to catch, stories about the best way to manage this moment are being told. That is, a poetry of *timing* of action in European governance is emerging as a bi-product, and at the same time a support, of the coordinated national activities that constitute European simultaneity:

> It is all a matter of tactics and negotiation, of putting your view forward in as clear a way as is ever possible in the process. The more efficiently you do that, the more impact it will have on the final outcome. The more quickly you formulate your position, the more quickly you get it in, the more likely you are to steer the eventual outcome in a direction which is in accordance with your preferences. (Research Unit, FCO)[51]

> Timing is a factor. The speed of events requires a rapid reaction. And the fact that you have to concert the result with 11 other member-states, maybe soon 16, means that you have to act fast to get everything settled. (Research Unit, FCO)[52]

> The quicker you act, and the quicker you get your views known, in the CFSP process, the more likely the final outcome will be tailored to your own thinking. This is not guaranteed of course, because if member-states feel strongly 'we do not go along with that'. It is better to get your views known sooner rather than later. (Multilateral Policy Section, FCO)[53]

The many explicit references to timing serve to create a feeling of urgency and executive ability. The choice of action in European governance is not mainly a story about *if*, but *when*, to enter activities. On the other hand, the new 'simultaneous activities' entails time constraints that leave less room for longer-term strategy, something which normally is associated to a prerequisite for timing:

> Time is always important. But the pace of events is so fast that you cannot very often choose your timing. You might plan to do something and something else happens. You say we launch an initiative in three weeks time and after a week someone makes it all out of date. You try to plan ahead as far as you can, but you have to be extremely flexible and being able to adapt to what you want to do. This is the kind of circumstances, so you might have to abandon an initiative, or put it forward, or adapt it. It involves quite a lot of flexibility, and imaginative thinking ... It does add a whole dimension to the work. (OSCE Division, FCO)[54]

Timing in European simultaneity is different: adaptable and defensive, instead of offensive? In any case, 'timing in EU' has become a centrally placed fiction in the life of civil servants, described with a very innovative and nuanced vocabulary:

> As for timing, it would depend on the individual case, there can be an advantage of getting your opinion in first. There can be an advantage of waiting to see what other states are thinking, and come in on either one side of the debate or the other. That would depend on individual decisions taken in each circumstance. (EUD, FCO)[55]

> I think the general conception is that once it [the proposal] is launched into the CFSP structure it may take a long time to come out at the end of it. Because there are so many uncertainties that come into play whenever you have twelve people sitting around the same table trying to agree on something. (Policy Planning Staff, FCO)[56]

These examples of ways to emplot timing clearly show that the description of practical routines have considerably more temporal content than the stories of national coordination outside European governance. There is a more even balance between spatial and temporal aspects in the imitation of contacts between colleagues. Might this new balance in fact be the main characteristic of late (post) modern European governance?

EUROPEAN PREDICTIONS

A fifth theme that helps imagining a European present, is the plots of (non-) *planning* and *prediction*. Civil servants create the feeling of simultaneity in European activity not only in their organisation of an inescapable 'now', but also by extensive discussion about particular ways of handling issues over time. The quotations below show that two different stories have to be reconciled when creating, and thinking, about the future beyond the moment of decision. On the one hand a story reproducing officials' experience of a reactive style of policy-making, in fact a story of a lack of a common future that could be subject to planning. On the other hand, the experience of a need of prediction has given rise to a plot of individual incremental collection of pieces of information (by means of identification with partners), that can make up a more coherent framework for the advance preparation of the up-coming moments of simultaneity in European governance. However, although the two themes concerning the control of coming time tell different stories, they both very effectively contribute to the imagining of European simultaneous activity and a European present. *Vis-à-vis* the external world, they create the feeling of joint simultaneous reaction. Internally they are oriented towards decision-making moments in time. In fact, they have in common the engendering of an image of a strong connection between EU member-state foreign ministries through their common problem of time management:

> One of the criticisms of CFSP – and we make the criticisms but we are not the only country – is that it has no strategic plan, no vision, no coherence. Well, there is a rhythm of meetings, but not of substance. There is a working group of EU-planners where people like me from the twelve states meet, or ought to meet once a month. It should, or could, perform the same kind of function that the one in national planning. It should be of help to the Political Committee [PoCo] so that the political directors could be looking ahead at issues: 'here is something on the horizon, make that into a problem, what can we in the EU do about it now?' That sort of forward-looking process, that has not developed yet. (Policy Planning Staff, FCO)[57]

> Well it [CFSP] is reactive at the moment … Again, there are the institutional problems, or whom they pick up the phone to, who they talk to, who is representing the

common foreign security policy, what is the policy? You know these questions are difficult for us to answer for the moment, so no wonder, partners for life, USA, are saying, what is it, where is it, who is it? So we are conscious that something needs to be done to give it a better profile. And you know, forward planning is part of that. So you are not talking necessarily about a kind of European Union planning, but some way of introducing the planning function. (Policy Planning Staff, FCO)[58]

As we have seen earlier, the techniques behind imagining a common CFSP 'now' seem to be rather effective: European simultaneous activity is perceived to be strong. However, truly joint efforts over extended time spans are perceived to be weak. There are very few traces of stories for the imagination of a common coming time. As discovered in chapter 2, there is very little of a future in European governance.

Instead of a common long-term calendar, the enforced simultaneity of the CFSP has brought forward a language of anticipation of EU partners' action in the well recognised, common moments of decision. The importance of *predicting* the other member-states' positions and actions has increased because of the CFSP:

There is a much bigger obligation for each member-state to be aware of the views and positions of its partners on particular questions. And to anticipate how they would react to a particular set of events around the world. You have to develop a knowledge of for example the German position to Eastern Europe, France on Africa etc. And your expert has to formulate a knowledge of the attitudes of other member-states in that particular area, what their particular priorities and objectives are likely to be. So that we, when we feel that we would disagree with their view, can try to influence them through the CFSP process to change it. (Policy Planning Staff, FCO)[59]

Future presents of civil servants are constructed in their narrations in terms of anticipation of member-state proposals, decisions, and moments of decisions:

Obviously we have – I am not sure what other countries have – ideas about what they want to do, what they might be able to run. And you then have to think, is this something we share with our partners or is it something that they are unlikely to like. And then of course on particular points one might phone up a colleague, whether just to find out where something has got to, or to discuss a problem as to how something should be handled. And that quite often happens with the presidency, for example, one time we want to know how they propose to handle something. Or if you are unsure about how to propose an initiative you might find out what other people thought informally first. (OSCE Division, FCO)[60]

However, there are great difficulties with this way of creating the future out of pieces of anticipated European presents:

And we cannot anticipate; there is going to be a summit in Budapest in early December, we will be there and most probably we will have to make a statement. We will have to write it, we will have to get everybody's OK, but do not know what to say. I cannot write it now because I do not know what the conference will produce.

The conference is happening now, any result … I will be writing it at one o'clock in the morning the night before, because we just do not know. We try to take care of it, but as I said you also have to be flexible and be able to change and adapt what we have done. (OSCE Division, FCO)[61]

EUROPEAN SKILLS

The fiction of new simultaneities are also discernible in the diplomats' stories of how they feel their profession has changed owing to the CFSP:

There is less scope for an individual officer of the foreign ministry to sort of take up an issue and bring it forward in the decision making process. One might say that the diplomat risks being more of a processor of paper than a 'thinker' in the CFSP process. (Research Unit, FCO)[62]

Now because of CFSP, he or she has to use all the time, multilateral skills, negotiation skill, coordination skills, and there is much greater demand on his or her what we call drafting skills, skills of exposition, writing and speaking in a way that will convince other people. So now every diplomat will have to develop these multinational skills and presentation skills which in the past a more limited number of diplomats had to develop. (Security Policy Department, FCO)[63]

The other big change, of course is in IT. The fact that information travels so fast now, and then the fax machine – that is the other big change that has more impact I would say. But it is all linked together. The turn around time for reaction is getting faster and faster, for everyday events not just for situations of crisis. (OSCE Division, FCO)[64]

While the tacit coordination of the nation-state required only the 'passive' awaiting of the sufficient time for differing views to be sorted out, coordinated simultaneity in European governance demands of civil servants their constant active engagement to achieve precisely that coordination. The reproduction of a feeling of being a link in an information chain which cannot be broken is very illuminating of a simultaneity which must constantly be borne in mind. The image of working simultaneously on a European concern is very effectively created by mention of the constant transmission of information, linking European governance colleagues together. This linkage is a striking analogue of the idea of a present which connects them and which they have in common, but which has to be upheld very actively. That the analogy is an apt one is confirmed by the significant new demands on the official to uphold CFSP simultaneity:

Sometimes with the work here you can be sent a paper in the morning by somebody asking you for comments by four o'clock. Obviously, it is quite short, that you have to look at something, a paper, and make your comment on it the same day within a few hours. (OSCE Division, FCO)[65]

The European present and the need to be present

The active now

This chapter has shown how European governance's different and strict timetables for different policy areas 'tear apart' the basis of the feeling of simultaneous activity within the established community of national central government. Thereby, European governance erodes one of the fundamentals of the nation as an 'imagined community': the confidence in a simultaneity of anonymous activity. In this process, a new conception of simultaneity is in the making.

In European governance, the idea of national homogeneous empty time is less adequate. The experience of action in terms of a national 'now' and a European 'then' gives way to other perceptions of reality. The past events are imitated and articulated in a way that makes the feeling of exclusive national simultaneity and the confidence in a nation acting as an organic whole lose ground. The time of a national interval is no longer experienced in European governance. The sequencing of action is in European governance not associated with tacit coordination and empty time, but built on conscious temporal calculations for action.

The individual ministry is before its action no longer given a 'national sequence' for awaiting and sounding out of other ministries' opinions for national action. Instead, it is believed that action in European governance has to be very actively coordinated in relation to European simultaneous events (meetings, actions, moments of declarations). Passive time is turned into active in interpretations of coordination within complex interaction patterns. The taken-for-granted national timetable in people's minds is in European governance replaced by images of 'European' speed, timing, deadlines and timetables engendering the fiction of strongly marked European decisional presents. This ideational development can be described as if we are taken from national to European simultaneity through European governance deadlines.

The themes of simultaneity in European governance can be summarised as poems of fatalistic time. The experiences of temporal events are imitated in the policy-makers' plot and organised in a story of 'fatalistic' time. The story is told in the form of the 'femme fatale' of the European Union whose time you cannot escape. You cannot do anything to change this time, it is laid upon you from outside, 'from Europe'. It is mainly characterised by its shortening of your available time for action. European time is more densely packed than nation-state time. The civil servants tell it in a way that makes you think that you cannot beat it; the only thing you can do is to learn it, adopt it and work out techniques for coping with it in your everyday work. A whole range of sub-themes constitute the narrative expression of these techniques. In order to win back time for calculating alternative actions, certain managerial skills and anticipation techniques are formulated.

The narratives of the coordination of European governance point towards a new construction of the simultaneity plot, different from a simultaneity defined as temporal coincidence. When political and administrative time is no longer experienced as empty, taken for granted, it is 'filled' – defined once again. When confidence is eroding, when 'the national clock' no longer appropriately refigures temporal experience, people start telling new stories about time. The coordination narratives express subtle but crucial shifts in the telling of simultaneity. In a close reading we discover that a whole poetic universal of coordination is elaborated in order to engender the idea of common 'national' action but, at the same time and in a complex interplay, also of uniform behaviour of the European Union *vis-à-vis* the external world. The stories contrast with the feeling of calendric coincidence that was the idea behind the tacit coordination in anonymity, which in turn helped to create the image of national homogeneity. The narratives of the image of simultaneity in European governance include new techniques for the emplotment of temporal experiences, analogous with the invention of the word 'meanwhile' serving the imagination of the nation.

Paradoxically, the concerns regarding the lack of a common European destiny seep into reality in themes such as 'something needs to be done to give it a better profile …, forward planning is part of that'. It is in this kind of 'innocent' temporal remark that clues about the particularities of the feeling of community in European governance can be found. Here again, maybe the most subtle, but most efficient, narrative 'trick' is the unclear and ambiguous connotation of 'we' and 'us' in the recapitulation of planning and prediction experiences: we, the Union, or we, the British? The horizon of the collectivity in question is blurred. Through these small and subtle narrative means, the image of simultaneous existence and activity of CFSP colleagues is incrementally built up. The epic structure is connecting people in the form of expressions such as 'common actions', 'common views'. Furthermore, it is often not clear to whom the word 'negotiation position' refers, national, CFSP or …? The condition for the anonymous steady clocking of a national community was a very clear understanding of the meaning of 'we'. Are we witnessing in the answers from officals only a first step towards a more fixed connotation of 'we', or a trend towards a permanent ambiguity of who 'we' are? How will this affect the possibility to think of, and thereby create, Europe? A constantly ambiguous Europe?

The enforced present for action

Instant communication and precise coordination between the units within the nation as well as European governance seem to be an important instrument for the image of 'unity' in actions *vis-à-vis* other member-states or the external world. The organisational pattern is very similar to the networks of today's 'virtual enterprise', which is often made up of relatively independent units which seek to *appear* as one when acting on the market (Mascanzoni, 1998).

The idea of a homogeneous empty time is being replaced by a simultaneity that is thought of as a *parallel series of enforced moments of exchanges and decisions*. This follows from the fact that the main narrative techniques behind the new simultaneity fiction is formed not as stories expressing temporal coincidence, but

as various 'enforcement instruments' (coordination, deadlines), their consequences (high-speed communication, shortened horizons, a professional role of
processing) and particular characteristics (advanced strategies of timing). New
metaphors are born out of this emplotment. The sequencing of everyday routines
is formulated in very suggestive – and, in comparison with the nation-state, vague
– terms like 'process', 'rhythm', 'speed' and 'flows'.

Simultaneity in European governance is felt not only as coincidental, in the
sense that events and actions just happen at the same time, but also as a 'coincidence' in which something both takes place *and* has some sort of a common
meaning. In the CFSP that meaning could be characterised as a coinciding pressure for active response. The sheer occurrence of various European events at the
same time is not a strong enough factor for the creation of a feeling of European
simultaneity. In European governance, coinciding events must be linked to
an action-related meaning. There is no sense of coincidence – i.e. there is no
coincidence – without narratives of concerns and actions. Something has to be
connected to the occurrence of a European event, something of direct interest
to the actor, for him or her to be consciously involved and thereby embraced
by the common calendar. Decisions and actions are very closely interwoven
with the image of the present. This is the strongly marked *decisional present* of
European governance.

It is generally felt that nobody – no member-state or individual officer – can
afford to refrain from participating in simultaneous European activities,
because of the risk of losing tempo and influence *vis-à-vis* other actors. As
already concluded, this simultaneity is not based on an empty time. Instead, it
points to the following historical line of development of the meaning of simultaneity: from a medieval sense of 'fulfilment', through the 'coincidental' notion
of national consciousness, to the *enforced simultaneity* of European governance
– that is, a fiction based on the feeling that constant *participation in the common
present is a pre-requisite for action*: a participative present. In this particular fiction of 'necessity', an interesting new nuance in the story of simultaneity
appears, namely that the very pace of decision-making has clearly gained
ground in determining policy results, at the cost of more substantial factors.
This fact is only confirmed by the general trend that space is replaced by pace as
the major determinant in international relations. In fact, the above analysis
points even further: it shows that ideas are also replaced by pace.

The imagined network of European collaborators
European governance timetables constitute an increasingly large part of the
civil servants' overall calendar. These timetables can and do play a role similar
to that of the press and national calendar in 'dating' time and in creating a sense
of identity among those whose work it guides. Because the timetables have
the crucial function of coordinating the activities of all the member-states, those
affected by them are highly aware of them and of the fact that they put the
same demands on colleagues in other member-states, and that the creation of

routines are replicated by European colleagues. These timetables thus give national civil servants occasion to see themselves as part of an imagined community of people actively engaged in European governance. And in *thinking* European they *create* Europe.

To what extent is this kind of simultaneity the origin of a broader community feeling within European governance, a European 'consciousness'? Well aware of the limitations of my elite-level case of central government, I believe that changes at this level are of great significance owing to their historically close links with broader patterns of state formation.[66] The question is whether the strongly enforced present of European governance is a sufficient component of a common time for that 'hypnotic confirmation of the solidity of a single community … moving onward through calendrical time', that Anderson (1983: 27) talks about. Can calendrical time, in Anderson's community-building sense, be built on a timetable for up-coming moments of decisions – European governance simultaneities? Or is something more required?

My empirical material gives some indication of a growing feeling of community among policy-makers involved in European governance. And I believe that already at this stage we are able to discuss interesting *differences* between the two conceptions of simultaneity with regard to their capacity to give birth to, and form, imagined linkages between people. One could, of course, see the present outlook on time in European governance as being in a state of transition: the cooperative pattern based on actively upheld simultaneity is over time going to turn into a community of tacit European simultaneity of a national style. However, the great complexity of European governance is a factor that speaks against this development, and in favour of an interpretation emphasising the historical uniqueness of the new conception of simultaneity and its consequences for imagining communities. Owing to its complexity and size, and, not least, the great number of stories and languages it includes – European governance may always need an element of enforcement of temporal disciplines for the coordination of people in time and space. Owing to the active enforcement of European governance simultaneity, connections between people may always be imagined of as being more ephemeral than those in a national community. Will there ever be a 'complete confidence' in a European governance or community time? Are we in European governance witnessing the imagined information society, where people's strong feeling of time as a human articulation ('EU timetables laid upon us') will always hamper fiction from seeping quietly into reality, in contrast to nation-state time? That is, a society where time is perceived less as cosmological, hence less in contradiction with its narrative epistemology.

The new type of simultaneity makes it possible to think about European governance colleagues as members not of a collectivity, but of a communication and decision-making network, connecting people by means of certain codes and procedures that are actively and constantly being recreated, making permanent participation necessary owing to the risk of exclusion. Consciously fabricated common points in time, instead of tacit coincidence. Net connection instead of community. *Collaboration* around concrete common concerns, instead of a consciousness of an invisible abstract community of common events. The actors feel forced to act simultaneously – in the common present – in European governance, which makes them think, and thereby creates Europe as an *imagined network of collaborators*.

Notes

1 Author's interview (Sw. 1) (18 March 1996).
2 For example, between the national and the international 'level' in a two-level game of mutual influence (Putnam, 1988).
3 See Giddens' theories of modern interaction discussed in chapter 4.
4 In Aristotle's *Poetics*, Ricoeur finds the points of departure for his elaboration of how time comes into being through 'emplotment' of temporal experience. Ricoeur divides this problem into two: the character of the 'mimetic activity' in itself and the very techniques of emplotment. When reproducing past events we *imitate* and *represent* human action. The imitation of action takes the form of a plot. There are various rules for the construction of a plot, i.e. for the organisation of events into a plot (so-called 'narrative rules'). Some of them make up standard 'types' of narrative organisation, for example the 'tragedy' and the 'comedy'. Compare Anderson's description of how national literature introduced a new standard narrative technique for the writing of novels, namely the telling of stories parallel in time (Anderson, 1983: 24–30). In his theory of narration (muthos), Aristotle includes the notion of a 'whole': 'Now a thing is a whole if it has a beginning, a middle and an end' (Ricoeur, 1984: 38). For each part of the whole there are certain rules. The tragic organisation has its own 'logic', the comedy another. Ricoeur interprets Aristotle as meaning to say that the rules are quite strict because the norms for the telling of a tragedy are formulated in terms of necessity and probability. Ricoeur draws the ontological conclusion that Aristotle's narratives 'are not features of some real action but the effects of the ordering of the poem' (1984: 39): 'To make up the plot is already to make intelligible spring from the accidental, the universal from the singular, the necessary or the probable from the episodic' (1984: 41)
5 For this study, twenty-five individual officials of various ranks and administrative affiliations were interviewed off the record and in depth for an average of an hour. The aim was to get the individual official to account for his or her experience of coordination in European governance. Extracts from approximately half of the total number of interviews are used in the analysis. As will be seen, the answers from the three EU states show a remarkable consistency with regard to patterns of internal national coordination and of simultaneity, which of course strengthens my assumptions. The extracts presented and interpreted below are chosen because of their particularly clear traces of conceptions of a present. Consequently, they are only highlights of the phenomena this project is designed to examine and should be placed in relation to the quite extensive material collected (around twenty-five hours of interviews). How significant are the highlights? The forms of coordination characteristic of a national administration, as expressed in Larsson's analysis (1986), could not be found in any of my interviews with European governance officials. All but two of them maintained that there is a great difference between the way interministerial relations are managed outside and inside European governance.
6 Author's interviews in the British and Swedish Foreign Ministries.
7 The figure is given by the European Commission, the unit for 'reunion de group de membres de la Commission'.

8   The figure is given by the European Commission, the unit for 'reunion de group de membres de la Commission'.

9   European Commission information: 'Etat de transposition des mesures du livre blanc. Situation par Etat membre (situation au 14/9/94)'.

10 Communication from the Commission: 'Legislate Less to Act Better: The Facts', COM (1998) 345 Final.

11 All data from Statskontoret (1996: 7: 91–112).

12 The data about United Kingdom and the Community/Union is collected from HMSO (Cm 2369) Developments in the European Community January–June 1993, *European Communities*, 5 (1993); HMSO (Cm 2525) Developments in the European Community July–December 1993, *European Communities*, 4 (1994).

13 HMSO (Cm 2369) Developments in the European Community January–June 1993, *European Communities*, 5 (1993): 44.

14 HMSO (CM 2369): 15.

15 HMSO (CM 2369): 45.

16 The information was given by the European Union Department (External) of the Foreign and Commonwealth Office, London (1995).

17 The information was given by the CFSP Unit of the Foreign and Commonwealth Office, London (1995).

18 Author's interview (St. 1) (19 October 1994).

19 Author's interview (St. 6) (21 October 1994).

20 Author's interview (St. 6) (21 October 1994).

21 Author's interview (Sw. 1) (18 March 1996).

22 Author's interview (Sw. 1) (18 March 1996).

23 Author's interview (St. 2) (27 October 1994).

24 Author's interview (Sw. 1) (18 March 1996).

25 Author's interview (St. 2) (27 October 1994).

26 Author's interview (St. 4) (25 October 1994).

27 Author's interview (St. 2) (27 October 1994).

28 Author's interview (St. 2) (27 October 1994).

29 Author's interview (St. 2) (27 October 1994).

30 Author's interview (Sw. 1) (18 March 1996).

31 Author's interview (Sw. 2) (7 September 1995).

32 Author's interview (Sw. 2) (7 September 1995).

33 Author's interview (St. 4) (25 October 1994).

34 Author's interview (St. 2) (27 October 1994).

35 Author's interview (Sw. 4) (5 September 1995).

36 Author's interview (Sw. 5) (15 August 1995).

37 Author's interview (Sw. 5) (15 August 1995).

38 Author's interview (St. 6) (21 October 1994).

39 Author's interview (Sw. 1) (18 March 1996).

40 Author's interview (Sw. 1) (18 March 1996).

41 The interview was made on 4 February 1994 over the telephone.

42 Author's interview (St. 1) (19 October 1994).

43 Author's interview (St. 6) (21 October 1994).

44 Author's interview (Sw. 4) (5 September 1995).

45 Author's interview (St. 1) (19 October 1994).

46 Author's interview (St. 6) (21 October 1994).

47 Author's interview (Sw. 1) (18 October 1994).

48 Author's interview (St. 5) (25 October 1994).

49 Author's interview (Sw. 3) (9 September 1995).

50 Author's interview (Sw. 3) (9 September 1995).

51 Author's interview (St. 1) (19 October 1994).
52 Author's interview (St. 1) (19 October 1994).
53 Author's interview (St. 7) (19 October 1994).
54 Author's interview (St. 5) (25 October 1994).
55 Author's interview (St. 2) (27 October 1994).
56 Author's interview (St. 4) (25 October 1994).
57 Author's interview (St. 4) (25 October 1994).
58 Author's interview (St. 4) (25 October 1994).
59 Author's interview (St. 1) (19 October 1994).
60 Author's interview (St. 5) (25 October 1994).
61 Author's interview (St. 5) (25 October 1994).
62 Author's interview (St. 1) (19 October 1994).
63 Author's interview (St. 6) (21 October 1994).
64 Author's interview (St. 5) (25 October 1994).
65 Author's interview (St. 5) (25 October 1994).
66 For this view of the relationship between public administration and the state see also Wessels (1990: 229).

4

The recurring past
Transformed horizons for policy planning

Planning without past

As noted in chapter 1, politics in the modern nation-state was firmly based on the notion of a linear time and history, from which political plans logically could be drawn. In European governance, there is no natural common history from which a future horizon logically follows. Chapter 2 also showed that the linear view of the future is seriously challenged in European governance owing to the abstract and vague formulations of coming time. In fact, all previous chapters in this book have shown that the horizon of the future is under transformation in European governance. At the same time, the need for better planning to counter-balance the feeling of loss of control has been stressed throughout the empirical material. So far, the implications for policy planning have only been alluded to in the empirical sections and touched upon in the analysis. In order to fully understand the relevance of European governance, we need to deepen our investigation of the implications for policy planning – of such importance in the modern welfare state. It was not only the view of the future that changed in the modern state conception of planning possibilities. According to the historians, maybe the most important explanation to the strong confidence in planning was the transformation of the long-term historical memory (chapter 1). How should the *longue durée* be defined in European governance? What are the originary points? How is it stretched into the future? Is it linear or circular, recurrent in character?

Given the lack of a written common past and planning in the 'polity' of European governance, analogous to the nation-state, the analysis calls for particularly careful considerations with regard to methods. In line with the arguments presented initially in this book, I have in the following chosen a method focusing on the practice of actors of European governance. That is, a method able to catch the logic of the practical past making, which is seen as both a medium and consequence of planning endeavours. What experiences are planning based on? How are planning horizons reproducing and changing the sense of the past? On the basis of what past can planning follow logically in European governance?

Sources of modern linear history

Irreversible time

Time in modern society and state derives its linear forms from its de-contextualised and commodified characteristics. In contrast to small, traditional societies, time is in modern social relationships separated from the substance of activities. The development of this form of time was due to the fact that time, like other phenomena, was 'industrialised', with the result that it was divided into uniform, quantifiable, countable units of clock time (Giddens, 1981). Time was in Anderson's (1983) term 'empty'. Its components were the same over an expanding geographical area and apprehended as having a constant constitution over history.

The creation of clock time was an expression of the commodification of time in industrial society. From having been determined by the work rhythm in traditional societies, time was exchanged as an abstract, context-free commodity. It was abstract clock time and it was its dominance over other social times that made possible, and characterised, the modern state's control over its citizens' time. The state's capacity to store information enabled the state to control, to surveil, as Giddens chooses to say, people's past and future. In the capitalist state it is quantified, commodified time that regulates and mediates the exchange values and the relationship between goods and labour. The consequence of this industrial time is, according to Giddens, that objective time in modern society has come to be seen as 'formless duration', a formless resource, conceptualised as a quantity. The dominant measure of time – that is, clock time – has become a reified objective reality (Giddens, 1981: 131). This apprehension of time implies that time in modern Western societies is linear, in contrast to the cyclical conception of time of traditional cultures. Owing to the fact that modern society understands time as an eternal adding of standardised time units and dates to 'history', time becomes irreversible. The same time never comes back. It is the social equivalent to Newtonian physics. Modern time is *irreversible*, whereas traditional time is reversible. The cyclical understanding of time prevalent in older societies derived not only from the fact that time was bound to the seasonal cycles of nature, but also from the lack of storage of information, a pre-requisite of the creation of linear history. For this reason, a longer past and future could, in Giddens' perspective, simply not exist for these societies.

Bourdieu (1979) has shown that traditional societies also hold an understanding of a distant future (un avenir), which should not be confused with the near future (le futur) of up-coming calculable possibilities. Other time researchers have criticised the tendency of what they regard as an overly schematic categorisation of historical societies as dominated by either reversible or irreversible (cyclical or linear) time. These scholars have pointed to the great variety within the time consciousness of every society (Adam, 1990). In fact, Giddens also recognises the repetitiveness of human action in his analysis of the reproduction of social systems over time, which however takes place within the framework of modern, linear clock time (Giddens, 1981: 17).

Out-stretched time

Longer-term horizons derive their form also from time's specific relation to space in modern societies. In earlier historical periods (i.e. before the eighteenth century) people were only socially integrated into society because of the predominance of co-presence in their interaction. Giddens makes a crucially important distinction between, on the one hand, time–space situations in which the persons involved in interaction are co-present and, on the other, those in which they are distanciated from each other. The two types of situation differ from each other with regard to modes of co-ordination of the actor's 'monitoring' and 'interpretation' of the meaning of action. In the former case, presences make it possible to talk about a co-monitoring of meaning. Communication in situations of absences has a very different character, e.g. the medium of transmission across contexts in time and space will often play a crucial role in meaning creation and interpretation. Time–space distanciation is thus defined as 'the conditions under which time and space are organised so as to connect presence and absence' (Giddens, 1990: 14). The co-presence of ancient societies meant that people's time–space relationship was not, in Giddens' terms, stretched out (Giddens, 1984). The consequence of modernity and its technology of communication and control is a continuous acceleration in time–space distanciation (Giddens, 1990). New media of time–space distanciation have been constructed; for example 'expert systems' creating the degree of 'trust' between actors (which was not a problem in situations of 'direct' communication of ancient society), that is necessary in their exchanges of meanings across time and space, by means of modern techniques (Held and Thompson, 1989: 279). During recent decades we have witnessed an extreme acceleration of the pace of alteration of spatial structures, i.e. time–space distanciation, owing to the computerisation of telecommunications and media-image systems (Virilio, 1988). Like commodified time, the conception of out-stretched time is of a linear character.

Simulated time

New information technology and computerised methods of analysis have enabled civil servants in central state bureaucracies to cope better with information and control and *create* linear horizons. With the new prediction techniques, longer-term political scenarios grounded on historical perspectives can be elaborated with greater precision (McLuhan, Quentin and Jerome, 1967; Ronfeldt, 1992). Among these techniques are methods of simulation used in order to counteract the higher tempo of information transmission and political events by keeping the basis for long-term planning (Virilio, 1986: 141). By the means of scenarios, coming events do not have to be of a recurrent nature, which logically would be the only features that can be successfully forecasted since a certain degree of knowledge based on past experiences must always be implied in analyses of coming time. In contrast, other studies have shown that the need to manage the information flood in Western bureaucracies as a result of the recent information revolution have made people detached from the past and thereby shortened their perspective on the future (Bell, 1977; Rifkin, 1989). This phenomenon has also been shown in earlier parts of this book.

Practical past

The role of the past

In the study of history or 'the past', the importance of remembering that structure, expressing long-term conditions for action, is no more than a method constructed by the researcher as an instrument for approaching, simplifying and explaining the complexity of human practice, has been stressed. In the view of Bourdieu and Giddens, structure should be seen as rules of conduct imbedded in human actions or 'dispositions'. Owing to the fact that they see action as the outcome of a structuration process over time, there is a need to theorise about time and the past as an integral part of all analysis of human action.

FORGOTTEN HISTORY

According to Bourdieu (1990), the structuralists err by assessing human practices only from the outside, from the viewpoint of an 'objective' structure constructed by the researcher himself. But Bourdieu also criticises subjectivism and empiricism for not providing sufficient and adequate material for social-scientific inquiry because they investigate only one level of social reality, namely, the actor's view of the situation or visible social phenomena, respectively. Like the structuralists, Bourdieu is convinced that there exist fundamental and generative aspects of social life which are invisible to the subject and can by the researcher be reached only through his own construction of them.

Bourdieu's epistemological solution advocates relating the objectivist knowledge of the researcher to the actors' own subjective experience of themselves and their situation. With Bourdieu's approach, the researcher constructs, via interpretation, an objective world of relations, an objective structure, in the same way as is done within traditional structural theory. The so-called 'structural method' is the same; it is the search for the social relations that generates the practice of agents. However, the structure under investigation should, according to Bourdieu, not be assumed in advance, and thereafter tested by means of empirical data. Instead it should 'crystallise' in the process of empirical examination, in what Bourdieu calls 'the second break'. By this he means that the researcher should try to situate herself in the position of the subject at the very moment when the act is taking place. In order to relate the agent's own 'feeling' of her practice and the objective structure constructed by the researcher, Bourdieu uses the concept of habitus, which consists of

> Systems of durable, transposable dispositions, structured structures predisposed to function as structuring structures, that is, as principles which generate and organise practices and representations that can be objectively adapted to their outcomes without presupposing a conscious aiming at ends or an express mastery of the operations necessary in order to attain them. Objectively 'regulated' and 'regular' without being in any way the product of obedience to rules. (Bourdieu, 1990: 53)

Dispositions are the result of experienced past patterns of action and reactions of other agents. They are an unconscious memory of similar situations – 'forgotten history' – forming the basis for the agent's capacity of 'knowing' how to go on, that is, her practical sense. Memory can be defined as the preservation of past experiences for future use. This unconscious capacity for action has been described by Bourdieu as the result of incorporation into habitus of the objective structures for future-oriented practices. Thus, habitus is shaped but not determined by social processes (Bourdieu, 1977: 78). In contrast to the theory of rational action, in which the agent consciously judges her alternatives of action, habitus *unconsciously* generates actions. However, a strategic act is an act by which the agent consciously tries to do something different from what, through habitus, she normally would do. With the concept of strategy, Bourdieu shows that it is indispensable to account for the subject's own view of her situation in order to fully explain actions. However, Bourdieu strongly emphasises that strategic calculations 'are first defined, without any calculation, in relation to objective potentialities, immediately inscribed in the present as things to do or not to do, to say or not to say, in relation to a probable, "upcoming future"' (Bourdieu, 1990: 53). In this way, he places the freedom of the subject within a 'framework of possibility'.

EVERYDAY PAST

A central question for Giddens is to show empirically how social systems are 'stretched across time and space'. Giddens talks about the time–space routinisation of social life – a bottom-up methodology:

> Locales and regions have to be understood in terms of their reflexive involvement with social organisation and social transformations. The example of the territorial character of the states is a case in point. As nations, states enter reflexively into how citizens organise their lives and how governments act. (Giddens in Held and Thompson, 1989: 280)

In contrast to Bourdieu's conception of structure as dispositions in some sense preceding action, Giddens localizes structure in the action itself. He argues that we should look upon structure as an integral part of human practice. According to Giddens, a structure is constituted by rules and resources that are both the medium and the outcome of action. By this 'duality of structure' Giddens means to say that 'social structures are both constituted by human agency, and yet at the same time the very medium of this constitution' (Giddens, 1976: 121). He conceptualises the agent–structure relationship as a process in which the agent 'draws upon' those rules and resources which are reproduced only through this very practice:

> In my usage, structure is what gives form and shape to social life, but it is not itself that form and shape – nor should 'give' be understood in an active sense here, because structure only exists in and through the activities of human agents. (Giddens, 1989: 256)

Giddens describes structuration similarly to Bourdieu, in terms of rules 'organising' practices and rules 'instantiated' in the act of the agent in the form of memory traces. Agency is central in Giddens' thinking on the past. 'Agency is "all there is" in human history. Agency is history, where "history" is the temporal continuity of human activities' (1987: 220). Giddens sees 'human beings as purposive actors, who virtually always know what they are doing (under some description) and why' (1989: 253). He talks of actors as 'knowledgeable agents'. Giddens wants to say that the agent is not determined by structure because she evaluates her situation and could in a historical perspective 'have done otherwise' (1987: 218), i.e. she could have drawn upon other rules and resources. In order to make his view clear Giddens argues for the use of the concept of human praxis in order to 'reject every conception of human beings as "determined objects" or as unambiguously "free subjects"' (1981: 54):

> Study of the 'everyday' or the 'day-to-day' forms a basic part of the analysis here, many seemingly trivial or mundane features of what people do being the actual 'groundwork' of larger-scale institutions. (Giddens, 1989: 298)

Recreating the past of their practice

> A question as innocuous in appearance as 'What next?', inviting an informant to situate two periods in relation to each other in a continuous time, which does no more than state what the chronological diagram does implicitly, has the effect of inducing an attitude to time which is the exact opposite of the attitude involved practically in the ordinary use of temporal terms and notions which, like that of a 'period', are not at all self-evident. (Bourdieu, 1990: 201)

The objective of the empirical study is to search for the structure that can explain how actors engaged in European governance relate to the past in their shaping of plans for the future. I use the ethnographic method of 'participant observation'. The aim of my observation of practices is to have the structure crystallise as a result of a gradually growing understanding of how the past is created and organised within European governance.

In the crystallization process, both objective and subjective components of time structures are included. My analysis is particularly inspired by Bourdieu's earlier investigation of the creation of calendars in smaller communities. Objectivist knowledge has in these studies taken the form of an interpretation of observed practices of sequencing, timing, temporal categorisation, illustrated in both texts and figures:

> Probably the only way to give an account of the practical coherence of practices and works is to construct generative models which reproduce in their own terms the logic from which that coherence is generated, and to devise diagrams which, through their synoptic power of synchronisation and totalization, quietly and directly manifest the objective systematicity of practice and which, when they make adequate use of the properties of space (up/down, right/left), may even have the merit of speaking directly to the body schema (as all those who have to transmit motor skills are well aware). At the same time, one has to be aware that these theoretical replications transform the logic of practice simply by making it explicit. (Bourdieu, 1990: 92–93)

In figure 1, one of the 'generative models', concerning the 'calendar' of the Kabyle people of Tunisia and Algeria, is given as an example. As can be seen, the figure contains both (Bourdieu's) objective and subjective (of the Kabyle people) terms for the reproduction of the seasonal rhythm.

I shall look upon the individual's conscious and unconscious knowledge of his past and temporal situation as facts. The forms of a temporal European governance structure are searched for, rather than postulated. In my investigation, I define the field to be investigated as the planning practices of a selected group of people (henceforth also called the informants) involved in European governance. For practical reasons, the study was limited to the everyday praxis of a selected group of officials within one ministerial department (called for

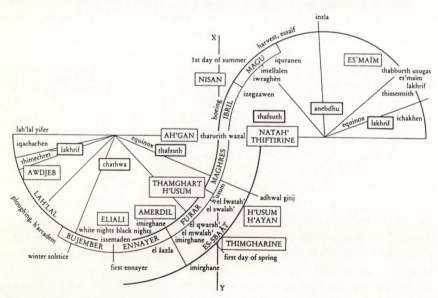

Figure 1 The abstract 'calendar'
Source: Bourdieu (1990: 203).

purposes of anonymity the 'Y department') of an EU member-state ('state X'). The group, made up of about twenty civil servants of various ranks and administrative levels, was studied during a period of two-and-a-half months. In my observation, I made note of informants' actions in time and their practical sense of 'how to go on' in planning over time. These are the aspects reproduced in the study below. To summarise: the past in European governance exists to the degree the studied actors attach importance to it. Its characteristics are 'pointed out' by the actors themselves. I put the structure of European planning together.

Subjective plans of European governance

In order to understand informants' own experience of their planning, we need to map out the official and unofficial EU timetables – the basis of subjective time in everyday work. This is the reason why I first describe the institutionalised timetables of European governance, in the form of the agendas of both the European Union and national ministerial meetings. Secondly, non-formalised subjective knowledge is exemplified and explained by the reproduction of an individual officer's conscious organisation of her everyday time in the form of private memoranda. In the next section, patterns of planning routines are described on the basis of my own objective observations of practice. In the last section, the objective and subjective facts are combined and decoded in terms of a coherent structure of past and planning in European governance.

Official EU timetables

The meetings of the Council of Ministers of the European Union are convened by the EU presidency on the initiative of the presidency, another member-state or the European Commission in Brussels. The presidency should inform EU partners of preliminary dates of the planned Council meeting seven months before it comes into office. The chair presents a working programme for the six months of its presidency at the time of its taking office. Owing to this fact, the official EU timetable is for the individual member-state given externally. The preliminary agenda for each Council meeting should be produced by the presidency and distributed to member-states and to the Commission fourteen days in advance of the meeting. Proposals for points on the agenda from member-states and the Commission should have been received by the Council Secretariat sixteen days in advance of the meeting. Today there are nineteen specialised EC Councils of Ministers. In 1994, the total number of formal Council meetings was ninety-one (including meetings for the specialised Councils: fifteen on Foreign Affairs, eleven on Agriculture, and eleven on Economy and Finance) while the informal meetings amounted to seven in 1992 (INNO/EU Information, 1994). In figure 2, extracts of the 'Calendario' (meeting agenda) of the Spanish presidency of the second half of 1995 is given as example.

CALENDARIO '95

BRUS/LUX	P. MUNICIPAL	JULIO		ESPAÑA	OTROS LUGARES	C. ORGANIZADOR
		1	SA			
		2	DO			
		3	LU	COMISION GOR. ESPANOL (MADRID)		
C.E. E.	4		MA			
PLENARIA COREPER II COREPER I		5	MI	COPO MALLORCA		
		6	JU			
		7	VI			
		8	SA		I	NICIO OBRAS
		9	DO			MODULO PERMANENTE
ECOFIN		10	LU		SESION DE ESTRASBURGO	
		11	MA			
COREPER II		12	MI			
COREPER I		1 3	JU			
COREPER I Event.		14	VI			
		15	SA	SEMINARIO TRANSPORTES PALMA MALLORCA		
		16	DO			FIN OBRAS MODULO PERMANENTE
AA.GG/AGRI		17	LU			
C. AA.GG/ AGRI		18	MA			
REGI ONE\$ CORE PER I		19	MI		ASEAN BRUNEI	
COREP ER II		20	JU			
COREPER I		2 1	VI			
		22	SA			
		23	DO			
PRESUPUESTO		24	LU			
		25	MA			
COREPER I COREPER II		26	MI			
		27	JU			
		28	VI			
		29	SA			
		30	DO			
		31	LU			

Figure 2 The Spanish presidency of the second half of 1995: 'Julio'
Note: PLENARIA = Plenary
PRESUPUESTO = Budget
Source: The Spanish Representation to the European Union, Brussels (January 1995).

A practice has developed whereby the presidency normally calls, in addition to the planned meetings marked in the programme, one extraordinary 'informal' Council during its time in office. The Coreper (Comité des représentants permanents) is made up of the ambassadors of the member-states based in Brussels and functions as the standing committee for the preparation of the Council's discussions and decisions based on proposals of the European Commission. Concretely, Coreper prepares the issues on the agenda for the next Council meeting. Coreper is also empowered to decide on certain questions. Coreper meets once a week. The task of the working groups of the Council is to prepare the proposals of the European Commission for Coreper and for eventual decision in the Council.

Specific timetables for particular issue areas are also established. One example is the timetable put forward during the British presidency for all meetings concerning the Commission's long-term work programme for the years 2000–2006 called 'Agenda 2000' (figure 3).

In the Union's CFSP, which has been characterised as foreign ministries working together intergovernmentally,[1] decisions are adopted by consensus. In decisions of a more operative nature, majority voting of the Council is envisaged. The common organs include the General Affairs Council (GAC: the meetings of foreign ministers) (meets once a month), and the Political Committee (PoCo), composed of the political directors of the foreign ministries of member-states (meets every two weeks). The leading role in making and coordinating policy between the CFSP and the Community is given to the GAC and the European Council (meets four times a year; the so-called 'summit meetings'). Since 1993, the European Council heads the three-pillar Union, which now acts as a whole. The Commission also has a right of initiative within the CFSP, and thus in practice constitutes its 'sixteenth' member. The European Parliament (EP) has a formalised status in relation to CFSP, through a duty of the Council to report to the EP about all CFSP issues (Maastricht Treaty establishing the European Union).

As seen in figure 2, the half-year agenda regulates the meetings of the PoCo (in French: COPO), Coreper, the Council and the GAC. Only a few committee and working groups (Wg) meetings are marked in the schedules. The many hundreds of EC Council and CFSP working groups are not included. Moreover, it is important to note that the Commission has a separate meeting schedule for its working groups, engaging thousands of national experts from the central governments of member-states. Council working groups meet regularly, on average once or twice a month, the frequency being of course highly dependent on the need and urgency within each policy area. The division of work between the groups follows traditional domestic policy dividing lines; in the Community there are Councils for agriculture, economy and finance, research, environment, internal market, transport, budget, etc. In the CFSP, regional (Asia, Central and Eastern Europe, etc.) as well as functional (disarmament, human rights etc.) sub-areas exist. In 1995, the CSFP working groups covered nearly every important foreign policy

COREPER *18.03*		Initial presentation of Commission proposals Mandate for Friends of the Presidency
Informal ECOFIN	19–20.03	Presentation by President Santer
Friends of the Presidency	23.03	Detailed presentation of Commission proposals on future financing and structural funds Proposed overall handling
COREPER	*25.03*	Possible lunch discussion
General Affairs Council	30.03	General discussion and procedure for handling this dossier at Council level
Agriculture Council	31.03	Presentation by Commissioner Fischler
Friends of the Presidency	31.03–01.04	
Friends of the Presidency	06–07.04	
COREPER	*08.04*	Presidency oral progress report
Friends of the Presidency	20.04	
ECOFIN Council 21.04		Presidency oral progress report
COREPER (special session)	*23.04* <u>am</u>	
Friends of the Presidency	23 <u>pm</u>–24.04	
General Affairs Council	27–28.04 <u>pm</u>	
COREPER (special session)	*05.05*	
Friends of the Presidency	07.05	
COREPER	*14.05*	Preparation for ECOFIN
Friends of the Presidency	14–15.05	
ECOFIN Council 19.05		Discussion of financial aspects
COREPER *20.05*		Preparation for General Affairs Council
General Affairs Council	25.05	Discussion of elements for report for Cardiff
Agriculture Council	25–26.05	Discussion of contribution to the report for Cardiff
COREPER (special session)	*02.06*	Discussion of draft report for Cardiff
ECOFIN Council	05.06	Discussion of contribution to the report for Cardiff
General Affairs Council	08.06	Finalisation of the report for Cardiff
CARDIFF EUROPEAN COUNCIL 15–16.06		
Friends of the Presidency	19.06	(poss.)
Friends of the Presidency	26.06	(poss.)

Figure 3 Agenda 2000: timetable

Note: Where necessary, the Friends of the Presidency may have recourse to specialist working groups (financial counsellors or the structural actions working group) to assist them.

Source: The UK Representation to the European Union, Brussels (February 1998).

area with the exception of those relating to defence. The aim of the working groups is mainly to prepare higher-level meetings, which usually take place in Brussels or, for the European Council, in a city of the chairing member-state. Both PoCo and Coreper have the power to decide in certain questions (as does, to some extent, the Wg as well) and prepare the Council meetings.

The preliminary agenda of the meetings of the three EC levels (Wg, Coreper and Council) is in practice normally distributed to member-states a month in advance, but can continuously be changed until the very date of the meeting. Sometimes the final version of the agenda is presented by the presidency as late as two days before the meeting is planned to take place (or even later). Information about exact meeting dates and agendas is transmitted by the presidency, in cooperation with the Council Secretariat in Brussels. At every stage of the preparations, member-states can also transmit information and proposals for new items on the agenda, common EU declarations, actions, etc. This is normally done through the formal network of information, but initiatives have often been prepared through informal contacts between member-states with similar views on some specific question.

Domesticised 'European' timetables

At the national ministerial level the Wg, Coreper and Council meetings are very important points of reference for daily work. In order to coordinate officers' preparation of the various EU meetings at the member-state level, internal time schedules for all ministries are created by the foreign ministry's EU secretariat. In these schedules are marked all preliminary EU meetings planned and foreseen by the EU presidency, all the internal coordination meetings of the foreign ministry's EU secretariat (which coordinates the national ministries' EU work), the consultation meetings with the parliamentary EU standing committee and internal deadlines for delivery of the individual desk officer's contribution to each of these EU meetings. This means that the desk officer who is responsible for the particular agenda point at Coreper or Council meetings (he/she usually takes part in Wg him/herself), must meet the deadline set by the EU secretariat in the so-called 'order' for material sent out two weeks in advance of the meeting in question.

The domestic timetable in the observed member-state is divided into two parts. The first includes the schedule of regular meetings, deadlines and other points in time to be observed by ministries (see figure 4).[2] Moreover, there are rules prescribing that a national preliminary reaction to a European Commission proposal should be ready at the latest five weeks after its presentation in the EU Council, that the basis of the instructions to the national representation in Brussels should be received by the EU secretariat two days in advance of the Coreper meeting, and that reports from meetings should be handed in at the latest twenty-four hours after their termination to the EU secretariat and other concerned ministerial units (author's interviews).

The second part of the domestic timetables comprise the more detailed plans for preparing high-level meetings of the Union. These plans, distributed by the foreign ministry to all ministries, usually contain the major events for the two months preceding each meeting, and a more detailed day-by-day schedule for the last fortnight, including information about all deadlines for material, dates of preparation meetings and of briefings. The procedures of the all-embracing schedule are similar but of another scale, with regard to Coreper and PoCo meetings. The EU secretariat structures the time of the observed informants with

Essen-summit: continuous preparations

The following timetable was fixed at the 'Essen consultations' of 23 November

25 Nov.	Deadline: if possible include material for the files (comprising final positions) (cf. order 15/11/94)
28–29 Nov.	General Affairs Council
30 Nov.–1 Dec.	The Council of Justice and Home Affairs
1 Dec., p.m.	Deadline: Memorandum for the Parliamentary EU committee (concerned officials are contacted separately)
1 Dec., p.m.	Deadline: filematerial 'Central and Eastern Europe'
1 Dec., evening	Deadline: filematerial 'Justice and Home Affairs' (possible preliminary material. Urgent report from the Council of Justice and Home Affairs through A. H., Perm. Rep. in Brussels)
2 Dec., p.m.	The Parliamentary EU committee is informed (by the Prime Minister)
2 Dec., a.m.	Briefing the Prime Minister
2 Dec.	Deadline: 'be on duty-telephonelists' for concerned Ministries (see below)
4 Dec.	The Prime Minister leaves for Budapest (directly from B. to Germany on 6 Dec.)
5 Dec.	Ecofin Council
5 Dec., at 10 a.m.	Second 'Essen consultations' (summons are distributed separately to concerned Ministries)
7 Dec.	Deadline: filematerial 'Growth and employment'
7 Dec., p.m.	The files are closed
8 Dec.	The Internal Market Council (Brussels)
8 Dec.	Completed files are transported to Düsseldorf
8 Dec., p.m./eve.	Briefing the Prime Minister about the files.

Figure 4 The ministry's internal timetable
Source: Internal material from an anonymous Ministerial Department (y) of an EU
         member-state (x).

very detailed directives of when and in what form their material should be
handed over to the central level of coordination. The half-year plan, the 'driving
scheme', is reproduced in figure 5 (for the sake of anonymity, names of persons
have been left out).

'Driving scheme' for the preparation of the General Affairs Council

1 Preliminary basis for decision to the Ministers
– The Minister for Foreign Affairs and the Minister for EU coordination shall on Mondays before each General Affairs Council meeting be provided with a preliminary compilation over all proposals for positions, to serve as a basis for discussions within the government and the Parliamentary Advisory Committee on European Union Affairs.

– The compilation is done by Div. 4 on the basis of information from each responsible unit.

The ordering of this material is issued in connection with the delivery of other remaining material. The contributions shall be written on a separate paper and be at our disposal (Div. 4) at 11.00 a.m., at the latest, on the delivery-day of the preliminary basis. Please state document number.

2 Political Committee
– 2.1 Material for the Political Committee (PoCo) will be ordered as soon as the agenda has arrived (according to the rules 7–10 days before the meeting). The deadline in the order will be set to 17.00 p.m. Wednesdays before the PoCo.

– 2.2. The pre-meeting for the exposition of the agenda for PoCo takes place on Friday at 10.00 a.m. in room 101. Units whose areas will be dealt with are expected to attend the meeting.

– 2.3. 'Last-minute-telegrams' and reports from meetings taking place after the deadline in the order may be delivered in an envelope at the latest the day before PoCo at 12.00 a.m. Mark the envelope 'XX To be collected'.

– 2.4. Oral report from PoCo takes place the day after every PoCo-meeting at 08.00 a.m. (thus, preliminary on 01/18, 02/02, 03/01, 04/05, 04/29, 06/07, 06/17) in room 100. The meeting is open for all heads of unit and officials at P, F and G who are affected by the preparations and/or will be responsible for the following-up.

– 2.5. Written report from PoCo will be distributed during the morning after the meeting (the ambition is to distribute it as early as at the 'report-meeting').

3 Coreper
– 3.1. Coreper (Brussels ambassadors) prepares all points on the Council agenda at meetings on Wednesdays (sometimes even on Thursdays) before the General Affairs Council. Proposals from PoCo to the Ministers are directed through Coreper.

– The final verification of instructions to Coreper takes place in the Coordinating Group for EU Relations, which meets on Tuesdays at 1.30 p.m. – 3.00 p.m. Due to the fact that the Coordinating Group for EU Relations meets on Tuesdays (simultaneously with PoCo), the verification of possible instructions to Coreper, concerning questions that have been dealt with in PoCo, will take place in a special procedure between Div. 4 and the EU Coordination Secretariat. Possible instructions should be sent to the Representation at the latest 30 minutes before the Coreper meeting. In the Council-file should always be enclosed a report from Coreper as a complement to the material (which is finalised before the Coreper meeting.

4 General Affairs Council
– 4.1. The Orders for the General Affairs Council will be issued as soon as a preliminary agenda has arrived (14 days before the meeting).

– 4.2. Division 4 issues a coordinated order including the full agenda of all units concerned at P.G. and possible other departments concerned. Possible extra orders from other Ministries are coordinated by F1. Common 'papers' should, when possible, be produced in cases when several departments/units/groups are concerned with the same item on the agenda.

Figure 5 The 'driving scheme'
Source: Y Department of EU member-state X.

Private European timetables

> People will not accept uncertainty. They will make an effort to structure it no matter how poor the materials they have to work with and no matter how much the experts try to discourage them. One way to structure uncertainty is to structure the time period through which uncertain events occur. Such a structure must usually be developed from information gained from the experience of others who have gone or are going through the same series of events. As a result of such comparisons, norms develop for entire groups about when certain events may be expected to occur. (Roth, 1963: 93)

In order to meet the deadlines prescribed in the ministry's formalised time-tables of European governance, many informants produce their own personal agendas to manage their interactions with national and EU colleagues. The schedules found among informants have often included written sketches of personal memoranda, written for the purpose of being transmitted on a personal basis to a possible successor at the same post within the ministry, thus with a high degree of accuracy.

I exemplify the non-formalised subjective time experience within the observed group with a schedule of the informant responsible for the EU coordination of ministerial colleagues and the dossiers for EU meetings. These tasks make this informant's situation somewhat different compared to that of other informants. However, even though the situation is special, it displays the care with which informants informally organise their week to structure periods of uncertainty and complexity. Much of the informant's knowledge of how to master 'the week' (in practice between seven and thirteen days) of a 'round' of meetings is learned in discussions with his or her predecessor and from written notes inherited when taking over the posting. The notes reproduced in figure 6 took the form of a private schedule that included a detailed list of nearly every task which had to be carried out at each date over the cycle of the round. The aim of the schedule is to help the informant to remember all steps necessary in order to meet the deadlines of the internal ministerial timetables. An extract of the private schedule is reproduced in figure 6.

Council

3/7   Check Telex: draft agenda
        Phone X for annotated agenda

        Orders
        1. EU Parliamentary Committee, files, background material, deadline 6/7
        2. EU Parliamentary Committee folder background material + speaking notes
        3. GAC folder (background memo and possible speaking notes + English version, informal meetings) deadline 13/7

        Meeting IU section with agenda, check with X (Y for agenda)

7/7   Deadline 1 copy EU Parliamentary Committee + 1 ex

        Summons to GAC coordination to section officials, head of department, heads of section, contact persons in V and U,
        Assistant head of department 12/7 15.00 M room.

10/7   Summons for briefing FM 14/7 8.00 in J room.
        To Head of department, assistant head, heads of division, Y, G, heads of concerned sections, coordinators, F.

        Summons to EU emb fax to EU emb + Comm's repr

        Deadline EU parliament Comm folder 2
        Check background memo the same to the Parl. standing comm.
        Plastic folder if something is missing
        No A-points in the folder
        Closing the folder S. checking
        Distribution to:
        F-G
        K
        other concerned (check with L)
        head of department, assistant head
        IO
        AOK
        JI
        DT
        EU-secretariat
        1 extra

Transmit speaking notes EU emb, coordinate with A for speaking notes

12/7   Coordination GAC 15.00 M room Head of department in lead
            Last contact with U
            Check the composition of delegation (YG, head of department, FM)
            Phone LO Parliamentary Committee and inform of participants from our
            ministry

13/7   Deadline GAC folder
            List of Content
            Practical arr. by repr.
            Check report of repr Paris meeting
            Check report PoCo Coreper
            No reference material
            Distribution to:
            FM, head of department, GH, check GL, EU secretariat, head of division
            5:3 archives, JP

14/7   8.00 briefing FM for Parliamentary EU committee
            9.00 Meeting with Parliamentary EU committee
            11.30 Briefing EU embassies
            Closing GAC folder
            definitive last deadline 16/7 12.00

Next week: communicate reports from Coreper, GAC.

Figure 6 The private EU timetable I (extract)
Source: Y Department of EU member-state X.

With the private schedule, the informant tries to rationalise her actions within the time limits of the EU timetables. Such a schedule mediates between the informant's subjective experience of EU time and the official deadlines. It structures the uncertainty of the informant's practical European governance time into a more manageable temporal situation. In the very process of making the schedule, the informant objectifies his or her inner time, that is, transforms the temporal aspect of unconscious practice into a *rationalised individual time* more in harmony with official EU time. The scheme contains time of various degrees of objectification. As can be seen, some of the conceptual tools used to give time structure are the same as those used in the official timetables: 'GAC', 'GAC consultation meeting'. Others – such as 'closing the folder', 'definitive last deadline'– are innovations, streamlined in order to express more accurately the situation in practice, and thereby to be of more use to the informant. Furthermore, the informant structures her working time with an additional personal schedule, namely the practical planning of preparations for Coreper (figure 7). As seen below, the events are to some extent simultaneous with her activities in the Council preparation.

Coreper

3/7   Order of folder, speaking notes (Eng.) deadline 6/7

        Produce list of content, incl. teleph. numbers

        Call for coordination 5/7 14.00

        Assistant head of department

        All officials

        G. H.

5/7   Coordination M room 14.00

6/7   Deadline: folder

        Remind officials, S department + coordinators GH and J.

7/7   Packing of folder. N supervises

        Definitive deadline 12.00

        Check reference documentation included

14.00   Folder ready

        Distribution of folder:
        G.H. 3 folders
        Head of department (or H)
        Brussels repr. 3 cop.
        the archive
        KL
        JF
        For attention GJ, LO, HK
        EU Secretariat

        Contact persons: YO HJK
        G2 G L
        F6 HO
        D8 GY
        U9 DL

Figure 7 The private EU timetable II (extract)
Source: Y Department of EU member-state X.

At a rationalised level the two schedules are separate although they overlap in time. However, as we shall discover, they are in practice representations and objectifications of the same social time, whose meaning is not fully discernible until its form is completed over time. This is a time not reducible to either official or private static abstractions of the logic of the informant's practice. On the one hand, private timetables mirror the practical mastering of planning that is necessary for the coordination of official meetings. On the other hand, these timetables affect the informant's dispositions by providing deadlines which give rise to an unconscious organisation of practice. However, the conscious rational division of tasks into two chains of meetings does not change the fact that the practical management of the situation is indivisible. The privately objectified schedule, which is created for the fulfilment of her responsibility as a whole, disposes the informant for a certain unconscious sense of handling parallel events in preparing the Council and Coreper meetings. These schedules are creatively transformed by habitus into customary dispositions. In order to fully understand this dialectic, I now turn to the unreflected, practised time that is invisible in official timetables and informants' rationalisations, but observable to me.

European pasts and plans in practice

The theoretical point of departure of this section is that practical planning and past making is different from the rationalised one of the informants. However, there is a close dialectical and overlapping relationship between objective categories used to coordinate practical life and the subjective calendars and well-established time units described above. In contrast to the other chapters of this book, where time is constructed on the basis of categories making sense on the level of ideas, this chapter deals with the practical sense-making of the passage of time in European governance. The representation of time by the logic of 'scientific' interpretation is here replaced by the logic of *practice*. A scientific logic brings order but thereby also brings division. The selected informants' subjective 'knowledge' of time is objectively interpreted in terms of my own conceptualisations. It is in the light of this interpretation that the meaning of European governance activities should be understood. The time forms gives European governance as a whole its form, 'as the order of a succession, and therefore its direction and meaning' (Bourdieu, 1990: 98). The method is to reunite planning practices to forms of a practical whole. Instead of assuming sub-categories of time, the point of departure in the following is the informants' own *sense* of their situation in time.

In practice, informants situate themselves in what could be described as different recurrent 'rhythms' of various time spans and characteristics. The rhythms are not scientific sub-headings, distorting the logic of practical planning, but are reproduced because they play a role in the informants' own structuring of the passage of time. That is to say that they are perceivable in the practical sense-making within the group of informants, taking place beyond the post-rationalisation of action under official time categories. The advantage of the concept of rhythm is that it puts emphasis on the strongly *cyclic* character of everyday work in European governance. In addition, the rhythm conception is used for reasons of clarity in this first descriptive phase of the search for a generative structure in the great richness of observed practices. In the perspective of individual officers, there are of course no sharp boundaries between these various rhythms in every-day endeavours. The rhythms are unconsciously woven into each other in the actor's overall planning oriented activities. This is also the reason why they are decoded as a whole in terms of coherent structure. As this structure will show, the meaning of each specific planning practice can be fully understood only when related to all the rhythms described, and their completion in time. Given this perspective, the initial description of facts in 'rhythms' strikes a fully acceptable balance between induction criteria, researchable categories and the demands of illustration. The rhythms largely correspond to various time spans: rhythms spanning over several years, half a year, a month, a week and a day.

The multi-year rhythm

ORDER OF EU PRESIDENCIES

One of the main horizons making up the informants' total planning situation emanates from the order of EU presidencies. One after the other, in alphabetical order, each EU member-country holds the presidency for a period of six months on a rolling schedule. For informants, this highly objectified temporal scheme constitutes some of the most certain knowledge there is of a more distant future for European governance. It creates the long-term cycle within which important future landmarks in European governance can be placed in time. The series pro-vides points of reference for predicting the main questions facing the Union in the future and the long-term development of the organisation as a whole. Each member-state is expected to take initiatives within areas of its special national interest during its presidency. The adaptation of practices to the long chain of presidencies is natural, considering that these differ from each other with regard to emphasis on policy issues and areas, thereby creating different determinants for national actions with respect to European governance over time. The infor-mants' knowledge of each partner's priorities constitutes an important compo-nent in national policy planning. In order to improve the conditions for taking national initiatives in European governance, these are attempted to be presented during presidencies which are expected to give priority to the same issues. Although the scheduling of future practices in accordance with presidencies does not play a prominent role in the determination of everyday practice, it consti-tutes, in a somewhat diffuse way, a more deeply lying practical sense of the mas-tering of longer time spans within European governance. The most important practical function of the multiyear schedule is the provision of convenient tem-poral points of reference for all kinds of practices and discourses relating to the past and future of European governance – for example, in the fixing of periods of particular practical importance: 'the Intergovernmental Conference will probably not begin during the Italian presidency, we should rather expect it to start at the end of the Irish, thereby entering its decisive moments not until Luxembourg comes into office the first half year of 1997.' Or in evaluations of and lessons for the presidential organisation: 'It was the efficiency and ability of the incumbent presidency to work out sensible compromises that paved the way for the successful accomplishment of the EU Summit of 197X.' Why have not more subjective – and, for practical purposes, perhaps more adequate and efficient – sequences been created? There are many reasons why the periodisation into chairmanships is so manifest in the temporal organisation at the level of individual practice.

The period of a chairmanship is a very useful time unit because, as mentioned above, even practical work varies greatly in character and intensity with the shifts in presidencies and follows similar routines within each presidency (certain standard operating procedures in relation to the beginning, carrying through and close of presidencies). For a quick routinisation of European governance practices, national administration is very much helped – and therefore very much influenced – by existing temporal division such as 'the clock of presidencies'. As noted by Luckmann (1991), even though subjectively organised time relations are to a large extent locally structured, they are highly influenced by objectified social categories (Luckmann, 1991: 160–161).

In European governance, the objectified presidency structure plays the role of a standard to adhere to, something which is very obvious in the process of the enlargement of the Union. This is one of the reasons why this structure infiltrates practical life to such a large extent; it is an easy scheme to naturalise and universalise for a new member-state. For practical reasons, and for the sake of simplicity, new members adapt to European governance time by learning the original practical structures, which over the past decades have become increasingly objectified. Like, for example, the election period in national political life, the EU presidency stands out as one of the most natural measures of periods in the Union's history and future. One important reason why abstract, formal principles of division so closely overlap with practical distinctions in time is that informants find practical justifications for them in their everyday work. What should be remembered, however, is the different meaning of the same notion in practice and in the abstract presidential timetable.

'IMPORTANT PRESIDENCIES'

Another practical consequence of the horizon created by the presidency cycle is the impact of *important* presidencies. These are the presidencies held during periods when it is planned to take important decisions – e.g. the end of 1996, beginning of 1997 (the IGC), 1999–2000 (the establishment of Economic and Monetary Union (EMU). Under these presidencies, the individual member-state needs to have a clear view of its position in areas in which important decisions are to be taken within the Union – it has to be ready for decision. Officials explicitly speculate about when a specific event is going to take place in terms of 'during which presidency'. In fact, evaluative statements about the achievements, capacity and role of various partners in the Union are to a considerable extent based on the experience of how they manage their presidencies – or, rather, their latest presidency. The series of presidencies into the future not only determines the general direction of European governance, but also the intensity of work for informants. Over the longer time span, the series creates an overarching rhythm of weaker and stronger intensity – e.g. fluctuations in the frequency of working group meetings, expectations of initiatives, greater or lesser tension between EU and national policy priorities. The influence of this rhythm is particularly palpable in periods when two resourceful and traditionally influential presidencies (for example, Germany and France) follow each other. The importance and influence of the presidency rhythm were confirmed in informants' descriptions of particular presidencies as being better 'organised' and 'efficient', with 'higher ambition' and 'without emphasis on national interest' than others. This implicitly pointed to practical implications for their own work: a well-organised presidency in some senses meant less confusion and higher predictability for them. Each member-state, especially the new ones, learns from the organisation of the various presidencies in order to carry out a successful presidency of its own. 'We should re-organise the ministry in line with what the Danes did for their successful chairmanship.'

'own presidency'

Moreover, the knowledge of the order of presidencies gives the officials the opportunity to begin to plan *their own presidency* at a very early stage. In the observed case, the presidency was occasionally mentioned in planning papers and referred to by informants when discussing the future. The informants were reminded of the time for the presidency in the evaluation of the on-going one, worked out by the EU unit of the ministry. The importance of a thorough planning of the EU chairmanship was often connected to discussions of the increasing workload owing to the Union: 'I shudder at the thought of our own presidency when imagining the heavy workload behind the ongoing presidency'. In this context, the need to draw on the experience of presidencies of other member-states was often underlined. Again, the importance of the cycle of the presidencies for the informants' daily praxis should not be exaggerated. The reason why the sense of the presidency does not play a more active practical role is that in the studied case it lay in a relatively distant future. The head of the EU unit reminds colleagues of the presidency in planning papers. In this way, it is reproduced as a vague point of reference in a distant future, affecting daily work to a smaller extent for most of the informants, and more directly in the case of the planning unit. Naturally, as the date draws closer, the conscious awareness of it will increase and preparations for it will become more intensive. This experienced 'certainty' of a coming period creates a strong disposition in officials' habitus to organise their practices in time before their own state holds the presidency. When reflected over, answers to questions of the following character would probably represent practice: 'How should we (I) have acted in the place of the ongoing chairmanships', 'What can we learn from this presidency in order to make ours successful?'

TREATY REVISIONS

Other natural horizons in the far past and future, which are more manifest but less frequently referred to in daily discussions, are the dates of reviews and revisions of EU treaties. When talking about future perspectives within their area of responsibility, many informants quite frequently referred to 'the next treaty revision'. This was the future reference point on which long-term thinking often focused. The 'IGC perspective' was used as an expression of long-term planning, and constituted, in combination with discourses involving 'Europe's future', the main reason and driving force behind the need to work out a clear definition of 'the national interest', sustainable in the long term. Certain informants felt that the IGC horizon created something new for national policy planning. It forced the ministry to formulate long-term goals in very concrete terms owing to the fact that the preparation and carrying out of the IGC takes the form of a negotiation in which national standpoints should be known as early as possible in order to influence the discussions. Moreover, utterances like 'the Conference gives a wider horizon' not only referred to a wider spectrum of concrete questions, but sometimes also evoked links between the informants' own work and a more long-term vision of the future. It was as if their practical knowledge and preparation of the Conference conjured up a feeling of taking part in a European future. Another point of reference with connotations of fundamental future change was 'the enlargement of the Union'. The entrance into the Union of new member-states was the future that was hoped for, even though this also entailed a risk that coordination problems within the Union would become even more difficult to manage.

My observations revealed that more or less the same brackets that are used to divide up the future are turned and extended backwards into the past. As noted, the experience of former presidencies plays a prominent role in the constitution of the past. The history of European governance is designated in terms of former presidencies as well as in relation to major policy action and events (the European Monetary System (EMS) 1979, the Internal Market Programme, the Single European Act (SEA) 1986, Maastricht, 1992) and national adaptation reforms.

PRACTICAL PARADOXES

An overriding tension in the multi-year rhythm can be observed. On the one hand, there is the strong *reactive* style towards European governance colleagues owing to the difficulties of coordinating the fifteen and the lack of common planning functions or common views of the future. This creates a temporal praxis of short horizons. On the other hand, the fact that negotiation procedures among EU members are established on a long-term basis and codified in calendars provides opportunities for pursuing national policy objectives towards other member-states over a longer period. 'The shadow of the future', as Axelrod (1984) calls it, is also long in the practical-sense conception of planning in European governance. The commitment to a *long-term cooperative relationship* is strong, and defection is not considered to be a viable option. The structure is therefore more stable and of greater importance compared to other forms of international and multilateral cooperation. The EU decision-making structure creates the need to clarify national long-term substantive interests in specific issue areas. There is a great need for practical planning *vis-à-vis* EU colleagues both for the long term and the more immediate future. It is generally recognised that a member-state is able, by means of good planning and well-elaborated strategies, to strengthen its own actions and initiatives *vis-à-vis* its EU partners, more so than in traditional international situations in which a more reactive attitude to the policies of other states is feasible. This results in longer time horizons of the informants: 'you need to know your partners' long-term planning.'

The semi-year rhythm

SIX-MONTH PROGRAMME

The most important point of reference in the half-year cycle of European governance is the visit of the foreign minister of the country holding the EU presidency. A visit is paid to each of the other fourteen member-states at which the minister gives an account in outline of what is planned for the period, and gives his or her colleague the opportunity to discuss priorities and EU developments in general. In practice, the half-year cycle of meetings (including working groups, Coreper and Council) begins for informants when the in-coming chairman presents his six-month work programme. Formally, this is done at the first GAC of the presidency. For my informants, the presentation of the programme is the most important event of practical consequence each half-year. The first item on the agenda of the initial GAC of the presidency is normally 'the programme of the xx presidency', which is presented orally by the chairing foreign minister. Thereafter, the other ministers are given an opportunity to express support for, and comment on, the various points of the programme. The president's speech is brought back home for careful evaluation at every unit of the ministry; what indications of major initiatives can be found within each policy area? The ministry's EU unit starts to work out the national half-year plan as a response to the programme, and distributes a schedule with deadlines for the six-month period within the ministry, as described above. A few days later the new chairman presents more detailed programmes for working groups in each area (see figure 3 for the timetable of 'Agenda 2000' of the British presidency).

At the beginning of each presidency, the EU unit of the ministry composes an internal memorandum concerning the expected priorities and initiatives of the presidency and the principal national positions within each priority area. The memo is based on the presidency's official programme, experiences of previous presidencies and earlier discussions of national policies.

RECURRENT AGENDAS

There is generally a strong regularity in the handling of EU questions over time, and particularly over a presidency; the agendas of every Coreper and Council meeting during a 'normal' term of office are almost identical. The individual informant follows the agenda item she is responsible for, and continuously updates her background notes and speaking notes for the ambassador and the minister before each meeting. One could say that this regularity makes the rhythm of the individual officer's routine less an outcome of 'real'-world events or policy concerns than the result of the dynamics of EU meetings. This rhythm predominates over other more natural policy rhythms that might be more appropriate for the solution of concrete policy tasks. However, the rolling meeting schedule of the Union creates a high degree of continuity in policy-making; it routinises the common policy-making procedures within the Union to a greater degree than that experienced in other instances of international cooperation. This is why the standard operating procedures within the observed group can to a large extent be understood by an investigation of the Union's meeting cycles. However, the logic of this half-year meeting cycle does not imply that informants know in advance exactly what will be taken up under each of the points on the agenda of the scheduled meetings. The presidency sets the agenda only two weeks in advance, and often in very broad and vague terms in order not to exclude the most recent developments under each item. New points may be added. After having learned what is on the agenda, the individual informant, working with the national representatives in Brussels and through informal channels, collects as much information as possible in order to make his or her briefing note for the meeting as up to date and relevant as possible.

SUMMITS

The other point of reference within the semi-year horizon is the summit meeting of the European Council. These summits, which end each presidency, play an important role in the development of the Union in the longer run, and great attention is therefore paid to them in the practical periodisation. The observed group plays an important role in the briefing of the prime minister before these Council meetings. The group produces a schedule for the entire government's preparation of the national input into the European Council (cf.figure 4). For many informants, it entails as much work as does an ordinary Council meeting, and its result and the implementation of its decisions are very closely monitored by the ministry. Thus, the half-year planning sequence originates not only from the working rhythm of the Council, but also from the meetings in the European Council .

The monthly rhythm

THE 'ORDER'

The informants often begin their account of the monthly round of EU meetings (Wg, Coreper, Council) with a reference to the provisional agenda sent out one or two months in advance by the president in office. The first practical thing to happen is that a preliminary order for contributions is sent out to informants responsible for issue areas affected by the questions scheduled for discussion according to the presidency's agenda. The national driving force that ensures that the monthly rhythm is maintained is the government's EU secretariat; it decides and controls the internal EU calendar, commissions the various files from concerned ministries, sets the deadlines, sees to it that they are met and produces the comprehensive background dossier for Councils and Coreper. It is the main channel by which the temporal forms of European governance are diffused into the ministries. The individual informant sometimes has the feeling that she is 'drowning' in orders as a consequence of the large number of EU meetings. She also has to prepare for meetings held in a purely national context, but it is easier to plan this work because national schemes are fixed longer in advance, often under strong influence by the informant, and are not as many in number. The qualitative differences in the temporal forms of European governance lie mainly in its quantitative characteristics: the regularity and high frequency of meetings. As described above, EU meetings are held at the level of working groups (Wg), ambassadors (Coreper) and ministers. In the observed ministry, three officials are busy full time with the internal coordination of EU activities. In practice, one of their tasks is to administer the preparation of the dossier put together for the minister before each of the EU meetings. The order for background material and the national position for each item of the agenda is sent out to the responsible desk officer two weeks before the meeting with a deadline for delivering the material to the EU secretariat, which puts the contributions together in the dossier (the 'Council folder' and 'Coreper', see figures 6 and 7).

THE 'FILE'

The EU secretariat's coordination work consists of seeing to it that their colleagues deliver material to the normally 15–20 points on the GAC meeting agenda (see figure 6), which most often equal the number of officials to coordinate them (sometimes one official is responsible for several agenda points). Owing to the many other engagements and tasks, informants often have difficulty meeting the deadlines. For this reason, the secretariat often sends out a reminder one week in advance of its deadlines. In order to standardise the contributions of officials and thereby make it easier for the ambassador and the minister to read and draw the operative conclusions from them, the order prescribes how 'the file' is to be written. The directives of the EU unit call for 'short and operative papers at a maximum of 1–2 pages'. The files should be formulated in a short, 'operative' manner, to provide a basis for an operative discussion aimed at concrete decisions of substance in Coreper and Council. It should begin with a well-argued national position, followed by the 'position of the question in the EU decision-making process', the present status of the presidency's proposal, when a decision is expected to be taken and, when 'necessary' (and if space permits), the standing of the subject-matter in general – 'a background'. However, it is very seldom that informants add a more detailed background note of the traditional type, including a historical perspective on the question and a more elaborated account of the reasons behind the initiation of the process in the first place. The main reason why this kind of background has fallen into disuse is practical; the desk officer has to save time in the face of many deadlines, and therefore keeps his briefing note short. Instead he devotes much time to mapping out partners' positions and to formulating the national position in a very concise way. The minister and other higher representatives have time to read only very short 'notes' before each item of the agenda. According to most informants, this tendency to divide policy questions into very short routine commissions is growing and with it a parallel increase in the number of issues in European governance. In addition, informants are asked to enclose several appendices to their papers; the reports of the last EU working group meeting (and, if relevant, Coreper meeting) produced by the national representative, and the Council secretariat, respectively; discussion and working papers ('non-papers') that have been circulated; telegrams from EU colleagues and from the European Commission; press releases; and official statements of relevance for the question. In other words, the contributions under each agenda point should be streamlined for a situation of multilateral negotiations with short time limits. According to the EU unit, the 'ideal instruction' to the minister should be included on 'one page'.

DEADLINES

The deadline for delivery to the government's EU secretariat is, as already mentioned, normally not set until three days before the Coreper or Council meeting. The ambassador's report from the meeting to all concerned is sent back home to the capital immediately or the day after the meeting.

The reason for the strictness regarding the meeting of deadlines is very practical: the coordination of fifteen administrations in time and space requires a very disciplined organisation at the EU and national levels. A date set for the meeting of fifteen ambassadors or ministers is for practical reasons very difficult – almost impossible – to change; the train, or more likely the plane, leaves for Brussels regardless of whether all the files for the minister's dossier have been delivered. The national representative in Brussels cannot be let down in the sense of not being provided with the best possible conditions – i.e. streamlined reports and position files – for a successful negotiation. At the moment a new schedule of deadlines is received, activities start gradually to shift into a new temporal rhythm; the order of priorities changes, the working day becomes longer. In fact, the main temporal units are constituted as the time between two EU deadlines.

European governance is characterised by the *deadlinification* of the temporal structure, generating the day-to-day institutional praxis of the observed informants. Their practical disposition of their time is largely grounded in a system of deadlines. Presidencies are perforated by regular Wg, High Level Officials Meetings (HLO) and Council of Ministers' meetings (CM), which yield objectified and implicit deadlines that shape the rhythm of informants' workday and week. Also, EU interaction through telecommunication is to a large extent based on deadlines or, in concrete terms, messages prescribing deadlines for responses to draft decisions from EU partners and Wg.

EU deadlines are decisive benchmarks in relation to which other temporal – but also non-temporal – aspects of the Union are defined. One of the main temporal units is constituted by the lapse of time between two deadlines. Other temporal actions are practically related to this principle of division. The deadlines thus become natural and universal points of reference. This is a very strong tendency because meeting EU deadlines is a pre-requisite for the general management of EU cooperation, but also of other policy areas owing to the fact that EU questions are often given high priority. This is the reason why the internal EU schedule is so strongly formalised and officialised. European governance strongly *erodes informants' temporal sovereignty*. Their reciprocal relations are often organised with reference to EU deadlines. A significant example is the temporal ordering of acts involved in the joint writing of a draft for a speech to be held at a CM. Drafts of this kind are produced by several officials in a concerted effort. Each officer is responsible for the part that concerns his or her field of competence. In this case the whole system of social relations is built up on strict deadlines. The co-writers meet the deadlines they more or less explicitly give to each other with great punctuality, because they are highly aware of the trouble that would result from not respecting them.

EU deadlines are thus everywhere, not only explicitly reproduced in formalised and private timetables, but in all activities: in written memoranda, in the allocation of time between all kinds of tasks, in determining the beginning and end of the working day, in lunch breaks, even in gestures; in short, in the routines of everyday life. The EU deadline is the fundamental principle of allocating time for the observed group of civil servants. Almost every other practice is practically related to this principle of division. It is around the deadlines that informants organise their activity in, and planning over, time.

THE 'PIPELINE'

One of the consequences of this character of the process is that, in practice, the decision-making procedure is temporally the reverse of what is implied by formal decision-making rules (cf. March and Olsen, 1989). It is more true to say that the Coreper and Council *confirm* the process than that they initiate and lead it, which informants' descriptions often tend to suggest by emphasising formal rules and decision: e.g. 'at the Council of January 14 it was decided to. Thereafter the implementation process starts'. Observed over a month's time, the questions have been handled in the pipeline (Wg, informal communications and meetings) often long before the presidency even puts them on an agenda. When it is time for a formal meeting, a consensus on a policy has often already been hammered out. This reverse process is accentuated by the fact that a successful outcome of a Council is regarded for political reasons as very valuable, not least for the presidency. Thus, in practice the formalisation of the problem is often made at the same moment a solution can be presented. Compared to national policy-making, where a formal decision of the government frequently sets off the process (for example, by establishing a Commission), formal decisions in the Union are most often taken once the road to consensus has already been travelled by the fifteen.

It is in relation to this 'pipeline' that informants function in time. They try to predict and control matters that flow through it as early as possible before formal meetings. Ideally they should be fully informed and involved from the very moment an issue is launched, which is of crucial importance for the medium-term allocation of resources within the ministry. The strong need felt by informants to foresee what will come up on the agendas of EU meetings is the result of the great importance of the Union for national policies generally; at EU meetings very important decisions may be taken, and considerable resources have to be devoted to anticipate them. In contrast to purely national issues, a question on the agenda of the Union requires that officers devote time to determining which meetings it may come up at as well as to foreseeing the positions of the other EU member-states.

The motto that the EU secretariat wants everybody within the government to learn and use to guide their work is, 'long-term planning, flexibility and anchorage of decisions'. As a result, informants concentrate their efforts on the next meeting but keep an eye on possible future extensions of the pipeline in alternative directions. For the overall result of the observed department, it is becoming as important to understand and predict the process and dynamics of decision-making in the Union, since these can deeply affect national political interests, as it is to make predictions about developments in national political life. The informants claim that it is more difficult to forecast what will happen in the politics of the Union than in national political life, but in practice there is just another kind of anticipation. To meet their deadlines, officers concentrate their attention on the meetings next to be held.

The planning future is *cyclified* into preparation rounds for 'presidencies', 'treaty revisions' and 'Coreper–Council meetings'. Owing to the largely informal nature of the decision-making process in the Union, anticipation is essential to gain influence: 'we need to be one step in advance of our EU partners' as informants put it. Therefore, it is becoming more and more important to listen to the other EU partners and to analyse their position before formulating a standpoint of one's own. There is subsequently less time available for independent in-depth study of an issue – including, for example, its relation to earlier national experience. Reacting on an ad hoc basis takes an increasingly large part in planning, with management of cooperation on a day-to-day, or at most monthly, basis. The monthly rhythm is from the informants' point of view 'the long term' where, relatively speaking, 'oceans of time' exist for preparation.

The weekly rhythm

COORDINATION CYCLES

European governance practices, as seen over a week's time at the ministry, can be exemplified by the work of the informant whose rationalised private timetable was examined in figures 6 and 7. As mentioned there, this official has the main responsibility for coordinating the background reports and files other informants prepare for EU meetings, and for reporting to the EU secretariat on the ministry's behalf. She functions as the timekeeper in the observed group; she orders the files, sets the deadlines and is responsible for making sure that they are met. She uses her private schedule to plan her actions and makes as rational use of her very limited time as possible. From an observer's standpoint, her practice might be characterised as 'crisis management', in the sense that at each individual moment she is completely absorbed in her immediate tasks. She describes her work as 'very stressful' but she skilfully manages her time in order to keep to the timetable – or, rather, to minimise the inevitable stress of the last few days before meetings.

In Bourdieu's terminology, her habitus is disposed by her private schedule (i.e. earlier experiences), thereby generating actions that manage the race to meet deadlines. At the conscious level she forgets about past and future actions in order to manage the complex present that is densely packed with responsibilities and activities. She does so in full and unconscious assurance that the past and the future, both of the nearest few days and a larger interval, are not lost, but exist both in her private objectified schedule and in her habitus. Thereby she can devote all her energy to the immediate present and to the many and complex and intense tasks, all to be completed 'now', with which her week is filled. As can be seen in the schedule, some of these consist of very short contacts with, for example, the head of department, to check on his or her preference for how a certain issue on an agenda should be organised and handled, or with others, often over the telephone, for information. Other reminders have to do with complex practical arrangements, such as booking flights for every member of the delegation to Brussels, and seeing to it that they all arrive on time for the current EU meeting.

In this private schedule, patterns of interaction can be discerned. The period covered is long enough to reveal a marked *recurrent pattern of practices*, which structures the informant's time, from the presidency's draft agenda for the GAC to the distribution of the meeting report. The calendar of tasks represents the fulfilment of the informant's overall responsibility to prepare for Council meetings. The chain of orders – deadlines – summons – closing the folder – distribution – coordination – orders – deadlines and so on forms a circle in which the informant is constantly situated. Moreover, several shorter loops can be observed. For example, 'the deadline – checks – distribution' loop of 10 July is repeated on July 13. As shown earlier, the officer manages the preparation of Coreper in accordance with a parallel schedule, including many tasks that are organised and carried out simultaneously with those in preparation of Council meetings.

The two sets of objectified routines are thus in practice woven together. The separate, but in practice overlapping, cycles of meetings create a strong disposition to organise nearly all practical matters in a *circular pattern*. This

organising principle of a never-ending circle of coordination, deadlines, commissions, control points and distribution is also applied within the ministry,
issues circulated for consideration within it eventually looping back to the
responsible official for finalization. The order of the informant's week is first and
foremost a circular rhythm.

The calendar of tasks serves both to order them temporally and to integrate
the separate steps into the harmonious whole expected by the collective of informants; 'my task is to prepare the Council meeting'. When reflecting on practice,
she often refers in her rationalising discourse to 'the short time limits' and 'the
deadlines' under which 'you are a slave'. The deadlines are made 'natural' points
of reference, 'points of orientation' over the week. The driving force behind the
process of naturalisation and universalization of the deadlines is very strong,
because to meet them is a prerequisite for managing other tasks at the ministry
efficiently and exerting influence in the decision-making process of the Union.

The private timetable exemplifies the strong tendency to objectify time routines in European governance, and the great extent to which practical planning
is determined by deadlines. In addition, deadlines play an important role in all
informants' discursive accounts of their own working situation over the week.
Informants point to the deadline system and the recurrent demand for material
for EU meetings as the features that distinguish their 'European' from their
'national' tasks. When alluding to the impact of cooperation in the Union on
their working situation, informants often express their dissatisfaction sponta-
neously, and reinforce it with gestures – 'All these EU orders will be the end of
me', 'I have no time for other things'.

The weekly deadlines determine the rhythm of the working day. They are
a decisive benchmark around which even national schedules and the timetables
of other international organisations are largely defined. For informants, the
main temporal unit is constituted by the lapse of time between two deadlines.
The private EU timetables mirror the administrative practices comprising the
concrete and complex exchanges and interaction between policymakers
involved in European governance. At the same time these timetables affect
praxis by creating deadlines around which administrative routines are organised, and which give rise to the experience of recurrent periods of intensification
and crisis management. As noted above, deadlines and recurrent rhythms are
also feature in, for example, the preparation of the national budget. But the
deadlines in European governance differ from these in quantity, regularity and
permanence; over and over again in an never-ending schedule they structure the
passage of informants' time. Contrary to what many informants' state – 'EU
business is like any other: a timetable to stick to', etc. – the sheer quantity of
deadlines makes a huge difference for practical routines. The short time limits
are most often not even reflected over: the deadlines simply have to be met.
Informants had assignments related to the national context as well, but these
were fixed longer in advance; to a far greater extent these tasks have for decades
been institutionalised and objectively 'written' into habitus. National time

demands less conscious consideration and is therefore experienced by the informants themselves as less stressful and more under control.

'MIDDLE-OF-THE-WEEK'

Another very decisive turning point in the transitional period into more intensive preparation work are the days in the middle of the week before 'the week' of the Coreper meeting on Wednesdays. These days are, in practice, the starting point of a new round of meetings, a monthly round including Coreper, Council, a meeting with the parliamentary standing committee on the Union, and various follow-up meetings. 'A meeting period' is for informants first and foremost defined practically: a time of intense activity. It is also contrasted to other periods in other respects. The EU meetings engage nearly all informants around one common event, which is normally not the case in other areas. People have to work very closely together; they consult each other in the preparation of each agenda point and brief one another about the results after the meeting. It is considered extremely important that views are harmonised. In this sense, the meeting system has a strong unifying and concentrating effect in terms of the creation of a common time framework within the group (and the entire ministry), but also between ministries. The process of concentration and intensification of work resembles an accelerating train: after a slow start it begins to roll ever faster, with an increasing number of colleagues on board, towards EU meetings.

Informants normally have a good practical sense of the *two* rounds of meetings lying ahead of them. As a matter of routine they prepare for up-coming rounds by reviewing the orders, schedules and files of earlier cycles. These documents constitute the structure on which the preparation of the new cycle is built. At this initial stage of the on-going cycle, the following round looms up in the distance as something the informants have in the back of their minds – or, rather, speaking with Bourdieu, in their habitus. This practical awareness can also result in concrete actions: early logistical coordination, for example that the minister is not double-booked on any of the meeting dates planned by the presidency. In practice, the EU decision-making process is constituted by a *constant* negotiation process out of which declarations and actions grow. EU policy is created in a continuous dialogue between European governance actors.

The daily rhythm: 1 – telecommunications

FREQUENCY

For those who take part in European governance the normal daily rhythm is largely determined by the telecommunication traffic and information from colleagues and counterparts. The first task of the day for informants is to read the *telegrams* that have come in since the previous evening, and to check whether any of them calls for action. This work is given priority over nearly every other duty because if there should be a need for action or an answer to any incoming telegrams, the margin of time is often limited to one or two days, although it may vary between 'the same afternoon' and fifteen days. Consequently, informants normally give top priority to handling questions raised in the information network of the Union. Only such matters as important national crises that have to be dealt with immediately go first. Owing to the fact that telecommunications (telephone, fax, telegrams, e-mail) have such a large impact on the way time is allotted during a day, a detailed description of them is called for. The other important determining factor for the daily rhythm – the *meeting cycles* – is discussed in the next section.

Telegrams are received by informants at set times during the day. The first 'package' arrives at about 9 o'clock, the second at noon and the last at 4 in the afternoon. Over a year, the average frequency with which telegrams are transmitted is more or less the same, only slightly lower during August – the main holiday period of most member-states of the Union. However, within the perspective of a week, the amount of information transmitted closely follows the meeting cycles described earlier in this chapter.

In addition to these cycles, the variation in frequency in the shorter, daily run depends, of course, on the specific policy in question. Sometimes, certain informants can receive up to twenty telegrams in one package, all of which must be read quickly but carefully since many messages are highly operative in character. This arrangement has many consequences on the way time is used in practice. The rhythm of the working day depends to a considerable extent on the moments at which the telecommunications are received, for they contain calls for action from colleagues in member-states or from the European Commission.

FORM

The form of telegrams varies from very short notices concerning confirmations of member-state participation in the next meeting, to longer arguments and proposals for action, reports of meetings, or new findings within the political area of concern. The number of pages (A4) may vary from one (e.g. confirmations) to 40–50 (e.g. yearly summaries of EU achievements in the field). Of course member-states send out many different types of initiatives and reactions. Many matters have already been worked out at the Wg level, and need only to be confirmed or amended via telecommunications. Others are initiated over the network. In the case of an EU declaration or statement, the deadline for an answer may be very short – perhaps only a couple of hours. Sometimes the call for action is formulated as a *procedure de silence* – i.e. if no answer is received from a member-state, this is interpreted as acceptance. This style of decision-making makes it very important for informants to be present at the office on a very regular basis in order not to miss any deadlines and to ensure that they have a substitute to watch over their area of responsibility should they go out.

LANGUAGE

The working language over the lines is either English or French. The information is formulated in a 'telegraphic', clear-cut, distinct, and concise language.

The sentences are short. Only well-known English and French diplomatic terms are used in order that those concerned can read them very quickly and 'operatively' without running the risk of misunderstanding. The language is mainly a reproducer, a carrier, of facts in the subject area. In longer messages, the initial lines contain a summary including the operative content. Thereafter the background of the issue or the national standpoint is given. The need to concretise the national position with diplomatic vocabulary results in a language that in its more 'technical' orientation loses much of the visionary potential of national politics in the area of negotiations. Positions are formulated in a clear-cut and very brief manner in order to narrow the possibilities of interpretation, and to be convincing in the telecommunication network. The language of telecommunications thereby tends to lose the long-term associations and visionary nuances of traditional policy formulations. Time affects language and substance.

HANDLING PROCEDURES

The operative character of messages results in a very action oriented approach by informants. As the cognisance of meeting deadlines changes the rhythm of activity at the department as a whole, an individual officer's situation suddenly changes at the moment of reception of an EU telegram, in need of a response of some sort. While the official reads the telegram and draws the conclusions about what response is needed, his or her sense of the situation switches into operative preparedness, a readiness to handle the issue. Often immediately after drawing the operative conclusion from incoming material, the desk officer starts to draft a national answer. With the new temporal rhythm turned on, the intensity of which depends on the prescribed deadline for answer, the officer first refers to earlier, similar messages or situations. If precedents do exist, they are studied in detail, and the parts that can be learned and drawn from are singled out. At the same time, the reaction of other EU partners is carefully taken into account. Thereafter begins the drafting of a reply telegram.

In some cases the individual attends to the issue independently. In others guidance from a higher level within the ministry is considered necessary. In many cases, comments on drafts of answers were obtained from the head of department. Most outgoing telegrams to EU colleagues are controlled by the EU unit before being sent off. The control regards both form and substance: the message or policy proposal should be consistent with earlier national positions and with the national policy in other areas; moreover it has to conform with the prescribed forms and structures of presentation, including the correct operative label (information, *pour action*, etc.) in the headline. The average duration of the procedure of having the draft checked by colleagues or a senior official is an hour or two after the individual informant has received the telegram. The exact time at which to transmit an answer via fax, telegram, or mail is a matter given strategic consideration; the right timing of the message enhances the chances for gaining national influence in the decision-making pipeline. According to informants, great political advantages may be gained if a message appears in the system in the 'right' order in relation to the answers of other member-states. In certain questions an association with partner X was preferred, in others with Y.

The *temporal consequences* of these constant negotiations are significant. The working day is punctuated by recurrent deadlines that have to be met in order to exert an influence on outcomes. Compared to purely national policy-making, the process of decision-making in European governance and the need for internal governmental coordination shortens the sequence of the handling of an issue, i.e. the time lapse between the first practical dealing with an up-coming question and its conclusion.

'TO THE POINT'

The system creates situations in which informants have to adopt and formulate a national stance very quickly – in some cases within policy areas in which the country in question traditionally lacks a more elaborated position. Moreover, national standpoints transmitted through the telecommunications system have to be more 'to the point than otherwise', as informants put it. Or as another expressed it, 'we need to be more to the point because we do not have time to seek support at a higher political level for every step we take'; 'we can no longer postpone the concretisation of national positions to the same degree as before', 'We now have to stretch our formulations as far as possible before asking for directives from our authorities'.

In this sense, the speedy process of decision-making via telecommunications makes the individual officer's work more independent. Each stance has to be very carefully formulated, because when it is sent to EU colleagues over the network, it is given political weight and directly becomes a negotiation standpoint, of which every word is evaluated by EU partners and bargained over in the traditional multilateral manner. The national position is often formulated in such a way that it could be inserted word for word into an official EU declaration. That is why the desk officer very quickly has to make sure, by means of intuition or directives from a higher instance, that the wording of the answer can be supported by the national authorities.

In practice the standpoint is often deduced from earlier policy formulations or from a general knowledge of national policy principles and 'the thinking' of those politically responsible. The patterns of communication by which European governance is carried on have created a new situation in which officers have to read, analyse, find support for and formulate positions at a higher speed than in the national context. There is less room for a 'rational choice' of policy when taking into account the temporal dimension of action, i.e. that the practice of EU officials proceeds through series of irreversible choices made under strong time pressure. Again, we see that the speed of decision-making affects the substance of policy: the demands on the form in which national views are presented influence the policy content.

Similar to earlier observations in this book, one consequence of the rhythms of the multilateral game of telecommunications is a strong *predominance of the present* on on-going action and planning. Officials allocate more time to investigating the current position of EU partners and to coordinating the national position. The focus on the present moment is also expressed in the character and substance of the various texts observed (telegrams, briefing notes, etc.). The interplay and intense negotiations between fifteen national ministries lead to complexity. In a national perspective, this has both positive and negative implications for time, including new possibilities of playing strategically with time in the process. The need for a speedy preparation of official national positions and the importance of timing are not only owing to the installation and use of communication networks between the capitals, but also to the complexity and specific logic of the multilateral game as such. It seems, however, that the characteristics of this logic are magnified owing to the high tempo in the decision-making process of European governance. (cf. Wallace, 1988, 1990). A qualitative difference between the EU communication system and more traditional procedures seems to be that the desk officer has to make up his or her mind more quickly, regardless of when he or she is planning to put forward the initiative. In practice, the informants function as links in an information chain. They have to handle each issue and transfer the information very quickly and clearly to the next stage in the decision-making process in order not to break the chain or cause problems for people further down the pipeline.

The daily rhythm: 2 – days before 'the meeting'
The days immediately preceding a meeting are a time of intense activity. As deadlines draw closer, informants increasingly use their working time to prepare their contributions. A few days (between three and five) before Coreper or Council meetings, the head of department has a briefing with all the desk officers that have contributed to the dossier for the meeting. The head goes through the agenda and poses questions to the responsible official in case he has found something unclear, or is requiring some additional background information. In order to provide the most up-to-date material, new information – for example, from the latest working-group meetings – is included in the issue specific file. The Council meeting often takes place only hours after a Coreper meeting, and many questions on the Council's agenda depend on its outcome. In consequence, all agendas of the working groups, Coreper and Council are in practice intertwined. Informants' internalisation of this rhythm on a daily basis create a strong practical disposition to order temporally their preparation of meetings according to this two-step rocket: the material produced for the Coreper file is designed to be easily transformed, whatever the outcome of the meeting, into a Council file. The practical effect of the simultaneity of preparations for meetings that subjectively succeed each other in time is that informants hardly distinguish between the formal decision-making status of the two (the Council is the instance at which decisions are formally taken). The practical simultaneity of meetings heightens the sense of an on-going process without distinguishable sequences, one that is completed over time not in steps, but in circles. The

rhythm of daily activity can be illustrated by deadline-day (normally a Friday; the Council meeting normally starts the following Monday see figure 8):

9.00	All resources of the observed unit, in terms of manpower, are devoted to the completion of the meeting dossier. For informants at the EU unit, it is at this point very difficult to combine other tasks with this phase of final preparation of the dossier. The stress factor is very high throughout the day.
9.00–16.00	Contributions are delivered. The most up-to-date information is included just before the deadline.
16.00	The files for the EU secretariat, to be forwarded to the representative in Brussels or to the minister, are put together in the dossier and a list of its contents as well as a check-list of practical information (departure time, hotel in Brussels etc.) are added. When the files are placed on the table, they are considered to be closed; only very important information is added after 16.00 hrs. There is an opportunity to add supplementary data concerning the development of an event during the weekend. The head of the EU unit collects possible supplements on Sunday evening, the evening before leaving with the minister for Brussels and the Council meeting. If the preparation has concerned the Council, i.e. the last meeting in 'the meeting round', the work of the informants is completed at least for that round. Before work on the next round gets under way, informants are given a short respite.

Figure 8 Deadline-day
Source: Y Department of EU member-state X.

To an observer it is clear that the working rhythm depends more on the calendar of EU meetings than on any other factor. Consequently, a mastery of the temporal dimension of European governance requires an ability to plan and foresee up-coming situations (agenda items, potential coalition partners etc.) in the rhythm of meetings. One of the components of what is regarded as high competence among the officials is clearly such mastery. No official escapes the rhythms of European governance.

Planning as anticipated decisions

From planning to preparation
Planning normally means to decide about future decisions. In European governance, to plan mainly means to *predict* when decisions will be taken in the complex of negotiations in which it is difficult to reach decisions about the next decision.

ONE STEP AHEAD

The past and the future are, in practice, marked off into the half-year periods of the EU presidencies, following each other in a never-ending rolling schedule. The six-month span is internalised as the medium-range horizon, for example, for predictions. It is on the basis of the presidency's work programme that the informant's sense of up-coming situations in a several-month-perspective is formed. The rolling working programmes stretching over several presidencies are not of the same practical importance. Little effort is therefore made to predict events beyond a half-year. The practical mastering of the temporal dimension of European governance requires a strong focus on the next EU meeting in order to foresee how issues will develop. Owing to the largely informal character of the decision-making process in the Union, this type of anticipation is seen to be essential for the *preparedness* needed at the moment of decision: 'in the negotiations, one needs to be one step ahead of the others.'

PREPARE FOR 'UP-COMING' EVENTS

Contrary to the reflected time of informants – that is, a time often in disorder – time is in practice very carefully planned in the short run. The importance of the right timing in the telecommunication traffic, and of a careful preparation for the next EU meeting, have resulted in complex routines evolved around the management of the present. In Giddens' terminology, the high degree of distanciation and complexity in the mediation of meaning between an increasing number of EU actors results in the extreme importance of timing, for example, with regards to the very issuing of certain telecommunications. The focus on the present is owing to the allocation of more time to the necessary investigation of European governance partners' positions on issues to be treated at coming meetings, and to national EU coordination.

The focus on the present is also expressed in the character and substance of various texts within the department, such as briefing notes and telegrams to EU partners. In order to master the internal coordination process (including a high number of telephone contacts with government and EU colleagues, many informal meetings with ministerial colleagues, the obtaining of directives from a higher level within the ministry), action is sometimes planned minute by minute. Nothing is allowed to fall outside this schedule because that would jeopardise the carrying through of the current round of meetings as a whole. The situation is often described as very 'stressful' and 'pressing'. In the most hectic days, informants refrain from activities involving the past and the future.

In order to be manageable, the complex present has to be free from as many considerations as possible beyond the 'now'. It is the next up-coming present, the next now, which habitus is mainly oriented towards, not the long-term consequences of decisions and future trends. In the complex present, the informant ignores the longer time horizons. As the date of an EU meeting date draws closer, his or her situation becomes increasingly more crisis-like. In the ordering of tasks, which from the outside seem to be very closely connected, the officer creates very clear boundaries between the respective 'immediates' in order to manage the many actions that have to be carried out in a very limited time span. The many contacts made with different persons point to the fact that the mass of information per unit of time that has to be given and received in order to master the process is great. Indeed, it is perceived to be greater than within 'national' policy-making. The private timetables over shorter periods exhibit the tension between the immediate need for 'crisis management' and longer-term planning (figures 6 and 7). The same tension is expressed in such utterances as 'we have to wait until this storm, this week, has blown over, then we have to sit down and formulate an overall policy'.

The historical background of EU issues is played down in planning in the sense that resources are shifted from writing reports concerning the origin of a particular question to strategic considerations relevant to the shorter horizons, needed in the multilateral game. The officials have to allocate their working time in a new way. Thus, the factors shaping the role of experience and the past are very practical. Owing to the constraints of time and extra work resulting from the Union, they simply do not have the time to produce reports and memoranda in a traditional way. Moreover, the continuous updating of briefing files for EU meetings is given priority over national areas, and takes considerable time. The practical conditions form another role of experience. There is less time for the past and the future in high-speed multilateral dealings. This is why calls for a stronger capacity of long-term planning at the national level, in order to counter-balance this development, are so strong among informants. The main future concern is to handle the up-coming meeting. The exception is the pre-diction of major events during the member-state's presidency. The planning of the presidency is made up to three to four years in advance.

Another reason, in addition to deadlines, why it is so difficult to reallocate time to activities beyond the present, is that informants constantly need to be '*on line*' in the EU telecommunication and multilateral network 'in case some-thing should turn up'. This phenomenon is a function of the strong irreversibil-ity of EU time: for those who do not participate at the prescribed moment, it is very difficult to change norms and decisions afterwards. The 'on-linification' diverts time from planning activities.

The snake in the wheel

The studied officials' practices proceed through series of irreversible, unconscious choices made under strong time pressure. Their practical sense of planning func-tions in urgency. The informant masters his or her time within the Union with-out thinking about it. The dynamics of the meeting cycles, the deadlines and the speed of decision-making create practically defined divisions, periods and time-horizons, i.e. 'boundaries of relevance' (Luhmann, 1985: 254). Habitus defines actions in relation to all of the overlapping rhythms.

The purpose of figures 9 and 10 is simply to give an overview of the plan-ning structure. In line with Bourdieu's methodological thinking, illustrative

Figure 9 The European governance calendar

models and diagrams should follow data, and not the other way around. The graphical illustrations of practical movements and generative structures have the advantage of speaking more directly to the reader's senses than the medium of written texts, which only add a level of distorting 'science' to practical logic. By combining objectivist and subjectivist facts, the decoded dynamics of the rolling meeting cycles of European governance are illustrated in figure 9. The national EU timetable is represented by a circle since the same procedural chain by which meetings are prepared recurs with a high degree of regularity over time. The circle also comes closest to practised time when including the official

EU timetable set by the presidency, which is the origin of the national timetable. Meetings of various kinds recur regularly on half-yearly basis. The 'snake' in the middle illustrates the never-ending circle of informants' practical organisation of time, defined in a dialectic relationship with the two simultaneous subjective timetables.

The model in figure 10 pictures an excerpt from the circle illustrated in figure 9. The informants experience a move over time between European and domestic schedules in the European governance calendar. *The subjective facts*: the official EU timetable regulates the meetings of Wg, HLO and CM. In the national timetable is marked official meetings, internal departmental coordination meetings, consultation meetings with the national parliament and internal deadlines for the delivery of the contribution to the high official's or the minister's dossier for HLO and CM. *The objective facts*: at each moment of action, informants via habitus simultaneously assess and draw on several time dispositions achieved through experiences of various parts of the calendar. Their mastering of the way to act in time involves, for example, strategic judgements of when a moment is ripe of action (policy initiatives, etc.). At such a moment, European governance actors simultaneously draw on the temporal structure of subjective components – a certain 'stage' in the national preparation and formalised EU schedules – and objective ones – the sense of the situation. Over time their habitus, which generates temporal practices, is disposed by the relating of the present and the future to past experiences. In the model, this process is illustrated as the objectivist snake's oscillation between simultaneous formal/subjective timetables and deadlines. Variations in the thickness of the snake depict shifts in the intensity with which work is experienced, and the 'waves' represent the shifting influence of European and domestic timetables and rhythms, respectively. The temporal snake perhaps constitutes the clearest and most telling evidence of 'planning' in European management of political relationships and problem-solving institutions beyond (not above) the state.

A few words on the ever-present risk of objectifying an illustrative model may be called for. The model sketched above must not be allowed to live a life of its own, e.g. by rigidly directing the search for generative structures. In other words, the model should not be allowed to put up mental obstacles to my decoding of observations or to my understanding of the real meaning of praxis. Since illustrative models are often abstract, it should be borne in mind that the conclusions drawn from it are also of an abstract nature. In other words, observing and constructing the logic of planning *through* these kinds of abstract models of illustration should be avoided. However, I believe my model, and the data it is built upon, closely correspond to a practice. It is my ambition that it displays the structure lying closest to the agent. I have therefore attempted to construct the scientific structure to make it coincide to the greatest possible extent with the forms of social time that can be said to have generated the dispositions incorporated by habitus. In this way, my illustrations give justification to the logic of planning in European governance.

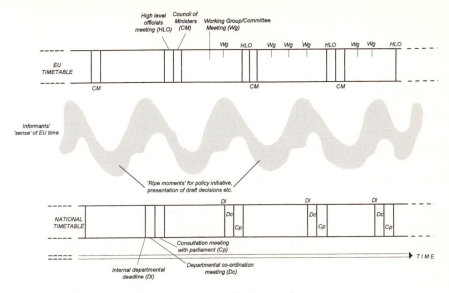

Figure 10 The European governance calendar (extract)

European circles of neomedieval time

Researchers of political space have referred to the new map of Europe as 'neome-dieval', with overlapping identities, authorities, sovereignties and jurisdictions (cf. von Bogdandy, 1993; Wæver, 1995; Diebert, 1996). Medieval time was the time of prophecies:

> According to the early Christian view, temporality could not be understood as a neutral chronology proceeding from some real or hypothetical origin (the creation, the founding of a nation, etc.). Rather, temporality had a center, a mid-point, from which it extended in opposite directions forward and backward. This center was the Incarnation. (Gross, 1985: 58)

In medieval consciousness, strongly influenced by the rhythm of the agri-cultural year, the church year and the mercantile year, time was also circular. The variation in rhythm, intensity and meaning of this time depended on the par-ticular period of 'the year' – that is, on a cycle of recurring temporal qualities brought up over and over again. As shown in this chapter, planning in European governance is structured by the experience of a *cyclic, high-speed, on-line time, sequenced by deadlines, and with a focus on complex presents that strongly domi-nate past and future.* The historical uniqueness of this time is that it is both cyclic and irreversible or 'strong'.[3] It is cyclical in form; the meeting rhythms and deci-sion-making procedures shaping time practices recur on a very regular basis over time. For the actors involved, it is irreversible in substance; meetings are added to meetings, decisions to decisions and substance to substance, regardless of whether someone is 'not on time'.

By reducing the chronological arrangement of their activities to 'meeting cycles and agendas' with little reference to specific dates or points in time, civil servants avoid measuring the succession of actions in relation to a 'ticking' of uniform units of time. This might be seen as the practical consequence of the more complex and difficult coordination of people entailed by European governance as compared to the governance of a nation-state, where a reliance on standardised clock time is sufficient both in theory and practice. The practical sequencing is also an expression of the generally recognised task oriented attitude towards work in European governance, in contrast to the state's time oriented fulfilment (discussed in chapter 2). Should this time be called unique, post-modern, or multitemporal (cyclic European time and linear, progressive, modern state-time existing simultaneously)? Or, are we witnessing a *neomedieval European temporality*: cyclic, centralised present, the crucial role of prediction in policy planning, or rather preparation?

Notes

1   The means of cooperation have been summarised as 'declarations politics, conference cooperation and diplomatic everyday cooperation with the overall aim of creating effective contact nets among the member-states' (Lindahl and Larsson, 1991: 90).
2   Figures 4–7 are verbatim reproductions of internal aide-memoires of the Y department, reflecting the nature of subjective planning horizons in European governance.
3   In contrast to 'weak' time, which links reversible sequences (Tilly, 1994: 5).

5

Institutional implications of European time

This book has revealed a unique temporal logic in the world view and practices of the management of political relationships and problem-solving institutions beyond the state in today's Europe. It has shown how European governance affects policy formulation, action and planning in the form of a changed status of political promise, new conditions for policy action and transformed planning horizons. The fundamental character of the three aspects of change justify a preliminary evaluation of the implications of my findings in relation to the current literature on European governance. The implications of European time will in this chapter be discussed in relation to the impact on public policy and administration, to explanations of changing conditions for democracy in the Union and to 'grand' theories of the historical significance of European governance.

European policy and administration for the moment

In the temporal logic of European governance a unique style of public policy-making is discernible. It is not only more complex, multilayered and of greater scale than governance in nation-states. It also represents new horizons and organisational rhythms for action and planning, including new ways of formulating political promise. Earlier research has touched upon this transformation when investigating decision-making, implementation and agenda-setting in the EU (e.g. Andersen and Eliassen, 1993; Richardson, 1996; Wallace and Wallace, 1996; Tallberg, 1999). However, even though it has been concluded that the 'policy style' generally constitutes something novel, rather than resembling that of any of the existing member-states, definitions and frameworks for its exploration have been surprisingly vague. There has been the 'hunch' of Schmitter and others that 'the enormous increase in the scale of governance will impose a logic of its own' (Schmitter, 1996: 145). The succesful revelation of a new temporal logic challenges many hypotheses of European public policy and administration. Two of the most central challenges are:

1   The style of policy-making in the Union may not be as issue-specific as some observers have expected (Majone, 1996; Wallace and Wallace, 1996; Kohler-Koch and Eising, 1999). On the contrary, the time of European governance to a high degree seems to shape all kinds of policy-making. The new temporal structure associated with European governance also challenges traditional explanations of EU policy outcome as only 'sub-optimal', awaiting future transformation into a more efficient 'normal' style.

2   The Europeanisation of national administration and policy-making may not be as uneven as is normally argued in research emphasising distinctive national patterns of adjustment to European governance (Bulmer and Paterson, 1987; George, 1992; Hanf and Soetendorp, 1998; Ladrech, 1994; Harmsen, 1999). The present work contradicts these findings in focusing on similarities of strategies and organisational adjustments by national administrations in coping with the new logic. Aware of the relatively narrow basis of my empirical material, the aim is to open up new complementary perspectives on the significance of European governance for public administration in Europe. Are the similarities among European bureaucracies greater in time than in space?

From national policy to European management

In evaluating the explanatory power of the logic of European governance, I will contrast it with examples of issue-specific network and governance explanations of European policy-making.

NETWORK QUALITY

Some observers hold that policy outcome in the Union can be explained by the type of network prevalent, which in turn is often argued to be dependent on the specific issue-area. Daugbjerg (1997) explains the more radical agricultural policy reform in Sweden in 1990 compared to that of the Community in 1992, as a result of differences in the *cohesion* of agricultural policy networks. The question is whether the cohesion of the network in this case has stronger explanatory power than the general logic revealed in the present study.

The reform proposals by the Swedish government did not meet the same resistance as those from the European Commission, owing to the fact that there was no consensus on the principle of state responsibility among Swedish farmers. This was the reason why the network was defined as 'not cohesive' by Daugbjerg. Thus, given the definition of 'cohesiveness' in this case, different outcomes might as convincingly be argued to be due to differences in beliefs between the Community and the Swedish farmers. In a later work, Daugbjerg (1999) also adds a second explanatory factor: 'The EC/EU is a highly fragmented political system in which it is difficult successfully to pursue fundamental reform of the CAP' (1999: 423). Thus, the policy style and outcome mainly had to do with the *general* organisational structure of the Union, in which members disagree over the appropriate policy instruments to apply. The temporal logic qualifies precisely the mechanisms at work in this fragmented system, and hence seems to be of stronger explanatory power than issue-specific parameters in this particular case.

The short horizons of the multilateral negotiation system and the difficulties in building on past experiences make all long-term policies a different game in European governance compared to the nation-state. The conditions for fulfilling a promise to work for reform are fundamentally different in European governance compared to national policy-making, indeed the promise does not have the same meaning. It means to work for better conditions for progress, that suddenly, and often very surprisingly, might be achieved. The way of making policy over time is fundamentally new.

'SUB-OPTIMAL' OUTCOME

The lack of strategic decision-making has been pointed out as one of main characteristics of European governance. Some have explained the 'sub-optimal' policy outcomes as a result of the interlocking of the two levels of government in the EU-system, where the short-term interests of each member-state still are considered to outweigh the benefits of common policies (Scharpf, 1988; Risse-Kappen, 1996). Others have labelled the EC policy style a policy of postponement (Schumann, 1991). The formulation and implementation of a long-term policy towards the Central and Eastern European (CEE) countries have been found to be seriously hampered by the troublesome and long-winded internal process of EU negotiation (Friis and Murphy, 1999). Other sector-specific studies have come to similar conclusions (Wallace and Wallace, 1996; Armstrong and Bulmer, 1998). The future horizon is often perceived as painfully short within the CFSP (Hill, 1996).

One of today's most important themes, both among theoreticians (Stubb, 1997) and practitioners (the flexibility clause of the Amsterdam Treaty), is the extent to which European governance will be differentiated in the future. It is the strong feeling of lost control that is probably one of the main reasons underlying the recent call of some EU states for a more flexible and reinforced integration of the Union (Jannings, 1997), for these kinds of arrangements would allow smaller groupings of states to take the lead in staking out a common destiny for all EU member-states. Furthermore, throughout the history of European integration, the Community and the Union have been seen by many as an incomplete federal state for which only one future is morally acceptable, namely further federalisation. The argument has in some analysts' view developed into a 'necessity discourse'. Gustavsson argues that today's long-term EU decisions are based on a teleological vision of the future (S. Gustavsson, 1993). Many scholars see strong parallels between the historical federalisation of the United States and the Union of today (McKay, 1996). In short, the particular style of governance in Europe has traditionally been defined in terms of protracted, segmented, complex, conservative and inefficient policy-making.

The 'sub-optimal' approach in explaining outcome, often implicitly, argues that there is, and should be, the possibility of more optimal policy solutions. That is, European governance is expected to resemble 'normal' policy-making in the nation-state. However, the argument could be turned the other way round. The fact that so many studies of different issue-areas over the years have come to similar conclusions with regard to the impact of European governance points to the strength and persistence of a specific style of European public policy. This book has shown that policy-making in European governance, rather than being sub-optimal, has a short-term logic of its own.

For example, the weakness of 'multilateral' external diplomacy could be better understood in relation to the short-term logic of circles of irreversible presents – the fundamental spatio-temporal limits to a European foreign policy. To what extent does the temporal logic show that 'flexibility' will not be as central to Europe's future as is often thought? Given the strong feeling of European simultaneity and the perceived need to participate in the first moment of decision-making,[1] can there be any differentiation without a strong centre and a hierarchy of members? To what extent would such an arrangement be acceptable to the EU member-states left outside the core of integrating states? In European governance, the future we have come to know in nation-state politics is lost, or at least is not the same. Historically, the definition of a community has in large part been based on the group of people that together decide on a common destiny. Will the European community of the twenty-first century be an exception? Or can we live with a post-state polity, locked in the present and without future? Or will the lack of leadership and a future eventually be perceived as increasingly unacceptable? An assessment of the situation will clearly gain analytical strength with an understanding of the temporal dimension of European governance.

I agree that many *politicians* may have a strong *interest* in presenting today's Union as 'sub-optimal' and the further integration of the Union as extremely valuable. In practice, however, the meaning of the future in the political process of creating, for example, the euro has always been dominated by extreme insecurity. As late as some months before the planned giant political step of deciding on the final process of establishing a common European currency, very few dared to say for sure whether this decision would be taken, let alone whether EMU would really be established. Predictions were pointing in many directions: how many states would join? This future of little expectation must be quite unique in political history. Given the unique character of European governance, to what extent do the scholars who compare the historical federalization of the United States and the Union of today draw anachronistic conclusions about Europe's federal future? It will also be interesting to determine whether or not the problems for participation owing to difficulties in keeping European levels interlocked in fact are mainly problems of coordination in time.

Jacobsson (1997), who is the one who hitherto has dealt most extensively with time in an EU policy context, believes that strategies in this context belong only to the present, implying 'the absence of a future and of Utopia', and the need for alternative 'competing futures'. In contrast, my work has shown that strategies for unforeseeable events in European governance unintentionally create a qualitatively different kind of future – a future of strategies made to make sense in response to the quickly up-coming row of approaching 'nows'; a future rooted in the need felt by stressed decision-makers for *alternative scenarios* worked out in advance, on the basis of which various strategies can be prepared. A future of strategies in which the horizon has not disappeared, but which has become a scheme devoid of progress and filled with stories of probable possibilities for more efficiency in the realisation of political goals. Furthermore, Jacobsson argues that the punctuality of the industrially based nation-state is giving way to temporal flexibility in a transnational European information society (1997: 175). This observation can in European governance be specified further: the need for flexibility is strong with regard to results, while punctuality is of increased importance when it comes to moments of decision. It is in this context the character of coming time in European governance as more insecure, less makable, and less visionary should be understood. It is in this *management* of the present that the connotations of progress have been lost. The images of the simultaneity, circularity and irreversibility in European governance only confirm the interpretation of a future already here. The new language collects experience and pictures future expectations in terms very similar to the language of state governance, but with a fundamentally new meaning.

EUROPEAN PUBLIC MANAGEMENT

The characterisation of the style of European public policy can take as a point of departure a 'Koselleckian' interpretation of the very concept of governance. I defined European governance partly as management of political relationships. The lexicographic definition of 'management' is 'handling', 'operation', or 'attendance', hence a term related to complex and problematic immediate concerns and solutions.[2] The temporal meaning of 'governance' is revealed through comparison with the concept of 'government', which is traditionally thought of, at least implicitly, as something providing 'leadership' and 'order' over longer periods of time.

All my empirical chapters support the interpretation that 'governance' has a strong connotation with the 'present'. In fact, the magnetic power of the present, shortening horizons of the past and the future, was perhaps the most significant finding in all three case studies. Consequently, European public policy can be characterised on the basis of the strongest time image of them all: the present of actors' interaction that has to be managed. The complexity and preponderance of the present in stories about European simultaneity left little room for the development of innovative narratives about the past and the future. Theoretically, the latter could have modified and simply replaced the traditional plots of a unitary past – a common history – that no longer made any sense. However, the temporal experiences were of a different nature than earlier ones. The 'empty' time of modern states was replaced by the 'filling' of time through European governance, and in the process there emerged an advanced language of coordination that refigured the experience of a complex organisation of direct, personal contacts and 'co-presences' (in Giddens' sense) with colleagues in European governance.

In European governance, 'when' is much more closely connected to 'why' and 'how' than it is in the governing of a state and therefore cannot be separated as easily from other aspects of action or taken for granted. The uniformity of the administrative organisation of time in the nation-state does not exist in European governance. Consequently, time considerations do not fade away and become 'forgotten'. In order not to give way to highly differentiated individual refigurations of temporal experience, stories about time have to be forcefully and actively told to make coordination meaningful. Furthermore, the practical management of political relationships and problem-solving institutions circled round moments of decisions. By internalised European calendars, deadlines and rounds of meetings, actors were able to focus their attention and deal with a greater number of issues per unit of time than they were outside European governance. The logic of the strong present is its irreversibility in practice, a feature which shapes action and, at the same time, is unconsciously used as a medium of action in the multilateral game through specific techniques of timing and anticipation. The system of rotating leadership in European public policy disposes actors to generate regular rhythms of intensification and moments ripe for action, with a sharp contrast between a future shorter, respectively longer, than half a year. The consciousness of an extended present, expressed in a 'possibility discourse', is only the semantic result of the shrinking dimensions of experience and expectation in European governance. And as in all presents, even though extended, actors found that they had little choice but to take part and try to make the best of the situation despite the limited room for manoeuvre.

In order to maintain the image of a control over future events, actors engaged in European governance try to draw on traditional temporal interpretations within administration. However, the creation of the many deadlines, the new tempo related to European simultaneity and the strong feeling of irreversibility of action make traditional ways of sequencing, predicting and planning increasingly awkward. To compensate for the experienced complexity of coordinating time and space and a low degree of predictability, actors develop notions of a very manifest simultaneity and a praxis of strongly routinised circles of day-to-day duties. The construction of a circularity of management situations makes the handling of rapidly approaching presents seem more calculable. In the place of the nation-state's ambition to control a 'makable' future has grown up a complex belief system for the management of extended presents. Circularity can engender presents that appear to be of a recurrent and more similar nature than would otherwise be the case, thereby providing a feeling of being better able to cope with the densely packed moments of choice and decision. Owing to the fact that the future is no longer planned, 'the future' traditionally associated with the state no longer exists in European governance. European management of public political life implies not only a *de-temporalisation* of the political language but also a *de-futurisation* of the characteristics of institutions and administration.

To conclude: 'governance' does not only better denote the new situation of European political rule in general, but also clearly bears witness to the new temporal dimension of public policy in Europe. Only further empirical research will be able to fully exploit the strong explanatory potential to which this section has given early evidence.

Cybereurocracy

Some observers have been puzzled by the fact that the homogeneous pressure of European policy-making has not resulted in a convergence of administrative structures among EU member-states: a common 'state model' (Wessels and Rometsch, 1996). Another line of research has put emphasis on the difference between governance and institutions. Despite the persistence of distinct national institutional arrangements, there has been a strong Europeanisation of national governance (Goetz, 1995). Here, it is generally acknowledged that new communication technology and modes of information processing often are applied in a way to conform to established bureaucratic practices. Institutional redesign occurs only when absolutely needed and only after a long period of maturation and acceptance of new patterns of communication and interaction. Even though expressed 'only' in new bureaucratic routines – cyberocracy – rather than in new institutions of government, the effects of the information revolution have been of historical magnitude (Ronfeldt, 1992). Organisational charts have never told the full story of how governmental work functions and significant change come about (Steiner, 1982). Important national adaptation to Europe has often been described as taking the form of 'attitudinal' change (Kerremans and Beyers, 1998: 33). Thus, the assessment of the impact of European governance on administration to a high degree depends on our perspective and emphasis on various indicators. The focus on 'visible' – in the positivistic sense – structural–institutional anomalies between the member-states should not be allowed to hide the European temporal logic of appropriate procedures.

The empirical findings presented in the present book have pointed to a very homogeneous European impact on national administration. National administration responds to the increasing pressure of managing European political relations and institutions by internalising a new logic of policy-making over and in time. Through the new logic is made visible a wide range of crucial organisational questions such as redirections of resources within bureaucracy, new demands on competence and handling procedures, routines and organs for the coordination of action. With the help of earlier empirical results, I will in this section explain some trends in this emerging *Cybereurocracy*. Trends that in the long term increasingly may come to characterise public administration in integrated Europe.

ANTICIPATION AND COORDINATION

The modern nation-state was built on future-creating institutions. It was their very prognoses and planning that created one uncontested future. The difficulties of making prognoses in European governance result in an outlook on coming time built on strategy and preparedness. The turn towards the present in people's mind might be interpreted as a result of the fact that there is no single producer of stories about visions of the future and memories of the past, as in the case of the nation-state. If the future is not told with the same emphasis and authority as before, it cannot be prognostised and planned to the same extent.

Somewhat paradoxically, the uncertainty creates an eagerness for the development of various methods and institutions of anticipation and simulation, in order to win back control (cf. Virilio's prediction (1986: 141) of the growing importance of simulation by the 'Research institute'). To *regain time* by means of anticipation is essential in order to be prepared in the present. One possible explanation for the planning units in European governance is that they are required by the specific political dynamics of European governance with its concomitant need of large amounts of information, and are made possible by new communication techniques that provide this information very quickly. In order to balance the more outstretched time–space distanciation in the 'inter-administrative' interaction, many new media have been set up to coordinate the creation of meaning (special communications networks and a high degree of informality within the field of international exchange, which traditionally is very formal). The administrative-organisational adjustments are ways to cope with the accelerating frequency of interaction between actors involved in European governance. The time component of the constitution of 'action context' is changing character, and is becoming more important in European governance.

The finely meshed network of communications and interaction through which Europe is governed seems to have a great impact on the form given to planning. National and European fields of action can to an increasing degree be linked together in time and space by means of information from both. The organisation of European governance constitutes a new medium of time–space distanciation, bringing European political actors together in time and space in a more regularised and systematic way. European governance is the medium of the interplay, providing opportunities for co-presences that facilitate the communication and interpretation of meaning. The new patterns of time–space routinisation emerging within the framework of European governance are the new locales of action that constitute the nucleus of new types of political organisation and institutions beyond the nation-state. As shown in this book, the temporal component of this locale can to a large extent be defined in terms of circles.

European governance intimates that its institutions are able to cope with the complex present: a bureaucratisation and technocratisation of politics are perceptible in the midst of the rapidity of political procedures. The democratic, parliamentary side of decision-making will have difficulty keeping up with the new pace. This study has shown that the perceived quantitative streamlining of the welfare state's institutions might imply a qualitative transformation. The new logic justifies a more prominent role for civil servants, negotiators and a technical juridical knowledge. First and foremost, the bureaucracy of European governance has to provide for coordination. The concern with central coordination appears to be a pressing issue for all European administrations (de Clausade, 1991; Hanf and Soetendorp, 1998; von Dosenrode, 1998; Luif, 1998: 125; Harmsen, 1999: 97).

The fact that EU deadlines are diffused deeply down into European and national bureaucracy has both centralising and decentralising effects. On the one hand, all European policymakers have to follow centrally decided time disciplinary norms and rules. On the other hand, there is less time for the individual department, group or official to be instructed from higher-level authorities which leads to decentralised autonomous policy-making. In attempts to ease the tension between the two trends, shifts of balance and concentration of powers are taken place within the central governmental structure.

CENTRALISATION

The primacy of coordination for simultaneous European action demands a top-down approach in the organisation of administration. There is an increasing pressure placed on the domestic system for implementing EU decisions in time. Countries like the Netherlands, France and Norway have developed increasingly more coordinated mechanisms for the strengthening of the implementation procedure downstream in order to speed it up and meet deadlines (Harmsen, 1999: 101; Soetendorp and Hanf, 1998: 43–45). Not only the mode of coordination but the extent of coordination has changed (Sverdrup, 1998: 160). As shown in chapter 3, national ministries have to be continuously supervised by means of centralised coordination. The fact that the common EU present is imposed and enforced by the necessity to participate in the given moment of decision enhances the need for coordination. In many of the EU member-states, but also in other administrations involved in European governance, there has been a need for *more personnel* in the central government:

> Since both the Co-Co [Coordination Committee for European Integration and Association Studies] and the Cabinet act under the pressure of the deadlines of the coming ministerial Councils in Brussels, another high-level coordination committee has been created in the Hague alongside the Co-Co. (Soetendorp and Hanf, 1998: 41)

Moreover, the workload on the personnel has increased (George, 1992; Ekengren and Sundelius, 1998: 139; Sverdrup, 1998: 157). Behind this need lies concern that the coordination of national actions in various EU institutions has been inadequate. The ministries have not been able to formulate clear and timely directives to all representatives managing European governance. The ministries are considered too small to function both as cabinet offices for the daily preparation of national positions and as more future oriented units. Expansion is needed in order to enable the national ministries to work more strategically, at the same time as they must cope daily with an increased overall workload owing to the membership. The reason for this approach given by governments is the need to improve the administrative capacity for a more proactive and potentially influential posture in prioritised policy areas (Ladrech, 1994; Hanf and Soetendorp, 1998).

It is often the Foreign Ministry of EU member-states that has become a strong advocate of the necessity of central coordination of external relations as a means toward enhancing national influence in the Union. It is argued that an effective membership requires such a centralising process, unless the national leadership is willing to accept a segmentation of the state into sector-defined and autonomously pursued interactions within the European networks.

The role of national EU coordinators sheds further light on the need for very active centralised coordination owing to externally imposed timetables. The coordinator's is often the role of the creator and upholder of those coherent national positions which are the pre-requisites for the image of national homogeneity. The importance and significance of this strongly inward-looking task is underlined by the limited extent to which this official is in contact with other member-states. There is no time 'to wait until every differing view has been settled' for a homogeneous national action. This is the main reason why the active interference of EU departments is needed. There is simply not enough time – no 'national interval' – for forging a tacit achievement of a complete confidence in autonomous simultaneous national activity. The result is that the traditional sequence of governmental actions now is broken up in the name of 'coordination' in all phases.

The shape and role of the EU departments reflect this task in coping with European time. The department for the European Union or the EU coordination secretariat at the ministry for foreign affairs or the ministry of finance is often the link between the national permanent representation in Brussels and the various ministries. It has the responsibility for ensuring that standpoints are prepared for all items on the agendas prepared by the EU presidency, and for finalising and transmitting official instructions to the representatives in Coreper and in Council meetings. Moreover, this department often has the responsibility for coordinating relations between the ministries and the national parliament, in particular the dialogue with its advisory committee on EU affairs (Luif, 1998; Sverdrup, 1998).

New catchwords are emerging to justify centralised coordination and counteract national difficulties in adapting effectively to European governance. In Austria, the permanent negotiation process in the Union has called for the elaboration of a 'comprehensive strategy' framing all Austrian action (Luif, 1998: 126). In Sweden, the aim of central coordination should be to form 'common outlooks' that can guide national representatives in the complex and decentralised European policy-making processes (Ekengren and Sundelius, 2002). The rationale behind these unifying concepts is that formalised and regularised central coordination is very difficult in the EU context. New government agencies, 'planning services', responsible for shaping such common outlooks across the many policy sectors of EU relations, are being set up in, for example, Greece (Christakis, 1998: 92), Ireland ('Institute of European Affairs') (Laffan and Tannam, 1998: 82), and Sweden (Ekengren and Sundelius, 1998: 143), and proposed in Austria (Luif, 1998: 126). Their purpose is to bring together diverse societal and corporate interests and prepare national directives for long-term strategic priorities.

DECENTRALISATION

A contrasting consequence of the high-speed European processes, giving less time for consulting central authorities, is that political actors are forced to act more independently and on mandates defined in advance. The short time for preparation functions as a force of decentralisation and informalisation of administration:

> An emphasis on the immediate to the neglect of the medium to long term is a feature of this administrative culture. Policy-making in Dublin tends to be reactive rather than active in nature. Position papers and negotiating tactics are worked out at each stage of the policy process. This policy style is reinforced by the Community's decision-making process which is dominated by negotiations and highly segmented. (Laffan and Tannam, 1998: 79)

The short time spans between EU meetings have challenged the logic of appropriate procedures in national administration. The high pace of decision-making in the Council has created difficulties for the tradition in many member-states of securing wide support for every decision, both within and outside the administration. There is simply less time for officials to anchor at home national actions in the Union, which leads to more *individual autonomy* and a more important role for flexible and less formal contacts (Wallace, 1971, 1974; Ekengren and Sundelius, 1998; Luif, 1998: 122).

A fundamentally new situation for policy-makers is created owing to the fact that matters cannot be 'left about'. There is no longer any 'automatic' autonomous national procedural logic. Time is always 'filled' with considerations. The feeling of a decentralised policy process is due to the experience of national activities as taking place simultaneously in separate fora. The question of how to synchronise national actions in time is as much a matter of coordinating decentralised negotiatiors in space.

Time constraints call for decentralised prediction praxis. With new tools, such as the 'loose threads' thinking described in chapter 3, smaller groups of officials are trying to create the feeling that their parallel 'national' activities in various EU organs are synchronised into homogeneous national initiatives and actions in all fora.

A serious strategic management dilemma is being faced in the member-state capitals: to be able to engage effectively, officials must be free to participate without being hampered by central coordination or control mechanisms. Coordination at the cabinet centre may restrict the ability to gain influence in those vital policy-shaping processes. The objective of maximising influence in the complex pre- and post-choice phases of European decision-making stands against the equally important ambition to gain bargaining leverage in the sometimes critical intergovernmental negotiations in the choice stage (Luif, 1998: 124). *New institutions* such as the Secretariat of State for the Community in the Spanish Ministry of Foreign Affairs (Morata, 1998: 103) are supposed to counteract the decentralising effects of European governance, and be able to speak with one voice. At the same time, the permanent delegations in Brussels, now representing all parts of the government, are growing. In the future, one may very well expect coordination problems between these decentralised mini-cabinet offices in place and the home-based senior officials.

PRIME MINISTERIALISATION

The Prime Minister has in many EU member-states noted the value of cabinet-level coordination of EU matters and suggested that its political direction could be elevated into his own office (Harmsen, 1999; Ekengren and Sundelius, 2002).

The position as Swedish State Secretary for EU matters in the Ministry for Foreign Affairs has been replaced by a State Secretary with the responsibility both for EU questions and international questions generally in the Office of the Prime Minister. The task of the new State Secretary and his staff is to solve conflicts between ministries, to coordinate EU issues of particular political salience, to coordinate the preparation of the meetings with the European Council, to lead the strategic thinking of the government on the long-term development of the Union, and to lead and coordinate the preparations of the Swedish EU presidencies. Owing to the reorganisation, the role of the Ministry for Foreign Affairs in making cross-ministerial political priorities in Swedish EU work has been weakened. The reorganisation could be interpreted as a step towards a more balanced administrative relationship between the Foreign Ministry, the Ministry of Finance and the Office of the Prime Minister, which earlier had to rely almost entirely on the Foreign Ministry resources and material.

In the Netherlands, the Prime Minister convenes the ministers principally concerned with European policy in the Council for European and International Affairs. The Prime Minister is responsible in the last instance for the coordination of European policy and to the Dutch parliament for problems of coordination. There has been a clear concentration of power in the hands of the Prime Minister owing to Dutch European policy-making (Harmsen, 1999: 94–97). The Danish Prime Minister has also been increasingly better organised to play a more active role in shaping EU policy. One of the main reasons for reorganising the Prime Minister's office has been the need to create a better capacity to control other ministries (von Dosenrode, 1998: 58–59). In Norway, the Prime Minister's Office plays the role of 'initiator, coordinator and controller', of the

EU process – 'a competent commentator providing deadlines and coordination of the "national interest"' (Sverdrup, 1998: 159–160).

In a similar way to trends in contemporary statecraft (see chapter 1), it looks as if the need for time calculations in strategic European governance planning implies a concentration of responsibilities to increasingly higher levels of political authority.

European democracy without a future

With regard to more specific areas of research, the implications of the new temporal logic for the explanation of democracy in European governance are considerable. Democracy in the European Union has during recent years engaged a growing number of debaters and researchers. The questions have concerned problems of representation (Hayward, 1995), the basic conditions for European democracy or the existence of a European demos (Weiler, 1999), democratic accountability (S. Gustavsson, 1998) and to what degree democracy can be reconciled with effective European governance (Andersen and Eliassen, 1996; Scharpf, 1999).

The dichotomy of democracy and time has also experienced a new-born interest. Here the issues have concerned the 'rhythms' (Goodin, 1998) and 'time constraints' (Linz, 1998) of democracy, as well as the time phases of democratisation processes (Schmitter and Santiso, 1998).

The two problem areas have not as yet been brought together. In fact, there has been a strong call for an application of the insights of the importance of the time dimension for democracy in systematic empirical research (Schedler and Santiso, 1998). The aim of the following is to demonstrate the usefulness of adding the time dimension in inquries and empirical research on democracy in European governance.

Time-efficient democracy

The temporal logic of European governance is closely related to the new view of democracy which the Union brought with it. The notion of what the central parts of democracy are is subtly interwoven with the three dimensions of European time outlined in this book.

From previously being defined mainly in terms of procedures, partly for demanding accountability, democracy in the Union has come primarily to concern the results and effectiveness of decisions (Jacobsson, 1997). Jacobsson presents the new expectations on the future in the Union as shaped by a new notion of democracy, defined in terms of efficient goal realisation (1997: 225–231). My work has shown that the temporal change is of such a fundamental nature that it should be taken as a point of departure in approaching today's problems of democratic deficit, rather than the other way around. In my perspective, a shift in the conception of democracy is only to be expected when social time has changed. An inverse treatment of the relationship between democracy and time is not important for reasons of causality, but it enhances our understanding of how democracy is made to make sense in the basic structures of European governance. The new temporal logic can provide explanations of the fundamental character of the limits to national democracy and answers to the question of whether supranational democracy can replace national 'rule-based' democracy. Or whether post-state time has forever changed the conditions for a democracy based on constitutional principles.

Democracy of unlimited time

Democracy has been described as 'government pro tempere'; 'the idea of electing someone for life to exercise effective power, or representatives for unlimited time (without ever having to stand again for election) does not fit into our thinking of democracy' (Linz, 1998: 19). All democratic accountability pre-supposes a lasting organisational framework for ensuring that the fulfilment of today's promises can be controlled in the future and that politicians can be held accountable and elected away (Weiler, 1999: 266). I have shown that the very basis of this mechanism – the existence of a long-term horizon – may be under transformation in European governance. This calls for a fundamental rethinking of the conditions for democracy.

The idea of demanding democratic accountability tomorrow for what is promised today is closely linked to the sense of a linear, stable and controllable 'future', in which the citizen votes knowing that the elected will be held liable at a given point of time in the future (the next election). In European governance the future is shortened and shaped into rapidly recurring but at the same time irrevocable decision-making situations, in which an opportunity missed is in practice an opportunity lost. This time structure makes it harder to reconsider decisions. To a great extent EU commitments mean that 'we shall do all we can but given the hard-to-predict negotiation game we cannot guarantee results'.

As shown, the high speed and strict dates involved in EU decision-making make it harder to maintain the time for national democratic deliberation. The idea that policy is shaped on the basis of a shrinking 'time interval' for deliberation at national level helps to strengthen the effectiveness view of democracy. That which has to be achieved – i.e. influence on the EU process in the time considered available for national preparations – overrides the traditional decision-making procedures. Increased focus on management of the present pre-supposes that procedural democracy can in some sense be taken for granted. In the Union those states defined in advance as 'democratic' can be allowed to devote a large proportion of their time to cooperating as effectively as possible. The ideology of cooperation is reaching member-states via the ideology of coordination, and because of time constraints it risks overriding procedural democratic ideals. Many decision makers risk being contemporary operators rather than long-term actors, prepared for complexities today and surprises tomorrow. The authority and capacity to deal with rapidly arising circumstances cannot be established in detail. The EU flow of information and coordination machinery puts pressure on politicians and civil servants to act as quickly as possible. A risk to which this situation gives rise is that the EU political actor becomes more and more disconnected from the past, from history.

In this system demanding political and democratic accountability does not mean determining whether the result has been achieved, but finding out whether the minister and negotiators did all they could. Was the line of negotiation effective? Is the result, however it was established, good? Democracy requires a calendar that is known in advance, with checkpoints and a period that is long enough to be considered surveyable. The pre-requisites for this long-term approach do not exist in European governance. This book has shown that the changes in the time structure may be so profound that any view of democracy other than effectiveness will find it increasingly difficult to gain a hearing in European governance. The new sense of time has made it more difficult to think about and argue for procedural democracy.

Whether we accept or oppose the change in the definition of democracy we have to take account of the new time conditions in the Union. If we want to oppose the viewpoint of effectiveness this involves building 'inertia' and opportunities for reappraisal into the system. If we would rather accept the increased emphasis on capability for democratic action and on results, the time perspective makes the consequences more clear – not least as regards the European concept of future and simultaneity.

From utopia to scenarios

The idea that the future can be equated with progress has played a central role in the democracy defined within the framework of the nation-state. The creation of expectations of when innovation ought to happen could explain the 'rhythms of democracy' (Goodin, 1998). The biggest long-term threat to national democratic participation may not be the high pace and rhythm of EU decision-making itself (Baldwin, 1996: 97–98; Sverdrup, 1996),[3] but the fact that there is less expectation of a future in European governance.

Optimism is diluted in the more neutral concepts about the future that originated in European governance. In the 'post-modern' time expressed by European governance the greater openness to the future does not mean increased expectations as in the modern nation-state, but a more abstract uncertain notion on the time ahead. The altered concept of time changes the view on the capacity and potential for change of politics. In European governance it is rather a question of whether not just lesser expectations of the future but also lesser expectations that some kind of time horizon *exists* that is significant for political action beyond the present. The significance of time is changed in the Union from being *progressive* to being mainly an *organisational principle*, a scheme. To what extent does democracy require a belief in the future? Can the future be created and not just predicted? What does it mean for democracy that the future in the Union is largely formulated as forecasts, strategies and scenarios? The choice between, not just the forecast of, alternative futures and utopias was a character-istic of the modern state. To what extent is this a condition for democracy? Fore-casts, strategies and scenarios produce looser kinds of alternative futures without the concreteness required for conceivable ideological and political solutions. Politics becomes more defensive in the sense that it is not creating a future but adapting itself to a future largely experienced as imposed by outside forces. The temporalisation of the political language that started in the 1800s seems to have slowed down. The sense of forward motion has been an important component of democracy. Can we imagine a democracy that builds on the choice between forecasts, future scenarios and strategies? A democracy that in the first place does not build anew but that is based on contingency, adaptation and alternatives for action that aim to fend off the flow of (European) events. Will the ideological differences between different forecasts and strategies increasingly resemble those between political programmes within the nation-state democracy? How will ide-ology and 'isms', traditionally building largely on forward motion, be influenced by a cessation in the time component in the political language of the Union? What will be the influence of removing ideology from the politics of democracy in European governance?

The central issues concerning the temporal conditions for democracy in the Union should now be summarised: Can and should we regain a modern nation-state temporal logic for democracy in the EU? Or should we assume that a post-modern logic has replaced the modern one in European governance and thereby fundamentally changed the bases of democracy, definitions, etc? What forms of democracy are best suited to the new structure of time and space that European governance creates?

A post-modern polity?

Post-modern community

The question is to what extent the sense of a European political simultaneity and 'contemporaneity' can lay the basis for a deepening of the European commu-nity, similar to the national community. Since the political 'now' seems to be experienced differently in the Union it is probable that its role in the creation of solidarity among those that comprise this present can come to look different. Earlier findings suggest an EU development in which political and cultural com-munity will be more separate than in the nation-state (Wæver, 1995).

European simultaneity emerges primarily in the EU's decision-making community. The EU decision-making community is forced to build on the sense of enforced simultaneity, partly because of the heterogeneity of the partic-ipants. It is however uncertain to what extent this feeling of simultaneity will come to be shared by broader social groups and be used as the basis of a more profound community. National politics and democracy was based on the idea of a national community that was both political and cultural. Underlying this idea was a sense of a common time context for all citizens. Will EU decisions come to be democratically based if citizens do not feel they are *natural* partici- pants in an EU simultaneity? Can a widened feeling of European simultaneity be 'enforced', as in the EU decision-making community? Or will it emerge slowly and naturally over time as in the nation-state? Or will we be able to live with *one* simultaneity in European governance and *another* uniting us in our cultural identity, reflecting our belonging to 'European multiple demoi' (Weiler, 1999: 344ff.)? What will European community and democratic anchor- age actually mean then?

European hierarchy for European simultaneity

Clear signs of the potential of combining time–space dimensions could be seen in an explorative study, in which I introduced the concept of European 'contact zone calendars' through a combination of everyday praxis in space and time (Ekengren, 1996a).[4] However, many questions are still waiting for answers.

To what extent are time and pace replacing territoriality and space as the most important factors for the organisation of political units? According to Giddens (1981), the breakthrough for the uniform measurement of time and 'empty time' came when time was linked to the modern state's uniformity of social organisation. What happens when polycentric European governance coincides with the strongly enforced, European-wide simultaneity? It seems reasonable to assume that the active upholding of simultaneity will continue in a 'system of interaction with no clear apex' (von Bogdandy, 1993: 27) because, even though there is no single place more central than any other, inter- action *between* centres must be coordinated within a common uniform time. What tools other than strongly enforced simultaneity are there in a polity of several centres?

To what extent will a permanent 'multiperspectival polity' (Ruggie, 1993) be able to agree in practice on decision-making simultaneity – a common time? Probably coordination in time in practice constitute the basis for the control of space. It is hard to think of simultaneity without hierarchy. Given my findings of a single perception of time in European governance and the fact that time has causal priority over space, as Giddens argues, can there exist a polycentric Euro- pean structure in people's imaginations? The centre that sets the timetable con- trols time and, logically, also controls space. A segmentation of time in European governance is very unlikely because somebody will always hold the power of producing the conditions of simultaneity: creating the timetables, etc. In the light of my findings, it might be more appropriate to assume a European governance structure of *shifting leading centres* than a polycentric Europe. It is the rotating EU presidency that produces the degree of temporal homogeneity needed for the complex coordination of contacts and meetings, which is greatly facilitated by the emergence of a single territorial 'meeting centre': Brussels. It seems that the timetables of European governance are a force for centralisation in both time and space.

Future research will also have to answer the question of whether European time will supplant state time. Can they co-exist simultaneously, in analogy to the Union and the state configurations of space (Nørgaard, 1994)? Chapter 4 showed that, at present, actors involved in European governance draw on time rules from the context of both national and European governance to determine when a moment is ripe for action. However, the two other case studies evidenced to the fact that European governance is most often given priority in time – that is, the notion of simultaneity in European governance tends to crowd out state time. European simultaneity is simply a much stronger story than state time, because it is more actively and extensively narrated than a form of time long taken for granted. To what extent can overlapping layers of territorial authority be combined with a European governance time that tends to be uniform and exclusive? What sense will people make of the different layers of political authority if post-state political units are distinguished to a larger extent in time rather than space? Does it matter whether European units are increasingly unlike in size and function (Wæver, 1994) when they are all operating in the same political time? Today, a common time may perhaps be a stronger source of identity than the feeling of common geographical borders.

I have shown that the perception of simultaneous administrative activity around the same issue is a very important factor in the imagination of networks among colleagues in European governance. To what extent do the images of a uniform time and space have to coincide before such a collegiate develop into a new imagined community? Or can a community be imagined in other ways than those already known to us? Or are we looking towards a future in which the predominant links between individuals – in all spatial and territorial contexts – take the forms of companionships over the 'net'? The final triumph of global simultaneity, and of time over space? To what extent is European governance time made to make sense as an answer to the expansion of contacts between actors in geographical space? Or should the relationship be thought of in the opposite direction: the new time consciousness is the origin of a perceived need to establish new patterns of contacts. Given a phenomenologically based view of time and space, to what extent is it possible to separate the two dimensions and set one of them logically prior to the other? How are European time–space images and practices related to global forms of governance? What is historically most significant and important: the extension of simultaneity or the very complexity of coordination in time and space? It is in those processes of spatial and temporal fusion that the evolving constitution of European governance should be found. More empirical research along these lines is urgently required.

Notes

1 See the debate about the establishment of an informal organ (EuroX) in EMU, limited to certain EU members.
2 See also modern literature in economics on time management, which is strongly focused on the efficient short-term handling of matters.
3 There might be ways to slow it down: see the Amsterdam Treaty's time rules for the EU Commission's presentation of proposals to national parliaments.
4 The model was obtained by a combination of new spatial contact patterns and changes in the time dimensions of the same sort that are examined in this book. The conclusion was that EU calendars tie officials together in time and space. As a consequence, it makes more sense for them to interpret their situation as characterised by a broader contact net with colleagues in other capitals *and* by new European time disciplines. The interactions between civil servants within the EU framework was said to constitute a new distinct space–time framework, including specific time–space relationships, shaping their routinised everyday practice.

BIBLIOGRAPHY

Books and articles

Adam, B. (1990) *Time and Social Theory*, Cambridge: Polity Press.

Adam, B. (1995) *Timewatch*, Cambridge: Polity Press.

Adler, E. (1997) 'Imagined (Security) Communities: Cognitive Regions in International Relations', *Millennium: Journal of International Studies*, 26:2, 249–277.

Amnå, E. (1981) *Planhushållning i den offentliga sektorn?*, Stockholm: PA Nordstedts & Söners förlag.

Andersen, S. and Eliassen, K. (eds) (1993) *Making Policy in Europe*, London: Sage.

Andersen, S. and Eliassen, K. (eds) (1996) *The European Union: How Democratic Is It?*, London: Sage.

Anderson, B. (1983) *Imagined Communities: Reflections of the Origin and Spread of Nationalism*, London: Verso.

Arendt, H. (1976) *Between Past and Future: Eight Exercises in Political Thought*, New York: Viking Press.

Arendt, H. (1978) 'Volume Two: Willing', in *The Life of the Mind*, One-volume edn, San Diego: Harcourt Brace.

Armstrong, K. and Bulmer, S. (1998) *The Governance of the European Single Market*, Manchester: Manchester University Press.

Axelrod, R. (1984) *The Evolution of Co-Operation*, London: Penguin Books.

Baldwin, R. (1996) 'Regulatory Legitimacy in the European Context: The British Health and Safety Executive', in G. Majone (ed.), *Regulating Europe*, London: Routledge, 83–105.

Bartle, I. (1999) 'Transnational Interests in the European Union: Globalization and Changing Organization in Telecommunications and Electricity', *Journal of Common Market Studies*, 37:3, 363–383.

Baudrillard, J. (1985) 'År 2000 kommer inte att äga rum. Efter historiens försvinnande: simulisationens makt', *Res Publica*, 1, 23–37.

Bell, D. (1977) 'Teletext and Technology: New Networks of Knowledge and Information in Post-Industrial Society', *Encounter*, 48:6, 9–29.

Benjamin, W. (1973) *Illuminations*, London: Fontana.

Bergström, H. (1987) *Rivstart?: om övergången från opposition till regering*, Doctoral dissertation, *Stockholm Studies in Politics*, 34, Stockholm: Tiden.

Bernitz, U. (1986) 'The EEC-EFTA agreements with special reference to the position of Sweden and other Scandinavian EFTA Countries', *Common Market Law Review*, 23, 567–590.

Blomberg, L. (1989) 'Långsiktig EG-politik saknas', *Dagens Nyheter*, 2 January.

Börzel, T. (1997) 'What's So Special About Policy Networks? – An Exploration of the Concept and its Usefulness in Studying European Governance', *European Integration online Papers* (EIoP), 1:16 http://eiop.

Bourdieu, P. (1977) *Outline of a Theory of Practice*, Cambridge, London, New York and Melbourne: Cambridge University Press.

Bourdieu, P. (1979) *Algeria 1960*, Cambridge: Cambridge University Press.

Bourdieu, P. (1990) *The Logic of Practice*, Cambridge: Polity Press.

Bovens, M. and 't Hart, P. (1998) *Understanding Policy Fiascoes*, New Brunswick and London: Transaction Publishers.

Brunsson, K. (1995) *Dubbla budskap – Hur riksdagen och regeringen presenterar sitt budgetarbete*, Stockholm: Department of Business Economics, Stockholm University.

Bulmer, S. (1986) *The Domestic Structure of European Policy-Making in West-Germany*, London: London School of Economics.

Bulmer, S. and Paterson, W, (1987) *The Federal Republic of Germany and the European Community*, London: Allen & Unwin.

Carey, J. W. (1988) *Communication as Culture*, Boston: Unwin Hyman.

Carlsnaes, W. (1992) 'The Agency–Structure Problem in Foreign Policy Analysis', *International Studies Quarterly*, 36, 245–270.

Carlsnaes, W. (1993) 'On Analysing the Dynamics of Foreign Policy Change: A Critique and Reconceptualization', *Cooperation and Conflict*, 28:1, 5–30.

Carlsson, I. (1989a) Inauguration speech at the seminar 'Europeisk gemenskap och vår välfärd – socialdemokratiska perspektiv', 1 September, Stockholm: The International Centre of the Swedish Labour Movement.

Carlsson, I. (1989b) 'Europa är större än EG', *Dagens Nyheter*, 5 December.

Carlsson, I. (1990) 'EG-medlemskap omöjliggörs', *Dagens Nyheter*, 27 May.

Cecchini, P. (1988) 1992, *Le défi*, Paris: Flammarion.

Checkel, J. (1998) 'The Constructivist turn in International Relations Theory', *World Politics*, 50 (January), 324–348.

Christakis, M. (1998) 'Greece: Competing Regional Priorities', in K. Hanf and B. Soetendorp (eds), *Adapting to European Integration. Small States and the European Union*, London: Addison-Wesley Longman, 84–99.

Christiansen, T. and Jørgensen, K. E. (1995) 'Towards the "Third Category" of Space: Reconceptualizing the Changing Nature of Borders in Western Europe', paper prepared for the 2nd ECPR Pan-Europoean Conference on International Relations, Paris.

Cohen, R. (1981) *International Politics: The Rules of the Game*, Essex: Longman Group.

Commission des CE (1985) *L'Achevement du marché interieur, Livre blanc de la Commission à l'intention du Conseil européen*, June.

Communication from the European Commission (1998) 'Legislate Less to Act Better: The Facts', COM (1998) 345 Final.

Connoly, W. (1974) *The Terms of Political Discourse*, 2nd edn, Oxford: Oxford University Press.

Cornett, L. and Caporaso, J. A. (1992) '"And Still It Moves!" State Interests and Social Forces in the European Community', in E.-O. Czempiel and J. Rosenau (eds), *Governance Without Government: Order and Change in World Politics*, Cambridge: Cambridge University Press, 219–249.

Cram, L. (1996) 'Integration Theory and the Study of the European Policy Process', in J. Richardson (ed.), *European Union, Power and Policy-Making*, London: Routledge, 40–58.

Czempiel E.-O. and Rosenau, J. (eds) (1992) *Governance Without Government: Order and Change in World Politics*, Cambridge: Cambridge University Press.

Daugbjerg, C. (1997) 'Policy Networks and Agricultural Policy Reforms: Explaining Deregulation in Sweden and Re-Regulation in the European Community', *Governance: An International Journal of Policy and Administration*, 10:2, 123–142.

Daugbjerg, C. (1999) 'Reforming the CAP: Policy Networks and Broader Institutional Structures', *Journal of Common Market Studies*, 37:3, 407–428.

de Clausade, J. (1991) *L'adaptation de l'administration française à l'Europe*, Collection des rapports officiels, Paris: La Documentation Française.

Der Derian, J. (1987) *On Diplomacy: A Genealogy of Western Estrangement*, Oxford: Blackwell.

Der Derian, J. (1992) *Antidiplomacy – Spies, Terror, Speed and War*, Cambridge, MA: Blackwell Publishers.

Dessler, D. (1989) 'What's at Stake in the Agent–Structure Debate?', *International Organization*, 43:3, 441–474.

Deutsch, K. et al. (1957) *Political Community and the North Atlantic Area*, Princeton: Princeton University Press.

Diebert, R. (1996) 'Typographica: The Medium and the Medieval-to-Modern Transformation', *Review of International Studies*, 22:1, 29–56.

Diez, T. (1997) 'International Ethics and European Integration: Federal State or Network Horizon', *Alternatives*, 22:3, 287–312.

Ds 1980:2 (1980) 'Förslag till utbildning för högre chefer i statsförvaltningen', Stockholm: Government Printing Office.

Ds 1992:96 (1992) 'Statsförvaltningens Europakompetens – Om behovet av kompetensutveckling hos myndigheterna inför integrationen', Stockholm: Government Printing Office.

Ds 1993:44 (1993) 'Statsförvaltningens internationalisering – En vitbok om konsekvenser för den statliga sektorn i Sverige', Stockholm: Government Printing Office.

Ds 1995:21 (1995) 'Samsyn och alliansförmåga – Hur regeringen, näringslivet, intresseorganisationer, regionala intressen och forskarvärlden behöver samverka för att stärka Sveriges position i EU', Stockholm: Government Printing Office.

Dunér, B. (1977) 'Autonomi: skiss till referensram och illustration av dess tillämpning', *Forskningsrapport*: Stockholm, The Swedish Institute of International Affairs.

Edelman, M. (1988) *Constructing the Political Spectacle*, Chicago: University of Chicago Press.

Eisenhardt, K. M. (1989) 'Making Fast Strategic Decisions in High-Velocity Environments', *Academy of Management Journal*, 32:3, 543–576.

Ekengren, M. (1994) 'Structures and Time in Foreign Policy Praxis', unpublished paper, Department of Political Science, University of Stockholm.

Ekengren, M. (1995) 'Statsförvaltningens "europeisering" i tid och rum–mot en postmodern terminologi', unpublished paper, Department of Political Science, University of Stockholm.

Ekengren, M. (1996a) 'Statsförvaltningens europeisering i tid och rum – En studie av den politiska tidens förändring till följd av EU-samarbetet', *Research Report* 25, Stockholm: The Swedish Institute of International Affairs.

Ekengren, M. (1996b) 'The Europeanisation of State Administration – Adding the Time Dimension', *Cooperation and Conflict*, 31:4, 387–415.

Ekengren, M. (1997) 'The Temporality of European Governance', in K. E. Jørgensen (ed.), *Reflective Approaches to European Governance*, Basingstoke: Macmillan, 69–86.

Ekengren, M. (1998) *Time and European Governance – The Empirical Value of Three*

Reflective Approaches, Doctoral dissertation, *Stockholm Studies in Politics*, 63, University of Stockholm.

Ekengren, M. and Sundelius, B. (1998) 'The State Joins the European Union', in K. Hanf and B. Soetendorp (eds), *Adapting to European Integration. Small States and the European Union*, London: Addison-Wesley Longman, 131–148.

Ekengren, M. and Sundelius B. (2002) 'Sweden', in B. Hocking and D. Spence (eds), *Integrating Diplomats: Foreign Ministries in the European Union*, London: Palgrave.

Erlander. T. (1961) 'Statement of Government Policy presented by the Prime Minister' (October) *Documents on Swedish Foreign Policy*, Stockholm: Government Printing Office.

European Commission information (1995) 'Etat de transposition des mesures du livre blanc. Situation par Etat membre (situation au 14/9/94)', European Commission, Unit for 'reunion de group de membres de la Commission'.

Fabian, J. (1983) *Time and the Other. How Anthropology Makes its Object*, New York: Columbia University Press.

Farr, J. (1989) 'Understanding Conceptual Change Politically', in T. Ball, J. Farr and R. L. Hanson (eds), *Political Innovation and Conceptual Change*, Cambridge: Cambridge University Press, 24–49.

Fraser, J. T. (ed.) (1968) *The Voices of Time. A Survey of Man's Views of Time as Understood and Described by the Sciences and the Humanities*, London: Penguin.

Friis, L. and Murphy, A. (1999) 'The European Union and Central and Eastern Europe: Governance and Boundaries', *Journal of Common Market Studies*, 37:2, 211–232.

Gahrton, P. (1988) 'Den svenske regering standser selv EF-politik', *Notat*, Folkbevaegelsen, Copenhagen, June, 4–6.

Garcia, J. E. (1990) 'Texts and their Interpretation', *Review of Metaphysics*, 42 (March), 495–542.

Geis, M. (1987) *The Language of Politics*, New York: Springer-Verlag.

George, S. (ed.) (1992) *Britain and the European Community – The Politics of Semi-Detachment*, Oxford: Clarendon Press.

Giddens, A. (1976) *New Rules of Sociological Method: A Positive Critique of Interpretative Sociologies*, London: Hutchinson; New York: Basic Books.

Giddens, A. (1981) *A Contemporary Critique of Historical Materialism: Vol. 1, Power, Property and the State*, London and Basingstoke: Macmillan.

Giddens, A. (1984) *The Constitution of Society*, Berkeley and Los Angeles: University of California Press.

Giddens, A. (1987) *Social Theory and Modern Sociology*, Cambridge: Polity Press; Stanford: Stanford University Press.

Giddens, A. (1989) 'A Reply to my Critics', in D. Held and J. B. Thompson (eds), *Social Theory of Modern Societies: Anthony Giddens and his Critics*, Cambridge: Cambridge University Press, 249–301.

Giddens, A. (1990) *The Consequences of Modernity*, Cambridge: Polity Press.

Gidlund, J. E. (1988) 'Reflexioner kring ett gränslöst Europa', *Tiden*, 2, 100–101.

Glaser, B. and Strauss, A. (1971) *Status Passage*, London: International Library of Sociology and Social Reconstruction.

Goetz, K. (1995) 'National Governance and European Integration: Intergovernmental Relations in Germany', *Journal of Common Market Studies*, 33:1, 92–116.

Goodin, R. E. (1998) 'Keeping Political Time: The Rhythms of Democracy', *International Political Science Review,* 19:1, 39–54.

Gross, D. (1985) 'The Temporality of the Modern State', *Theory and Society*, 14:1, 53–82.

Gumbrecht H.-U., Lüsebrink H.-J., and Reichardt, R. (1983) 'Histoire et langage: travaux allemands en lexicologie historique et en histoire conceptuelle', *Revue d'histoire moderne et contemporaine*, Tome xxx, April–June, 192–195.

Gustavsson, J. (1998) *The Politics of Foreign Policy Change – Explaining the Swedish Reorientation on EC Membership*, doctoral dissertation, Lund: Lund University Press.

Gustavsson, S. (1993) 'Fortsatt framgång för majoritetsprincipen?', in U. Bernitz *et al.*, *Vad Betyder EG?*, Stockholm: SNS förlag, 265–295.

Gustavsson, S. (1998) 'Double Assymetry as Normative Challenge', in P. Koslowski and A. Follesdal (eds), *Democracy and the EU*, Berlin: Springer-Verlag, 108–134.

Haas, E. (1958) *The Uniting of Europe*, London: Stevens.

Hägerstrand, T. (1968) *Innovation Diffusion as a Spatial Process*, Chicago: University of Chicago Press.

Hamilton, C. B. and Stålvant, C.-E. (1989) 'A Swedish View of 1992', The Royal Institute of International affairs, Discussion Paper 13, London: Chatham House.

Hanf, K. and Soetendorp, B. (1998) 'The Netherlands: Growing Doubts of a Loyal Member', in K. Hanf and B. Soetendorp (eds), *Adapting to European Integration. Small States and the European Union*, London: Addison-Wesley Longman, 36–51.

Harmsen, R. (1999) 'The Europeanization of National Administrations: A Comparative Study of France and Netherlands', *Governance: An International Journal of Policy and Administration*, 12:1, 81–113.

Hayward, J. (ed.) (1995) *The Crisis of Representation in Europe*, London: Frank Cass.

Held, D. and Thompson, J. B. (eds) (1989) *Social Theory of Modern Societies: Anthony Giddens and his Critics*, Cambridge: Cambridge University Press.

Hermansson, C.-H. (1987) 'Sverige, Europa, Världen', in C. Hamilton (ed.), *Europa och Sverige – EG-frågan inför 90-talet*, Stockholm: SNS förlag, 153–169.

Hernes, H. (1987) *Welfare State and Woman Power – Essays in State Feminism*, Oslo: Norwegian University Press.

Hill, C. (ed.) (1996) *Actors in European Foreign Policy*, London: Routledge.

HMSO (Cm 2369) (1993) Developments in the European Community January–June 1993, *European Communities*, 5.

HMSO (Cm 2525) (1994) Developments in the European Community July–December 1993, *European Commmunities*, 4.

Hollis, M. and Smith, S. (eds) (1990) *Explaining and Understanding International Relations*, Oxford: Oxford University Press.

International Political Science Review (1998) 'Thematic Issue: Time and Democracy', 19:1.

Jachtenfuchs, M. (1995) 'Theoretical Approaches to European Governance', *European Law Journal*, 1:2, 115–133.

Jachtenfuchs, M. (1997) 'Conceptualising European Governance', in K. E. Jørgensen (ed.), *Reflective Approaches to European Governance*, Basingstoke: Macmillan, 39–50.

Jachtenfuchs, M., Diez, T. and Jung, S. (1998) 'Which Europe? Conflicting Models of a Legitimate European Political Order', *European Journal of International Relations*, 4:4, 409–445.

Jacobsson, K. (1995) 'Konstruktionen av det nödvändiga: EU-debatten som offentligt samtal', *Häften för Kritiska Studier*, 28:2, 55–68.

Jacobsson, K. (1996) 'Den historiska fantasin. Om erövrandet av det förflutna och konstruktionen av framtiden. Eller: vår bästa tid är nu', unpublished paper, Department of Sociology, Uppsala University.

Jacobsson, K. (1997) *Så gott som demokrati Om demokratifrågan i EU-debatten*, Umeå: Boréa Bokförlag.

Jacobsson, K. and Øygarden, G. A. (1996) 'Ekonomernas Guernica: Rädslans metaforer och produktionen av mening', *Sociologisk Forskning*, 2–3.

Jannings, J. (1997) 'Towards a More Flexible Europe – Governance in Greater Europe', paper, Wilton Park and College of Europe Conference, Natolin, Warsaw, 19–23 May.

Jansson, P. (1991) *Säkerhetspolitikens språk*, doctoral dissertation, University of Linköping.

Jerneck, M. and Stenelo, L.-G. (1996) *Bargaining Democracy*, Lund: Lund University Press.

Jönsson, C. (1990) 'Den transnationella maktens metaforer: Biljard, schack, teater eller spindelnät?', in G. Hansson and L.-G. Stenelo (eds), *Makt och internationalisering*, Stockholm: Carlsson Bokförlag, 127–147.

Jönsson, C., Elgström, O. and Strömvik, M. (1998) 'Negotiations in Networks in the European Union', *International Negotiation*, 3:3, 319–344.

Jørgensen K. E. (1997a) 'Introduction', in K. E. Jørgensen (ed.) *Reflective Approaches to European Governance*, Basingstoke: Macmillan, 1–12.

Jørgensen, K. E. (1997b) 'PoCo: The Diplomatic Republic of Europe', in K. E. Jørgensen (ed.), *Reflective Approaches to European Governance*, Basingstoke: Macmillan, 167–180.

Jørgensen, K. E. (ed.) (1997c) *Reflective Approaches to European Governance*, Basingstoke: Macmillan.

Kapstein, E. B. (1993) 'Correspondence: Territoriality and Who Is Us?', *International Organization*, 47:3, 501–505.

Karvonen, L. and Sundelius, B. (1987) *Internationalization and Foreign Policy Management*, Aldershot: Gower.

Kelstrup, M. (1992) 'European Integration and Political Theory', in M. Kelstrup (ed.) *European Integration and Denmark's Participation*, Copenhagen: Political Studies Press, 13–58.

Keohane, R. O. (1989) *International Institutions and State Power*, Boulder, San Francisco and Oxford: Westview Press.

Keohane, R. O. and Hoffmann, S. (eds) (1991) *The New European Community. Decision Making and Institutional Change*, Boulder: Westview Press.

Keohane, R. O. and Nye, J. (1975) 'International Interdependence and Integration', in F. Greenstein and N. Polsby (eds), *Handbook of Political Science*, Reading, MA: Addison-Wesley, 363–414.

Kern, S. (1983) *The Culture of Time and Space 1880–1919*, Cambridge, MA: Harvard University Press.

Kerremans, B. and Beyers, J. (1998) 'Belgium: The Dilemma between Cohesion and Autonomy', in K. Hanf and B. Soetendorp (eds), *Adapting to European Integration. Small States and the European Union*, London: Addison-Wesley Longman, 14–35.

Kjaer, P. (1996) *The Constitution of Enterprise*, doctoral dissertation, *Stockholm Studies in Politics*, 56, University of Stockholm.

Kleiboer, M. and 't Hart, P. (1995) 'Time to Talk? Multiple Perspectives on Timing of International Mediation', *Cooperation and Conflict*, 30:4, 307–348.

Klein, B. (1990) 'How the West was One: Representational Politics of NATO', *International Studies Quarterly*, 34, 311–325.

Kohler-Koch, B. (1997) 'The Strength of Weakness: The Transformation of Governance in the EU', in L. Lewin and S. Gustavsson (eds), *The Future of the Nation-State*, Stockholm: Nerenius & Santérus, 169–210.

Kohler-Koch, B. and Eising, R. (eds) (1999) *The Transformation of Governance in the European Union*, London: Routledge.

Kooiman, J. (ed.) (1993) *Modern Governance, New Government–Society Interactions*, London: Sage.

Koselleck, R. (1983) 'Time and Revolutionary Language', *Social Research*, 50:3.

Koselleck, R. (1985) *Futures Past: On the Semantics of Historical Time*, Cambridge, MA: MIT Press.

Koselleck, R. (1988) *Critique and Crisis – Enlightenment and the Pathogenesis of Modern Society*, Oxford: Berg.

Koselleck, R. (1989) 'Time and Revolutionary Language', in R. Schürman (ed.), *The Public Realm*, New York: Stony Brooks, NY: SUNY Press, 297–306.

Krause, K. (1998) 'Critical Theory and Security Studies: The Research Program of "Critical Security Studies"', *Cooperation and Conflict*, 33: 3, 298–333.

Ladrech, R. (1994) 'Europeanization of Domestic Politics and Institutions: The Case of France', *Journal of Common Market Studies*, 32:1, 69–88.

Laffan, B. and Tannam, E. (1998) 'Ireland: The Rewards of Pragmatism', in K. Hanf and B. Soetendorp (eds), *Adapting to European Integration. Small States and the European Union*, London: Addison-Wesley Longman, 69–83.

Larsson, G. (1988) 'Dags för arbetarrörelsen att upptäcka EG och Europa', *Statsanställd*, 29, 7–9.

Larsson, T. (1986) *Regeringen och dess kansli*, Lund: Studentlitteratur.

Lewin, L. (1990) *Upptäckten av framtiden – En lärobok i politisk idéhistoria*, Stockholm: Norstedts.

Lindahl, R. and Larsson, L.-G. (1991) *Det europeiska politiska samarbetet – EPS*, Stockholm: SNS Förlag.

Lindberg, L. and Scheingold, S. (1970) *Europe's Would-Be Polity*, Englewood Cliffs, NJ: Prentice-Hall.

Linz, J. J. (1998) 'Democracy's Time Constraints', *International Political Science Review*, 19:1, 19–37.

Luckmann, T. (1991) 'The Constitution of Human Life in Time', in J. Bender and D. Wellbery (eds), *Chronotypes: The Construction of Time,* Stanford: Stanford University Press, 151–166.

Luhmann, N. (1976) 'The Future Can Not Begin: Temporal Structures in Modern Society', *Social Research*, 43:1, 130–152.

Luhmann, N. (1982) *The Differentiation of Society*, New York: Columbia University Press.

Luhmann, N. (1985) *A Sociological Theory of Law*, London: Routledge & Kegan Paul.

Luhmann, N. (1990) *Political Theory in the Welfare State*, Berlin: Gruyter.

Luif, P. (1995) *On the Road to Brussels – The Political Dimension of Austria's, Finland's and Sweden's Accession to the European Union*, Austrian Institute for International Affairs, Wien: Braumüller.

Luif, P. (1998) 'Austria: Adaptation through Anticipation', in K. Hanf and B. Soetendorp (eds), *Adapting to European Integration. Small States and the European Union*, London: Addison-Wesley Longman, 116–130.

Lundmark, L. (1984) *Det förflutnas makt. Om sociala tidsbegrepp och samhällsförändring*, Arkiv studiehäften, 14, Lund: Arkiv för studier i arbetarrörelsens historia.

Maier, C. S. (1987) 'The Politics of Time: Changing Paradigms of Collective Time and Private Time in the Modern Era', in C. S. Maier (ed.), *Changing Boundaries of the Polit-*

ical. Essays on the Evolving Balance Between the State and Society, Public and Private in Europe, Cambridge: Cambridge University Press.

Majone, G. (1996) *Regulating Europe,* London: Routledge.

March, J. G. and Olsen, J. P. (1989) *Rediscovering Institutions. The Organisational Basis of Politics,* New York: Free Press.

Marks, G., Scharpf, F., Schmitter, P. and Streeck, W. (eds) (1996) *Governance in the European Union,* London: Sage.

Mascanzoni, D. (1998) 'Flexibilitet nyckelordet i Italien – virtuella företag ökar konkurrenskraften', Nätverksföretag – innovativt, flexibelt och virtuellt, *Sveriges Tekniska Attachéer,* Stockholm: Nordisk Bokindustri.

Matlary, J. H. (1995) 'New Forms of Governance in Europe? The Decline of the State as the Source of Political Legitimation', *Cooperation and Conflict,* 30:2, 99–125.

Matlary, J. H. (1997) 'Epilogue: New Bottles for New Wine', in K. E. Jørgensen (ed.), *Reflective Approaches to European Governance,* Basingstoke: Macmillan, 201–213.

Mayer, P., Rittberger, V. and Zürn, M. (1993) 'Regime Theory – State of Art and Perspectives', in V. Rittberger (ed.), *Regime Theory and International Relations,* Oxford: Clarendon Press, 391–430.

McKay, J. (1996) *The Rush to Union,* Cambridge: Cambridge University Press.

McLuhan, M. (1964/1973) *Understanding Media,* London: Routledge & Kegan Paul.

McLuhan, M., Quentin, F. and Jerome, A. (1967) *The Medium is the Message,* New York: Random House.

Metcalfe, L. (1993) 'Trends in European Public Administration', in *Statsförvaltningens internationalisering,* Ds 1993:44, Bil. 1, 1–29.

Mitrany, D. (1966) *A Working Peace System,* Chicago: Quadrangle Books.

Morata, F. (1998) 'Spain: Modernization through Integration', in K. Hanf and B. Soetendorp (eds), *Adapting to European Integration. Small States and the European Union,* London: Addison-Wesley Longman, 100–115.

Moravcsik, A. (1991) 'Negotiating the Single European Act: National Interests and Conventional Statecraft in the European Community', *International Organization,* 45:1, 19–56.

Moravcsik, A. (1998) *The Choice for Europe. Social Purpose and State Power from Rome to Maastricht,* Ithaca: Cornell University Press.

Mörth, U. (1996) *Vardagsintegration – La vie quotidienne – i Europa, Sverige i EUREKA och EUREKA i Sverige,* doctoral dissertation, *Stockholm Studies in Politics,* 54, University of Stockholm.

Nassehi, A. (1994) 'No Time for Utopia: The Absence of Utopian Contents in Modern Concepts of Time', *Time and Society,* 3:1, 47–78.

Neufeld, M. (1993) 'Interpretation and the "Science" of International Relations', *Review of International Studies,* 19:1, 39–61.

Neumann, I. (1994) 'A Region-Building Approach to Northern Europe', *Review of International Studies,* 20:1, 53–74.

Nørgaard, A. S. (1994) 'Modernity v. Post-Modernity in International Relations: Coming to Terms with the "New" EC?', *Cooperation and Conflict,* 29:3, 245–287.

Nowotny, H. (1992) 'Time in Social Sciences. Theoretical and Empirical Approaches', in M. Dierkes and B. Biervert (eds), *European Social Science in Transition,* Boulder: Westview Press, 481–525.

Nuttall, S. (1992) *European Political Co-Operation,* Oxford: Oxford University Press.

Olsson, H. and Pettersson, L. (1987) 'Arbetarrörelsen och EG', in C. Hamilton (ed.),

Europa och Sverige – EG-frågan inför 90-talet, Stockholm: SNS Förlag, 170–191.

Olsson, J. and Svenning, O. (1988) *Tillhör Sverige Europa?*, Stockholm: Författarförlaget.

Onuf, N.G. (1994) 'The Constitution of International Society', *European Journal of International Law*, 51:1, 1–19.

Pijpers, A., Regelsberger, E. and Wessels, W. (eds) (1988) *European Political Cooperation in the 1980s – A Common Foreign Policy for Western Europe?*, Dordrecht: Martinus Nijhoff Publishers.

Pinder, J. (1968) 'Positive Integration and Negative Integration – Some Problems of Economic Union in the EEC', *World Today*, 24:March, 88–110.

Pinder, J. (1991) *European Community – The Building of a Union*, Oxford: Oxford University Press.

Proposition 1987/88:66 from the Swedish Government (1987) 'Sverige och den västeuropeiska integrationen', Stockholm: Government Printing Office.

Putnam, R. D. (1988) 'Diplomacy and Domestic Politics: The Logic of Two-Level Games', *International Organization*, 42:3, 427–460.

Reichardt, R. (1985) 'Einleitung', in R. Reichardt *et al.* (eds), *Handbuch politisch-sozialer Grundbegriffe in Frankreich 1680–1820*, Vol. 1/2, Oldenburg: Brigitte Schlieben-Lange, 39–148.

Richardson, J. (ed.) (1996) *European Union – Power and Policy-Making*, London: Routledge.

Ricoeur, P. (1975) *The Rule of Metaphor*, London: Oxford University Press.

Ricoeur, P. (1984–88) *Time and Narrative*, Vol I–III, Chicago: University of Chicago Press.

Rifkin, J. (1989) *Time Wars: The Primary Conflict in Human History*. New York: Simon & Schuster.

Risse-Kappen, T. (1996) 'The Nature of the Beast', *Journal of Common Market Studies*, 34:1, 53–80.

Ronfeldt, D. (1992) 'Cyberocracy Is Coming', *The Information Society*, 8:4, 243–296.

Rosenau, J. (1990) *Turbulence in World Politics. A Theory of Change and Continuity*, New York: Harvester Wheatsheaf.

Rosenau, J. (1997) *Along the Domestic–Foreign Frontier. Exploring Governance in a Turbulent World*, Cambridge: Cambridge University Press.

Rosenau, J. and Czempiel, E.-O. (eds) (1992) *Governance Without Government: Order and Change in World Politics*, Cambridge: Cambridge University Press.

Roth, J. (1963) *Timetables: Structuring the Passage of Time in Hospital Treatment and Other Careers*, Indianapolis: Bobbs-Merrill.

Ruggie, J. G. (1983) 'Continuity and Transformation in the World Polity: Toward a Neorealist Synthesis', *World Politics*, 43:2, 261–285.

Ruggie, J. G. (1989) 'International Structure and International Transformation: Space, Time and Method', in J. Rosenau and E.-O. Czempiel (eds), *Global Changes and Theoretical Challenges: Approaches to World Politics for the 1990s*, Lexington, MA: Lexington Books, 21–35.

Ruggie, J. G. (1993) 'Territoriality and Beyond: Problematizing Modernity in International Relations', *International Organization*, 47:1, 139–174.

Ruggie, J. G. (1998) *Constructing the World Polity. Essays on International Institutionalisation*, London: Routledge.

Sandemose, J. (1986) 'Vad tid är?', *Häften för kritiska studier*, 2.

Scharpf, F. (1988) 'The Joint-Decision Trap: Lessons from German Federalism and European Integration', *Public Administration*, 66:3, 239–278.

Scharpf, F. (1999) *Governing in Europe – Effective and Democratic?*, Oxford: Oxford University Press.

Schedler, A. and Santiso, J. (1998) 'Democracy and Time', *International Political Science Review*, 19:1, 5–18.

Schlesinger, J. A. (1994) *Political Parties and the Winning of Office*, Michigan: University of Michigan Press.

Schmitter, P. (1969) 'Three Neo-Functionalist Hypotheses about International Integration', *International Organization*, 23: 1, 161–166.

Schmitter, P. (1996) 'Imagining the Future of the Euro-Polity with the Help of New Concepts', in G. Marks, F. Scharpf, P. Schmitter and W. Streeck (eds), *Governance in the European Union*, London: Sage, 121–150.

Schmitter, P. and Santiso, J. (1998) 'Three Temporal Dimensions to the Consolidation of Democracy', *International Political Science Review*, 19:1, 69–92.

Schneider, G. (1991) *Time, Planning, and Policy-Making. An Evaluation of a Complex Relationship*, Bern: Peter Lang.

Schöttler, P. (1989) 'Historians and Discourse Analysis', *History Workshop*, 27, 37–65.

Schumann, W. (1991) 'EG-Forschung und Policy-Analyse – Zur Notwendigkeit, den ganzen Elefanten zu erfassen', *Politische Vierteljahresschrift*, Heft 2 (June), 232–257.

Scott, A. (1982) *The Dynamics of Interdependence*, Chapel Hill and London: University of North Carolina Press.

Sjöblom, G. (1987) 'Anteckningar om politisk tid', in L.-G. Stenelo (ed.), *Statsvetenskapens mångfald – Festskrift till Nils Stjernquist*, Lund: Lund University Press, 255–267.

Sjöstedt, G. (1973) *OECD – Samarbetet: funktioner och effekter,* doctoral dissertation, Department of Political Science, University of Stockholm, Stockholm: Rotobeckman.

Skinner, Q. (1988) 'Meaning and Understanding in the History of Ideas', in J. Tully (ed.), *Meaning and Context: Quentin Skinner and his Critics*, Cambridge: Polity Press, 29–67.

Skowronek, S. (1997) *The Politics Presidents Make – Leadership from John Adams to Bill Clinton*, Cambridge, MA and London: The Belknap Press of Harvard University Press.

Smith, S., Book, K. and Zalewski, M. (eds) (1996) *International Theory: Positivism and Beyond*, Cambridge: Cambridge University Press.

SOU 1979:61 (1979) 'Förnyelse genom omprövning', Swedish Government Official Report.

SOU 1983:39 (1983) 'Politisk styrning – administrativ självständighet', Swedish Government Official Report.

SOU 1992:96 (1992) 'Statsförvaltningens Europakompetens – Om behovet av kompetensutveckling hos myndigheterna inför integrationen', Swedish Government Official Report.

SOU 1993:80 (1993) 'Statsförvaltningen och EG', Swedish Government Official Report.

SOU 1995:132 (1995) 'Utvidgning och samspel – Förhållandet småstat-stormakt: svenskt identitetsbyte', Swedish Government Official Report.

SOU 1996:6 (1996) 'Ett år med EU – svenska statstjänstemäns erfarenheter av arbetet i EU', Swedish Government Official Report.

Statskontoret 1996:7 (1996) 'EU-medlemskapets effekter på svensk statsförvaltning', Stockholm: Statskontoret Printing Office.

Steinbruner, J. D. (1974) *The Cybernetic Theory of Decision*, Princeton: Princeton University Press.

Steiner, Z. (1982) 'Introduction', in *The Times Survey of Foreign Ministries of the World*, London: The Times, 27–30.

Stenelo, L.-G. (1980) *Foreign Policy Predictions*, Lund: Lund University Press.

Stenelo, L.-G. (1990) 'Den internationaliserade demokratin', in G. Hansson and L.-G. Stenelo (eds), *Makt och Internationalisering*, Stockholm: Carlsson Bokförlag, 273–363.

Stern, E. (1992) 'Information Management and the Whiskey on the Rocks Crisis', *Cooperation and Conflict*, 27:1, 45–96.

Stone Sweet, A. and Sandholtz, W. (eds) (1998) *European Integration and Supranational Governance: State, Culture, and Ethnicity in Comparative Perspective*, Oxford: Oxford University Press.

Stråth, B. (1990) 'Introduction – Production of Meaning, Construction of Class Identities, and Social Change', in B. Stråth (ed.), *Language and the Construction of Class Identities*, Gothenburg: Gothenburg University Press, 1–11.

Stubb, A. (1997) 'The 1996 Intergovernmental Conference and the Management of Flexible Integration', *Journal of European Public Policy*, 4:1, 37–55.

Sundelius, B. (1976) *Nordic Cooperation: A Dynamic Integration Process*, doctoral dissertation, The Faculty of the Graduate School of International Studies, University of Denver.

Sundelius, B. (1978) *Managing Transnationalism in Northern Europe*, Boulder: Westview Press.

Sundelius, B. (1995) 'Sverige bortom småstatsbindningen: litet men smart i ett internationaliserat Europa', in SOU 1995:132 *Utvidgning och samspel*, Swedish Government Official Report, 61–85.

Sundelius, B., Stern, E. and Bynander, F. (1997) *Krishantering på svenska – teori och praktik*, Stockholm: Nerenius & Santérus Förlag

Svenning, O. (1988) 'Den europeiska integrationen förbättrar fackets möjligheter till ideologisk förnyelse', *LO-tidningen*, 67:39, 7.

Sverdrup, U. (1996) 'Europeanisation of the Heavy Rhythms of the Nation-State – The Emerging Temporal Order in Europe', paper presented at the CORE seminar 'The Study of European Integration: Domestic and International Issues', Humlebæk, Denmark, June.

Sverdrup, U. (1998) 'Norway: An Adaptive Non-Member', in K. Hanf and B. Soetendorp (eds), *Adapting to European Integration. Small States and the European Union*, London: Addison-Wesley Longman, 149–166.

Swedish Christian Democrats (Kristdemokratiska samhällspartiet, Kds) (1993) 'Principprogram för gemenskap och människovärde'.

Swedish Christian Democrats (1995) 'Europapolitiskt handlingsprogram'.

Swedish Environmental Party (Miljöpartiet, Mp) (1994) 'Partiprogram'.

Swedish Environmental Party (1995) 'Mot EU – Miljöpartiet de grönas plattform inför valet till EU-parlamentet 95-09-17'.

Swedish Foreign Ministry: Green Book ('Grönbok') (1994) 'Sverige och den västeuropeiska integrationen – sammanfattning av konsekvensutredningarna, 1–6', Stockholm: Government Printing Office.

Tallberg, J. (1999) *Making States Comply*, Doctoral dissertation, Lund University.

Taylor, P. (1990) 'Functionalism: The Approach of David Mitrany', in A. J. R. Groom and P. Taylor (eds), *Frameworks for International Cooperation*, London: Pinter, 125–138.

Thompson, E. P. (1967) 'Time, Work-Discipline and Industrial Capitalism', *Past & Present*, 38, 56–97.

Thompson, J. B. (1989) 'The Theory of Structuration', in D. Held and J. B. Thompson (eds), *Social Theory of Modern Societies: Anthony Giddens and his Critics*, Cambridge: Cambridge University Press, 56–76.

Thrift, N. (1988) 'Vivos Voco. Ringing the Changes in the Historical Geography of Time Consciousness', in M. Young and T. Schuller (eds), *The Rhythms of Society*, London: Routledge, 53–94.

Tilly, C. (1994) 'The Time of States', *Social Research*, 61:2, 267–294.

Tonra, B. (1997) 'The Impact of Political Cooperation', in K. E. Jørgensen (ed.), *Reflective Approaches to European Governance*, Basingstoke: Macmillan, 181–198.

Trägårdh, L. (1990) 'Varieties of Volkish Ideologies. Sweden and Germany 1848–1933', in B. Stråth (ed.) *Language and the Construction of Class Identities*, Gothenburg: Gothenburg University Press, 25–54.

Vertzberger, J. Y. (1986) 'Foreign Policy Decisionmakers as Practical–Intuitive Historians: Applied History and its Shortcomings', *International Studies Quarterly*, 30:2, 223–247.

Vertzberger, J. Y. (1990) *The World in Their Minds: Information Processing, Cognition, and Perception in Foreign Policy Decisionmaking*, Stanford: Stanford University Press.

Virilio, P. (1984) *Guerre et Cinéma: Logistique de la Perception*, Paris: Editions de l'Etoile.

Virilio, P. (1986) *Speed and Politics*, New York: Semitexte(e).

Virilio, P. (1988) *La Machine de Vision*, Paris: Christian Bourgois.

von Bogdandy, A. (1993) 'The Contours of Integrated Europe', *Futures*, 25:1, 22–27.

von Dosenrode, S. (1998) 'Denmark: The Testing of a Hesitant Membership', in K. Hanf and B. Soetendorp (eds), *Adapting to European Integration. Small States and the European Union*, London: Addison-Wesley Longman, 52–68.

Wæver, O. (1994) 'Resisting Post Foreign Policy Analysis', in W. Carlsnaes and S. Smith (eds), *European Foreign Policy – The EC and Changing Perspectives in Europe*, London: Sage, 238–273.

Wæver, O. (1995) 'Identity, Integration and Security: Solving the Sovereignty Puzzle in EU Studies', *Journal of International Affairs*, 48:2, 389–431.

Wallace, H. (1971) 'The Impact of the European Communities on National Policy-Making', *Government and Opposition*, 6:4, 520–538.

Wallace, H. (1973) *National Governments and the European Communities*, London: Chatham House.

Wallace, H. (1988) 'The Best is the Enemy of the "Could": Bargaining in the European Communities', paper, London: Royal Institute of International Affairs.

Wallace, H. (1990) 'Making Multilateral Negotiations Work', in W. Wallace (ed.), *The Dynamics of European Integration*, London and New York: Pinter, 213–228.

Wallace, H. (1999) 'Whose Europe is it Anyway? The 1998 Stein Rokkan Lecture', *European Journal of Political Research*, 35:3, 287–306.

Wallace, H. and Wallace, W. (eds) (1996) *Policy-Making in the European Union*, Oxford: Oxford University Press.

Wallace, H. and Young, A. (eds) (1997) *Participation and Policy-making in the EU*, Oxford: Clarendon Press.

Wallace, W. (ed.) (1990) *The Dynamics of European Integration*, London and New York: Pinter.

Weiler, J. H. H. (1999) *The Constitution of Europe*, Cambridge: Cambridge University Press.

Wendt, A. E. (1987) 'The Agent–Structure Problem in International Relations Theory', *International Organization*, 43:3, 335–370.

Wendt, A. E. (1992) 'Anarchy is What States Make of It', *International Organization*, 46:2, 391–425.

Wendt, A. E. (1995) 'Constructing International Politics', *International Security*, 20: 1, 71–81.

Wessels, W. (1990) 'Administrative Interaction', in W. Wallace (ed.), *The Dynamics of European Integration*, London: Pinter, 229–241.

Wessels, W. and Rometsch, D. (eds) (1996) *The European Union and Member-States – Towards Institutional Fusion?*, Manchester: Manchester University Press.

Wind, M. (1996a) 'The Rules of Anarchy: N. G. Onuf', in O. Wæver and I. Neumann (eds), *The Future of International Relations. Masters in the Making?*, London and New York: Routledge.

Wind, M. (1996b) 'Towards a Post-Hobbesian Order. A Constructivist Theory of European Integration – Or How to Explain European Integration as an Unintended Consequence of Rational State Action', *EUI Working Paper*, Fiesole: European University.

Wind, M. (1996c) 'Rediscovering Institutions: A Reflectivist Critique of Rational Institutionalism', in K. E. Jørgensen (ed.), *Reflective Approaches to European Governance*, Basingstoke: Macmillan, 15–35.

Young, O. (1994) *International Governance. Protecting the Environment in a Stateless Society*, Ithaca and London: Cornell University Press.

Zartman, I. W. (1985) *Ripe for Resolution: Conflict and Intervention in Africa*, New York: Oxford University Press.

Åberg, C.-J. (1988) 'Europa – en ny rond', *Tiden*, 3, 137.

Internet addresses

www.pcf.fr/accueil.html
www.archi.it/fidia/forza.italia/welcome.htm
www.labour.org.uk/
www.parti-socialiste.fr/
www.tory.org.uk/
www.verts.imaginct.fr/
www.ulivo.it/

Index

References to figures and tables are in *italics*; those for notes are followed by 'n'.

Åberg, Carl Johan 23, 24
action *see* political action
Adam, B. 15, 16, 69, 84, 104
Adler, E. 17, 18
administration 145–6, 149–51
  anticipation and coordination 152–3
  centralisation 153–5
  decentralisation 155–6
  networks 14–15
  prime ministerialisation 156–7
  temporal dimensions 7–8
administrative language 29–30
  competencies 55–8
  political action 45–8
  projects and processes 53–5
  sources 31
  timing 59–60
agency–structure relationship 18, 20–1, 105
  Bourdieu 105–6
  Giddens 106–7
Agenda 2000 111, *112*
Amnå, E. 8
Andersen, S. 71, 145, 157
Anderson, B. 67, 69, 71, 72, 80, 81, 98, 99n, 103
anticipation 4, 47–8, 152
Aristotle 73, 99n
Armstrong, K. 14, 147
attitude 41–3
Augustine 73
Austria 154, 155
autonomy
  individual 155
  national 33, 35, 37, 38, 62
Axelrod, R. 124

Baldwin, R. 159
Bartle, I. 14
Begriffsgeschichte 25–6
Bell, D. 105
Benjamin, W. 69
Bergström, H. 7
Beyers, J. 151
Blomberg, Leif 34, 61

Book, K. 17
Börzel, T. 14
Bourdieu, P. 16, 19, 107, 120, 131, 140–1
  forgotten history 105–6
  irreversible time 103–4
  Kabyle calendar 108, *108*
Bovens, M. 51
Brunsson, K. 7
budgetary deadlines 7–8
Bulmer, S. 14, 67, 146, 147
bureaucracy *see* administration
Bynander, F. 10

calendar *see* timetables
Caporaso, J. A. 16
Carey, J. W. 8
Carlsnaes, W. 20, 21
Carlsson, Ingvar 24, 35–6, 61, 62
causality 19–20, 41
Cecchini, P. 33
centralisation 153–5
Checkel, J. 18
Christakis, M. 155
Christiansen, T. 18
circular view of time *see* cycles
clock time 103
Cohen, R. 38–9
cohesiveness 146–7
coincidence 72
collaboration 99
Comité des représentants permanents *see* Coreper
Commission *see* European Commission
common agendas 80
Common Foreign and Security Policy (CFSP)
  blurred borders 81–4
  common agendas 80
  Coreu 79–80
  deadlines 86–8
  official timetables 111–12
  overlapping timetables 84–6
  predictions 92–3
  rhythms 88–9

routines 80
skills 94
speed 89–90
timing 91–2
communications 8, 58
see also telegrams
comparative outlook 28
competencies 30
administrative language 55–8
political language 55
confidence 68
construction 53
consultation reflex 80
continuity 46–8
cooperation 124–5, 144n
coordination
bureaucracy 153
cycles 130–3
future 47–8
national ministries 81–6
present 67–9
co-presences 71
Coreper
official timetables 111, *112*, 113
private timetables 118, *119*
Coreu (Correspondence Européenne)
79–80, 86
Cornett, L. 16
Council of Europe 39–40
Council of Ministers
official timetables 109, *110*, 111–13
private timetables *117–18*
crisis management 10
cybereurocracy 151–7
cyberocracy 8, 151
cycles 6, 7, 120, 143
coordination 130–3
meetings 134, 137–8, *138*
planning 130
Czempiel, E.-O. 16

daily rhythms 133–8
Daugbjerg, C. 14, 146–7
de Clausade, J. 153
deadlines 86–8, 150
budgetary 7–8
centralisation and decentralisation 153–6
monthly rhythms 128–9
decentralisation 153, 155–6
decisional present 88–9
democracy 2, 157
time-efficient 157–8
of unlimited time 158–9
Denmark 156
Der Derian, J. 9–10

Dessler, D. 17
Diebert, R. 143
Diez, T. 13, 15
diplomacy, language 38–9
direction 34
discursive homogeneity 26–7
distinct events 6

Edelman, M. 8
education 57–8
effect 41
efficiency 31
Eisenhardt, K. M. 8
Eising, R. 14, 15, 16, 146
Ekengren, M. 10, 17, 19, 39, 71, 153, 155,
156, 161
Elgström, O. 14
Eliassen, K. 71, 145, 157
encyclopaedias 26, 29
enforced present 96–7, 98
English language 29, 134–5
Erlander, Tage 32, 35
European Commission 33
official timetables 111, *112*
European communications 58
European competence 55–7
European education 57–8
European encyclopaedia 29
European governance 145–6
administration 149–57
democracy 157–60
language 61
past and planning 120–38
policy-making 146–9
political action 40–8
political time 10
post-modern polity 160–2
present 68–9, 71, 73–5, 86–94, 95–7
projects and processes 49–55
reflective approaches 15–21
subjective plans 109, *110*, 111–14, *112*,
114, *115–16*, 116–20, *117–18*, *119*
temporal dimension 11–15
timetables 75–80, 97–8, 140–2, *141*, *143*
timing 59–60
European reflex 56
European simultaneity 74, 91, 92–3, 94,
95–6, 148, 149, 160–2
enforced 96–7, 98
everyday language 26, 29
everyday past 106–7
expectation 3, 26, 38, 43, 45, 61, 63
European competence 57
European education 57
projects and processes 53–4, 55

experience 3, 38, 43, 44, 45, 52, 62–3
    European communications 58
    European competence 56–7
    European education 57

Fabian, J. 16
files 127–8
foreign ministries 74–5, 154
    see also Common Foreign and Security
      Policy
forgotten history 105–6
French language 29, 31, 134–5
Friis, L. 14, 147
future 1, 2–3, 11, 149, 150–1
    competencies 55–8
    and democracy 159–60
    evolving oligopoly 32–7
    ex ante evaluation to scanning 23–4
    exploring 24–7
    international politics 38–40
    political action 40–8
    in political history 3–5
    political promise 61–4
    projects and processes 48–55
    research model 27–31
    Sweden 23–4
    timing 59–60
    uncertainty 152

Gahrton, P. 34
George, S. 67, 146, 153
Giddens, A. 25, 51, 150
    clock time 103, 104, 161
    structure 105, 106–7
    time–space distanciation 71, 104, 139
    timetables 75
Gidlund, J. E. 34
Glaser, B. 59
Goetz, K. 151
Goodin, R. E. 157, 159
governance 21–2n, 149
    see also European governance
grammar 38–9
Greece 155
Gross, D. 4–5, 25, 143
Gumbrecht, H.-U. 26, 28
Gustavsson, J. 28
Gustavsson, S. 147, 157

Haas, P. M. 17
habitus 106, 131, 140, 142
Hägerstrand, T. 21n
half-year rhythms 125–6, 139
Hanf, K. 146, 153, 154
Harmsen, R. 15, 146, 153, 156

Hart, P. 't 10, 51, 69
Hayward, J. 157
Held, D. 104
Hermansson, C. H. 34
Hernes, H. 6
Hill, C. 147
historical time 25
Hollis, M. 20
homogeneity 26–7, 28
human rights 39–40
hyper-mediated diplomacy 9

identity 15
independent events 72
individual autonomy 155
international politics
    future 38–40
    present 70–1
international relations (IR) theory 17, 18,
    20
Ireland 155
irreversible time 103–4
Italian language 29

Jachtenfuchs, M. 1, 13
Jacobsson, K. 10, 28, 51, 149, 157
Jannings, J. 147
Jerneck, M. 10
Jerome, A. 104
Jönsson, C. 14
Jørgensen, K. E. 13, 15, 17, 18, 19, 20
Jung, S. 13

Kabyle people 108, *108*
Kapstein, E. B. 13–14
Keohane, R. O. 17
Kern, S. 69, 70, 85
Kerremans, B. 151
Kleiboer, M. 10, 69
Klein, B. 18
Kohler-Koch, B. 13, 14, 15, 16, 146
Koselleck, R. 28, 45, 53
    anthropological categories 30
    experiences and expectations 38
    instrument and meaning 52
    projects 49
    temporalisation of political language 3–4,
      25–6, 27, 29, 63
Krause, K. 18

Ladrech, R. 146, 154
Laffan, B. 155
language 26
    Council of Europe 39–40
    diplomacy 38–9

experience and expectation 29–30
future 61
Swedish 27–8
telecommunications 134–5
see also administrative language; political
  language
Larsson, G. 35
Larsson, T. 67, 68
last judgement 3
legal Europe 55
legislation 41
Lewin, L. 25
lexicography 26, 29
linear view of time 6
  overlapping timetables 84–5
  sources 103–5
Linz, J. J. 157, 158
longue durée 4–5, 102
Luckmann, T. 123
Luhmann, N. 4, 5, 45, 63, 140
Luif, P. 79, 153, 154, 155, 156
Lüsebrink, H.-J. 26, 28

Majone, G. 13, 146
management 149
March, J. G. 129
Marks, G. 13, 16
Mascanzoni, D. 96
Matlary, J. H. 14, 18, 19, 20
McKay, J. 147
McLuhan, M. 69, 104
meeting cycles 134, 137–8, *138*
middle of the week 133
ministries
  blurred borders 81–4
  see also foreign ministries
modernity 62–3
monthly rhythms 126–30
Morata, F. 156
Mörth, U. 16, 71
multilevel governance 13, 16
multitemporalism 6
multi-year rhythms 121–5
Murphy, A. 14, 147

narrative view of time 72
Nassehi, A. 5, 51
nation-states
  administration 151–7
  language 61
  policy-making 146–7
  political action 40–2, 45–6
  present 67–9, 81–6
  projects and processes 48, 53–4
  timetables 113–14, *114, 115–16*

timing 59–60
  see also ministries
national autonomy 33, 35, 37, 38, 62
national encyclopaedia 29
national simultaneity 67–8, 69, 71, 95
neomedieval time 143–4
Netherlands 156
networks 14–15, 146–7
Neumann, I. 18
Nørgaard, A. S. 12, 162
Norway 156–7
Nowotny, H. 6, 16
Nuttall, S. 79, 80

official timetables 109, *110*, 111–13, *112*
Olsen, J. P. 129
Olsson, H. 34–5
on-linification 140
Onuf, N. G. 18
Øygarden, J. A. 51

pace 2, 9, 89–90, 161
participant observation 107, 108–9
past 3, 102–3
  European governance 120–38
  irreversible time 103–4
  practical 105–8
Paterson, W. 146
Pettersson, L. 34–5
Pijpers, A. 80
pipeline 129–30
planning 92, 102–3, 150
  as anticipated decisions 138–44
  European governance 109, *110*, 111–14,
    112, 114, 115–16, 116–20, *117–18, 119*,
    120–38
pluritemporalism 6
points 6
policy-making 15, 145–6
  network quality 146–7
  sub-optimal outcome 147–9
policy style 14
political action 30
  administrative language 45–8
  political language 40–5
  see also timing
political consciousness 28
political future *see* future
political language 29–30
  competencies 55
  de-temporalisation 151
  political action 40–5
  projects and processes 48–53
  sources 31
  timing 59

political present *see* present
political promise 61–4
political time
  bureaucratic 7–8
  categories 30
  European governance 10
  past, present and future 3–6
  statecraft 9–10
possibilities 42, 61, 62
post-modernity 11, 63, 159, 160–1
practice 120
prediction 92–4, 138–44, 150
preparedness 61, 63
present 67–9, 149, 150
  Anderson 72
  European governance 71, 86–94, 95–9
  European governance calendar 75–80
  fiction 81
  international 70–1
  management 149
  nation-state 81–6
  in perspective 69–70
  predominance 136–7
  Ricoeur 73
  see also simultaneity
presidencies 150, 161
  countries' own 123
  important 122–3
  official timetables 109, *110*, 111
  order 121–2
  six-month programme 125
prime ministerialisation 156–7
private timetables 116–20, *117–18, 119*
  coordination cycles 130–2
processes 30
  administrative language 53–5
  political language 50–3
prognosis 3, 45
progress 2, 3–5, 25, 61
projects 30
  administrative language 53–5
  political language 48–50
promotion 41, 43–4
Proposition 1987/88:66 (Sweden) 33–4
public management *see* administration

qualities *see* competencies
Quentin, F. 104

rationalistic perspective 17
reactive style 124
recurrent agendas 125–6
recurrent pattern of practices 131
reflective approaches 17, 18–21
Regelsberger, E. 80

regularity 125–6
Reichardt, R. 26, 29
representiveness 26
republic 25–6
rhythms 88–9, 120–1, 157
  daily 133–8
  monthly 126–30
  multi-year 121–5
  semi-year 125–6
  weekly 130–3
Richardson, J. 14, 145
Ricoeur, P. 5, 73, 99n
Rifkin, J. 105
Risse-Kappen, T. 13, 16, 147
Rometsch, D. 15, 151
Ronfeldt, D. 8, 104, 151
Rosenau, J. 16, 21n, 70
Roth, J. 116
routines 80
Ruggie, J. G. 10, 18, 19, 20, 70, 161
  modern political forms 11–12, 13–14

Sandholtz, W. 14
Santiso, J. 157
Scharpf, F. 13, 147, 157
Schedler, A. 157
Schlesinger, J. A. 7
Schmitter, P. 13, 16, 145–6, 157
Schneider, G. 6
Schöttler, P. 26
Schumann, W. 147
Scott, A. 70
semi-year rhythms 125–6, 139
simulation 104–5
simultaneity 67–8, 69–70, 71, 72, 80, 95
  see also European simultaneity
skills 94
Skinner, Quentin 64n
Skowronek, S. 6
Smith, M. 20
Smith, S. 17, 20
Social Democratic Party (Sweden) 32, 33–4, 36, 37
socio-historical semantics 25, 26, 29
Soetendorp, B. 146, 153, 154
sovereignty 33, 35, 37
space 1, 2, 9, 11, 161, 162
speed 2, 9, 89–90, 161
statecraft 9–10
Steiner, Z. 151
Stenelo, L.-G. 10
Stern, E. 10
Stone Sweet, A. 14
strategy 34, 37, 41, 44–5, 62, 106
Stråth, B. 26

Strauss, A. 59
Strömvik, M. 14
structure 18, 20–1, 105
    Bourdieu 105–6
    Giddens 106–7
Stubb, A. 147
sub-optimal policy outcomes 147–9
summits 126
Sundelius, B. 10, 153, 155, 156
Svenning, O. 35
Sverdrup, U. 10, 153, 154, 157, 159
Sweden
    bureaucratic politics of time 7, 8
    centralisation 154
    ministries 76–7
    political future 23–4, 32–7
    prime ministerialisation 156
Swedish language 27–8
    sources 30–1
synchronic analysis 29
systemic simultaneity 70

Tallberg, J. 145
Tannam, E. 155
telegrams 140
    Coreu 79–80, 86
    form 134
    frequency 133–4
    handling procedures 135–6
    language 134–5
    to the point 136–7
tempo 88–9, 150
Thompson, J. B. 104
Tilly, C. 10
time 1–3, 161–2
    bureaucratic politics 7–8
    and democracy 157–60
    irreversible 103–4
    narrative view 72
    out-stretched 104
    in political history 3–6
    reflective approaches 19
    simulated 104–5
time–space distanciation 71, 104, 152
timetables 46, 97–8, 107–8, *108*, 161

adapting to 78–80
deadlines 86–8
domesticised European 113–14, *114,*
    115–16
European governance 75–80, 140–2, *141,*
    143
indicators 75–8
official European 109, *110*, 111–13,
    112
overlapping 84–6
private European 116–20, *117–18, 119*
timing 30
    administrative language 59–60
    European simultaneity 91–2
    political language 59
Tonra, B. 79, 80
Trägårdh, L. 26
treaty revisions 124

United Kingdom 77–8
United States 5–6, 147
Utopia 51

Virilio, P. 9, 104, 105, 152
vocabulary 38, 39
von Bogdandy, A. 12, 143, 161
von Dosenrode, S. 153, 156

Wæver, O. 12–13, 18, 143, 160, 162
Wallace, H. 13, 14, 16, 71, 75, 76, 137, 145,
    146, 147, 155
Wallace, W. 14, 71, 145, 146, 147
war 9–10
weekly rhythms 130–3
Weiler, J. H. H. 157, 158, 161
Wendt, A. E. 17–18, 20
Wessels, W. 15, 75, 76, *76*, 80, 151
Wind, M. 18, 19
working groups 111, 112, 113

Young, A. 16
Young, O. 18

Zalewski, M. 17
Zartman, I. W. 10